Making Gluten-Free Living Easy!

D0830547

Cecelia's Marketplace
Kalamazoo, Michigan

www.CeceliasMarketplace.com

Gluten/Casein Free

GROCERY SHOPPING GUIDE

2010 EDITION

Dr. Mara Matison
Dainis Matison

khP

Kal-Haven Publishing

Cecelia's Marketplace
Gluten/Casein Free Grocery Shopping Guide

by Dr. Mara Matison & Dainis Matison

khP

Kal-Haven Publishing
P.O. Box 20383
Kalamazoo, MI 49019 U.S.A.

ISBN 978-0-9794094-5-5

2010 Edition

Printed in the United States of America
Cover illustration: Lilita Austrins

CONTENTS

About the Authors

The co-author of this book, Dr. Mara Matison, received her Doctor of Dental Surgery degree from University of Detroit Mercy, and her Bachelor of Arts degree in Psychology from Villanova University. Her husband and co-author, Dainis Matison, received his Master of Science degree in Information Technology and Bachelor of Arts degree in Finance from Ball State University. They are both members of Celiac Disease Foundation, Celiac Sprue Association, Gluten Intolerance Group, and Talk About Curing Autism. These are nationwide organizations that support people with celiac disease, gluten intolerance, gluten sensitivitiy and autism.

Cecelia's Marketplace was established by both Mara and Dainis in 2006, soon after Mara was diagnosed with celiac disease. The couple struggled with Mara's huge lifestyle change, which included adhering to a strict gluten-free diet. Shopping trips to the grocery store were very frustrating. Spending time calling food manufacturers to find out if products were gluten-free seemed like a daily routine. They knew there had to be an easier way, so they decided to compile a gluten-free grocery shopping guide. Since then, Mara has also been diagnosed with a casein and soy intolerance, which brought about the need for the *Gluten/Casein Free Grocery Shopping Guide* and the *Gluten/Casein/Soy Free Grocery Shopping Guide*.

Thanks to all three of Cecelia's Marketplace Grocery Shopping Guides, grocery shopping now has become easier for not only the authors, but also their families, friends and thousands of grocery shoppers nationwide.

Preface - Note to the Reader

Cecelia's Marketplace Gluten/Casein Free Grocery Shopping Guide has been written to help people that are in search of gluten-free and casein-free (GFCF) products. Whether you are on a GFCF diet, prepare GFCF meals for yourself or others, or just enjoy eating GFCF foods, this book is for you. It will help guide you to easy grocery shopping and eliminate the frustration and headaches that you've experienced trying to find GFCF products. This guide is also great for restaurant owners, chefs, dieticians, family members, husbands, wives, friends, and others who shop for, or prepare GFCF foods. For those that are not familiar with GFCF cooking or GFCF dining out, we have included three sections in the front of the book: *What is Gluten & Casein, Clean Kitchen Tips,* and *Gluten/Casein Free Dining Out*.

We have alphabetized our *Gluten/Casein Free Grocery Shopping Guide* to help you quickly find brand names of the GFCF products. The guide is easy to use: just pick a product, look it up, and you'll have GFCF brands at your fingertips. This book is small enough so that it can be carried with you to the grocery store when searching for products. Use it anytime, anywhere. In addition to the grocery shopping guide, there is a section in the back of the book that lists GFCF over the counter (OTC) medications. GFCF shopping has never been easier. Treasure this book and enjoy all the GFCF foods that are available!

Due to periodic changes in ingredients and new products, *Cecelia's Marketplace Gluten/Casein Free Grocery Shopping Guide* will be updated annually. Look for the new edition every year.

A percentage of our proceeds are donated to nationwide nonprofit organizations that support people with celiac disease, gluten intolerance, autism, and other food sensitivities.

Dr. Mara Matison
Dainis Matison

Acknowledgments

There are many people that have contributed to the creation of this book. The support from our family and friends has made this journey more enjoyable. Lauma for data research and editing, Lilita A. for editing, cover illustration, and all the gluten-free meals that kept us going; Mik for editing, critiquing and successful business strategies; Ray for all the reference materials and guidance to becoming successful entrepreneurs; Ligita supporting us and all the delicious gluten-free recipes along the way; Lija, Liana, Annette, & Leah for data collection; Lilita M. for showing us 'The Secret'; Velta and Ilga for believing in us; Jonnie Bryant for all the publishing advice and knowledge; Dr. Heidi Gjersoe for the diagnosis and support; Larisa Kins for book page layout & cover design; Jeff Matson at Creative Group for logo design; Natural Health Center for the wonderful gluten-free book signing events; Dr. Arnis Pone, Dr. Jason Ham, Kal-Haven Publishing, McNaughton & Gunn, and all our fellow "celiacs" for all the support.

Warning - Disclaimer

What is Gluten & Casein?

Gluten is a special type of protein that is most commonly found in wheat, rye, and barley. It is comprised of two main protein groups: gliadins, and gluteins. People who have celiac disease, gluten intolerance, or gluten sensitivity may suffer from chronic digestive problems when ingesting foods that contain gluten. Gluten is found in most cereals, breads, pastas, soups, and pizza crusts. It may also be hidden in foods such as seasonings, salad dressings, sauces, additives and natural flavors.

Casein is a protein found in milk. It is a phosphoprotein, which is a collection of proteins bound to phosphoric acid. Casein is found in products containing milk, such as cheese, butter, cream, yogurt, ice cream and any other derivative of milk. Many people suffering from celiac disease or gluten/casein intolerance cannot properly digest this protein.

Maintaining a strict gluten/casein free diet has shown to greatly improve the symptoms of celiac disease, and gluten/casein intolerance. After gluten and casein are eliminated from the diet, the digestive tract begins to heal and the symptoms normally start to disappear after a few weeks.

Autism research has shown that the body's failure to break down gluten and casein proteins may have an effect on the body, similar to that of morphine or other opiates. For this reason, some experts on autism recommend a gluten/casein free diet for those suffering with autism[1]. Please note, the authors of this guide do not either agree or disagree with this recommendation.

1. http://www.webmd.com/brain/autism/gluten-free-casein-free-diets-for-autism

Clean Kitchen Tips

It is very important prior to preparing a gluten/casein free (GFCF) meal, to clean the surrounding area including, pots, pans, utensils and any other items being used. Bread crumbs, flour particles or other gluten or casein containing foods left in the cooking area can potentially contaminate a GFCF meal.

Here are some tips to help prevent gluten and casein contamination:

- Use an uncontaminated sponge to wash all working surfaces with soap and water.
- Clean and inspect pots, pans, utensils, cutting boards and other kitchenware for gluten or casein residue.
- Use clean kitchen hand towels.
- If grilling, place aluminum foil over the grilling area.
- Use squeeze bottle mustard, ketchup, peanut butter, jelly/jam, or other condiments to prevent cross-contamination.
- Avoid using wooden utensils. Gluten and/or casein residue can stay embedded in wooden utensils and cutting boards.
- Use a separate toaster for GFCF bread, rice cakes, etc..
- In commercial kitchens, if using latex/rubber gloves, make sure the gloves are not coated with powder (starch).
- Do not deep fry foods in contaminated oil (e.g. from breaded chicken wings, breaded chicken tenders, mozzarella sticks).

Gluten/Casein Free Dining Out

Nationwide restaurant chains offering *gluten-free menus:

Austin Grill
Biaggi's Ristorante
Bonefish Grill
Bugaboo Creek Steakhouse
Carino's Italian Grill
Carraba's Italian Grill
Charlie Brown's Steakhouse
Cheeseburger In Paradise
Chili's Grill & Bar
Claim Jumper Restaurants
Fleming's Prime Steakhouse & Wine Bar
Legal Sea Foods
Romano's Macaroni Grill
Ninety Nine Restaurant
Old Spaghetti Factory
On The Border Mexican Grill
Outback Steakhouse
P.F. Chang's China Bistro
Pasta Pomadoro
Pei Wei Asian Diner
Pizza Fusion
Uno Chicago Grill
Weber Grill Restaurant
Wildfire Restaurants
Z. Tejas Southwestern Grill

*These menus are only gluten-free. Please explain to the wait staff that the meal needs to be gluten-free and also casein-free.

Other Products Available
by Cecelia's Marketplace

Grocery Shopping Guides:
Gluten-Free
Gluten/Casein/Soy Free

Other Products:
GF Dining Out Cards
Gluten-Free Safety Labels

FREE Email Sign-Up:
Gluten-Free Product of the Day

For **Product Alerts** or more information about our products please visit us online:

www.CeceliasMarketplace.com

Our Data Collection

The product information in this book was collected between May 2009 - December 2009. The information was received from product manufacturers and major supermarkets via internet, e-mail, phone, mail or product labels.

The Food and Drug Administration (FDA) has proposed to define the term "gluten-free" as containing less than 20 parts per million (ppm) gluten. This regulation was scheduled to be issued in 2008. Some food manufacturers have already begun testing their products for the presence of gluten. Those products that have not passed this test have been excluded from this book. Currently, not all companies test their products, therefore, we cannot guarantee that all the products listed in our book are less than 20 ppm gluten.

Casein is the protein found in milk products. Milk is one of the top eight allergens recognized by the FDA. Products containing any form of milk have been excluded from this guide. This includes casein, caseinate, lactose, and any other milk derivative.

Those products that have been manufactured in the same facility as gluten or casein, but indicate that they thoroughly wash their lines between products have been included. We have tried our best not to include products from manufacturers that do not take measures to prevent cross-contamination.

For more information on our data collection and up to date product alerts, please visit our website www.CeceliasMarketplace.com.

Symbols

Certified/Tested Gluten-Free Products

&

Gluten-Free Facilities

There are some companies that manufacture their products in a dedicated gluten-free facility or environment. Some products also go through strict guidelines and vigorous testing by either the Celiac Sprue Association (CSA) Recognition Seal Program or the Gluten Intolerance Group (GIG) Gluten-Free Certification Organization to be verified as gluten-free. In this guide we have marked these manufacturers and products with the following symbols:

▲   - manufactured in a dedicated gluten-free facility or environment

●   - verfied, tested, or certified gluten-free by either the CSA Recognition Seal Program or the GIG Gluten-Free Certification Organization

Celiac Sprue Association ®

This book is dedicated to:

All those in search of gluten/casein free products.

Gluten/Casein Free
Grocery Shopping Guide (A-Z)

A A

Almond Beverage... see Nut Beverages

Almonds... see Nuts

Amaranth
  Arrowhead Mills ▲ - Whole Grain
  Bob's Red Mill ▲ - Organic Flour
  Nu-World Foods -
    Amaranth Side Serve (Garlic Herb●, Savory Herb●, Spanish Tomato●)
    Bread Crumbs●
    Flour●
    Pre Gel Powder●
    Puffed●
    Seed●
    Starch●
    Toasted Bran Flour●

Anchovies
  Crown Prince - Flat In Olive Oil, Rolled w/Capers In Olive Oil
  Crown Prince Natural - In Pure Olive Oil, Paste

Angel Hair Pasta... see Pasta

Animal Crackers... see Cookies

Apple Butter
  Eden Organic - Apple, Apple Cherry, Cherry
  Fischer & Wieser - Texas Pecan (Apple, Peach)
  Lucky Leaf
  Manischewitz
  Musselman's

Apple Cider... see Cider

Apple Cider Vinegar... see Vinegar

Apple Rings
  Lucky Leaf - Spiced
  Musselman's - Spiced

Apples... *All Fresh Fruits & Vegetables Are Gluten/Casein Free*   **A**

    Lucky Leaf - Sliced

    Musselman's - Sliced

Applesauce

    Albertsons - Cinnamon, Natural, Original

    Appletime - Natural

    Baxters - Bramley Apple Sauce

    Beech Nut Baby Food - Applesauce (Stage 1 Fruits, Stage 2 Fruits)

    Eden Organic - Organic Apple (Cherry, Cinnamon, Regular, Strawberry)

    Food Club Brand - Applesauce (Chunky, Cinnamon, Mixed Berry, Natural, Original, Strawberry, Unsweetened)

    Full Circle - Organic (Cinnamon, Sweetened, Unsweetened)

    Great Value Brand (Wal-Mart) -

        Applesauce Glass Jar (Cinnamon, Regular, Unsweetened)

        Applesauce Plastic Cups (Cinnamon, Natural, No Sugar Added, Regular)

        Canned Applesauce Regular

    Hannaford Brand - Cinnamon, Original, Unsweetened

    Home Harvest Brand - Natural, Regular

    Hy-Vee - Applesauce, Cinnamon, Light w/(Mixed Berry, Strawberry), Natural

    Kroger Brand - Plain

    Lucky Leaf - Cinnamon, Natural, Regular

    Meijer Brand - Chunky, Cinnamon, Mixed Berry, Natural, Organic (Cinnamon, Sweetened, Unsweetened), Original, Regular, Strawberry

    Midwest Country Fare - Home Style, Natural, w/(Cinnamon, Peaches, Raspberries, Strawberries)

    Momma's Old Fashioned Applesauce - Original Flavor

    Mott's - All Varieties

    Musselman's - Chunky, Cinnamon (Lite, Regular), Golden Delicious, Granny Smith, Healthy Picks (Blueberry Pomegranate, Cupucacu Key Lime, Raspberry Acai), Homestyle (Cinnamon, Regular), Lite Fruit 'N

A Sauce (Cherry, Grape, Orange Mango, Peach, Raspberry, Strawberry), McIntosh Apple, Organic (Regular, Unsweetened), Regular, Sesame Street (Cherry), Totally Fruit (Apple, Peach, Strawberry), Unsweetened

Nature's Goodness Baby Food - Applesauce (Stage 1, Stage 2)

O Organics

Publix - Chunky, Cinnamon, GreenWise Organic Unsweetened, Old Fashioned, Unsweetened

Safeway Brand - Cups, Natural, Sweetened

Spartan Brand - Cinnamon, Natural, Peach, Raspberry, Regular, Strawberry

Stop & Shop Brand - Applesauce (Chunky, Cinnamon, Mixed Berry, Natural, Strawberry)

Trader Joe's - Chunky Spiced Apples

Wegmans Brand -

Applesauce (Chunky, Cinnamon, McIntosh, Mixed Berry, No Sugar Added, Peach Mango, Regular)

Natural Applesauce No Sugar Added

Sweetened Applesauce

Winn Dixie - Cinnamon, Sweetened, Unsweetened

Woodstock Farms - Organic Applesauce (Apricot, Blueberry, Cinnamon, Mango, Raspberry, Regular)

Apricots... *All Fresh Fruits & Vegetables Are Gluten/Casein Free*

Albertsons - Canned

Del Monte -

Canned/Jarred Fruit (All Varieties)

Fruit Snack Cups (Metal, Plastic)

Food Club Brand - Canned Unpeeled Apricot Halves

Hy-Vee - Unpeeled Halves

Meijer Brand - Halves Unpeeled In Pear Juice

Publix - Canned Halves Unpeeled (In Heavy Syrup, Water & Artificial Sweetener)

S&W - All Canned/Jarred Fruits

A

Stop & Shop Brand - Heavy Syrup, Island Apricots In Light Syrup, Splenda

Winn Dixie - Unpeeled Halves In Heavy Syrup

Artichokes... *All Fresh Fruits & Vegetables Are Gluten/Casein Free*

Birds Eye - All Plain Frozen Vegetables

Native Forest - Artichoke Hearts (Marinated, Quartered, Whole)

Reese - Artichokes (Marinated, Regular)

S&W - All Plain Canned Vegetables

Safeway Select - Marinated Artichoke Crowns

Spartan Brand - Artichoke Hearts (Marinated, Regular)

Trader Joe's - Artichoke Hearts In Water

Wegmans Brand - Artichoke Hearts (Halves & Quarters, In Brine, Marinated Quartered), Marinated Long Stemmed

Winn Dixie - Artichoke Hearts

Asparagus... *All Fresh Fruits & Vegetables Are Gluten/Casein Free*

Albertsons - Cuts & Tips, No Salt Spears, Whole Spears

Birds Eye - All Plain Frozen Vegetables

Cascadian Farm - Organic Frozen Asparagus Cuts

Del Monte - All Plain Canned Varieties

Food Club Brand - Canned Whole Asparagus

Great Value Brand (Wal-Mart) - Canned (Cut Spears, Extra Long)

Green Giant - Canned Spears, Cut Asparagus

Hannaford Brand - Cuts & Tips, Whole Tall

Hy-Vee - Cut Spears

Kroger Brand - All Plain Vegetables (Canned, Frozen)

Laura Lynn - Cut Asparagus

Meijer Brand - Canned Cuts & Tips

Native Forest - Green (Cuts & Tips, Spears), White

Nature's Promise - Organic Asparagus Spears

S&W - All Plain Canned Vegetables

Safeway Brand - Canned Cut

A

Spartan Brand - Cut

Stop & Shop Brand - Asparagus (Spears, Tips & Cuts)

B

Trader Joe's - All Plain Frozen Vegetables

Wegmans Brand - Cleaned And Cut Tips, Cut Spears & Tips

Woodstock Farms - Organic Frozen Whole Baby Asparagus

Avocado... *All *Fresh* Fruits & Vegetables Are **Gluten/Casein Free**

Avocado Dip... see Guacamole and/or Dip/Dip Mix

B

Baby Food

Beech Nut -

Cereal (Rice)

Stage 1 Fruits (Applesauce, Chiquita Bananas, Peaches, Pears)

Stage 1 Meats (Beef & Beef Broth, Chicken & Chicken Broth, Turkey & Turkey Broth)

Stage 1 Vegetables (Butternut Squash, Tender Golden Sweet Potatoes, Tender Sweet Carrots, Tender Sweet Peas, Tender Young Green Beans)

Stage 2 Desserts (DHA Plus Apple Delight)

Stage 2 Dinners (Apples & Chicken, Chicken & Rice, Chicken Noodle, Homestyle Chicken Soup, Macaroni & Beef w/Vegetables, Pineapple Glazed Ham, Sweet Potatoes & Chicken, Turkey & Rice, Vegetables & Beef, Vegetables & Chicken)

Stage 2 Fruits (Apples & Bananas, Apples & Blueberries, Apples & Cherries, Apples w/Mango & Kiwi, Apples w/Pears & Bananas, Applesauce, Apricots w/Pears & Apples, Chiquita Bananas, Chiquita Bananas & Strawberries, DHA Plus Apple Delight, DHA Plus Apple w/Pomegranate Juice, DHA Plus Banana Supreme, Guava, Mango, Papaya, Peaches, Peaches & Bananas, Pears, Pears & Pineapples, Pears & Raspberries, Plums w/Apples & Pears)

Stage 2 Rice Cereal (Apples w/Cinnamon)

Stage 2 Vegetables (Butternut Squash, Carrots & Peas, Corn & Sweet

Potatoes, Country Garden Vegetables, DHA Plus Butternut Squash w/Corn, DHA Plus Garden Vegetable, DHA Plus Sweet Potatoes, Mixed Vegetables, Sweet Corn Casserole, Sweet Potatoes & Apples, Tender (Sweet Carrots, Sweet Peas, Young Green Beans), Tender Golden Sweet Potatoes)

Stage 3 Dinners (Country Vegetables & Chicken)

Stage 3 Fruits (Apples & Bananas, Chiquita Bananas, Homestyle Apples Cherries Plums, Homestyle Cinnamon Raisins & Pears, Homestyle Peaches Apples & Bananas, Homestyle Pears & Blueberries)

Stage 3 Rice Cereal & Pears

Stage 3 Turkey Rice Dinner

Stage 3 Vegetables (Green Beans & Corn & Rice, Sweet Potatoes)

Earth's Best Organic Baby Food -

1st Beginner First Foods (Apples, Bananas, Carrots, Pears, Peas, Sweet Potatoes)

2nd Antioxidant Blends (Apple Butternut Squash, Banana Mango, Carrot Tomato, Sweet Potato Apricot)

2nd Dinners (Chicken & Brown Rice, Rice & Lentil, Summer Vegetable, Sweet Potatoes & Chicken)

2nd Fruits (Apples, Apples & Apricots, Apples & Bananas, Apples & Blueberries, Apples & Plums, Bananas, Bananas & Peaches & Raspberries, Pears, Pears & Mangos, Pears & Raspberries, Plum Banana Brown Rice Fruit & Whole Grain Combinations)

2nd Gourmet Meals (Chicken Mango Risotto, Creamy Chicken Apple Compote, Sweet Pea Turkey & Wild Rice)

2nd Seasonal Harvest Blends (Sweet Potato Cinnamon, Pumpkin Apple)

2nd Vegetables (Carrots, Corn & Butternut Squash, Garden Vegetables, Green Beans & Rice, Peas & Brown Rice, Sweet Potatoes, Winter Squash)

3rd Dinners (Vegetable Beef Pilaf)

3rd Fruits (Banana & Strawberries, Chunky Orchard Fruit)

Whole Grain Rice Cereal

B Gerber Baby Food -

1st Foods Fruits & Vegetables (Applesauce, Bananas, Carrots, Green Beans, Peaches, Pears, Peas, Prunes, Squash, Sweet Potatoes)

2nd Foods Desserts (Banana Yogurt, Fruit Medley)

2nd Foods Dinners (Apples & Chicken, Beef & Beef Gravy, Chicken & Chicken Gravy, Chicken & Rice, Ham & Ham Gravy, Pears & Chicken, Sweet Potatoes & Turkey, Turkey & Turkey Gravy, Veal & Veal Gravy, Vegetable Beef, Vegetable Chicken)

2nd Foods Fruits & Vegetables (Apple Blueberry, Apple Strawberry Banana, Apples & Cherries, Applesauce, Apricots w/Mixed Fruit, Banana Mixed Berry, Banana Orange Medley, Banana Plum Grape, Banana w/Apples & Pears, Bananas, Carrot Apple Mango, Carrots, Garden Vegetable, Green Beans, Mango, Mixed Vegetables, Peaches, Pear Pineapples, Pears, Peas, Prunes w/Apples, Smoothies (Hawaiian Delight, Peach Cobbler), Squash, Sweet Potatoes, Sweet Potatoes & Corn)

3rd Foods Desserts (Fruit Medley Dessert)

3rd Foods Dinners Vegetable (Beef, Chicken, Turkey)

3rd Foods Fruits & Vegetables (Applesauce, Banana Strawberry, Bananas, Carrots, Green Beans w/Rice, Peaches, Pears, Squash, Sweet Potatoes)

DHA (Apple Blackberry, Apples & Summer Peaches, Banana Mango, Banana Pineapple Orange Medley, Butternut Squash & Harvest Apples, Farmers Market Vegetable Blend)

Graduates Finger Foods (Apple Wagon Wheels)

Graduates For Toddlers (White Turkey Stew w/Rice & Vegetables)

Graduates Fruit (Diced Apples, Diced Peaches)

Graduates Fruit Strips (Apple, Strawberry, Wildberry)

Graduates Fruit Twists (Apple & Strawberry, Strawberry & Grape)

Graduates Juice Treats (Fruit Medley, Tropical)

Rice Single Grain Cereal

Gerber Organic Baby Food -

1st Foods (Applesauce, Bananas, Carrots, Pears, Sweet Peas, Sweet Potatoes)

B

2nd Foods (Apple Strawberry, Applesauce, Bananas, Pear & Wildberry, Sweet Potatoes)

Brown Rice Whole Grain Cereal

Mini Fruits - Apple, Banana Pineapple, Banana Strawberry

Homemade Baby - Baby Tex Mex●, Just (Apples●, Green Beans●, Pears●, Peas●, Squash●, Sweet Potatoes●), Piwi●, Squapples●, Yummy Yammies●

Meijer Brand -

Gluco Burst Arctic Cherry

Little Fruit (Apple, Strawberry Banana)

Little Veggies Corn

PND Bright Beginnings Vanilla Soy

Nature's Goodness Baby Food -

Stage 1 Fruits & Vegetables (Applesauce, Bananas, Carrots, Green Beans, Peaches, Pears, Peas, Prunes, Squash, Sweet Potatoes)

Stage 2 Desserts (Banana Pudding, Cherry Vanilla Pudding, Dutch Apple, Fruit Dessert, Mango Fruit, Papaya Fruit, Tutti Frutti)

Stage 2 Dinners (Apples & Chicken, Apples & Ham, Beef & Beef Gravy, Broccoli & Chicken, Chicken & Chicken Gravy, Green Beans & Turkey, Sweet Potatoes & Turkey, Turkey & Turkey Gravy, Turkey Rice Dinner, Vegetable Dinner (Bacon, Beef, Chicken, Ham))

Stage 2 Fruits & Vegetables (Applesauce, Apples & Blueberries, Apples & Pears, Apples Strawberries & Bananas, Apples w/Squash, Apricots w/Pears & Apples, Bananas, Bananas w/Apples & Pears, Bananas w/Mixed Berries, Carrots, Corn & Sweet Potatoes, Green Beans, Mixed Vegetables, Peaches, Pears, Plums w/Apples, Prunes w/Pears, Pumpkins w/Pears, Squash, Sweet Peas, Sweet Potatoes)

Stage 2 Rice Cereal (& Peaches, w/Applesauce)

Stage 3 Desserts (Bananas & Strawberry w/Tapioca, Bananas w/Tapioca)

Stage 3 Dinners (Green Beans & Rice)

Stage 3 Vegetable Sweet Potatoes

B

O Organics -

Stage 1 (Applesauce, Bananas, Carrots, Peas, Sweet Potatoes)

Stage 2 (Apple Apricot, Apple Banana, Apple Wild Blueberry, Applesauce, Bananas, Carrots, Mixed Vegetables, Peach Rice Banana, Pear Raspberry, Pears, Peas & Brown Rice, Prunes, Squash, Sweet Potatoes, Summer Vegetables)

Stage 3 (Sweet Potato Chicken Dinner, Vegetable Beef Dinner, Vegetable Lentil Dinner)

Baby Formula

Enfamil - Soy Infant Formula (ProSobee Lipil)

Hy-Vee - Baby Formula (Soy), Pediatric Electrolyte (Fruit, Grape, Regular)

Neocate - Infant (DHA & ARA, Regular), Junior (Chocolate, Tropical, Unflavored), Nutra, One +

Nestle Good Start -

Gentle (Soy Plus 2)

Soy DHA & ARA

Supreme (DHA & ARA)

Publix - Infant Formula (Soy)

Similac - Soy Formula (Isomil Advance, ProSobee Lipil)

Bacon

Applegate Farms - Natural (Canadian, Dry Cured, Peppered, Sunday, Turkey), Organic (Sunday, Turkey)

Black Label

Butterball - Turkey (Lower Sodium, Regular, Thin & Crispy)

Dietz & Watson - Canadian Style

Farmer John - Low Sodium, Quick Serve Fully Cooked

Garrett County Farms - Classic Sliced (Dry Rubbed, Turkey), Sliced (Applewood, Canadian Style), Thick Sliced Dry Rubbed, Turkey Peppered

Global Gourmet - Irish Bacon

Great Value Brand (Wal-Mart) - Hickory Smoked, Peppered, Turkey Bacon

Hannaford Brand - Maple, Sliced (Lower Sodium, Regular)

B

Honeysuckle White - Smoked Turkey Bacon

Hormel - Canadian Style, Fully Cooked, Microwave, Natural Choice (Canadian, Original)

Hy-Vee - Applewood, Double Smoked, Hickory, Hickory Smoked Fully Cooked, Lower Sodium, Maple, Peppered, Sweet Smoked

Jennie-O - Extra Lean Turkey, Turkey

Jimmy Dean - Fully Cooked Slices (Hickory Smoked, Maple), Premium Bacon (Hardwood Smoked Turkey, Lower Sodium, Original, Thick Slice)

Jones Dairy Farm -

    Canadian●

    Old Fashioned Slab Bacon●

    Sliced (Cherrywood Smoked●, Regular●, Thick●)

Meijer Brand - Lower Sodium, Regular

Old Smokehouse - Applewood, Maple Peppered, Original

Oscar Mayer - America's Favorite, Center Cut, Hearty Thick Cut, Lower Sodium, Natural Smoked Uncured, Ready To Serve (Bacon, Thick Cut)

Publix - All Varieties

Safeway Brand - Hickory Smoked, Lower Sodium, Regular

Shelton's - Turkey Breakfast Strips

Smithfield - Brown Sugar, Center Cut 40% Lower Fat, Cracked Peppercorn, Maple, Natural Hickory Smoked (Regular, Thick Sliced)

Wegmans - Fully Cooked Natural Smoked, Uncured Applewood Smoked

Wellshire Farms - Bacon (Bulk Maple, Classic Sliced Dry Rubbed, Classic Sliced Turkey, Dry Rubbed Center Cut, Fully Cooked Hickory Smoked, Natural, Pa Pork Applewood Smoked, Sliced Beef, Sliced Canadian Brand Turkey, Sliced Canadian Style, Sliced Dry Rubbed, Sliced Maple, Sliced Pancetta, Sliced Peppered Dry Rubbed, Sliced Peppered Turkey, Thick Sliced Dry Rubbed, Whole Pancetta)

B **Wellshire Organic** - Organic Bacon (Dry Rubbed, Turkey)

Winn Dixie - Hickory Sweet Sliced (Lower Sodium, Regular, Thick, Thin)

Bacon Bits

Hormel - Bacon (Bits, Crumbles, Pieces)

McCormick - Bac'N Pieces (Bits, Chips)

Oscar Mayer - Real Bacon Bits

Publix - 100% Real Bacon Pieces

Wellshire Farms - Salt Cured Bacon Bits

Winn Dixie - Bak'N Bits, Imitation Bacon Bits

Bagels

Enjoy Life▲ - Bagels (Cinnamon Raisin●, Classic Original●)

Gluten-Free Creations▲ - Berry●, Cinnamon Raisin●, Everything●, Onion●, Plain●

Kinnikinnick▲ - Tapioca Rice (Cinnamon Raisin, New York Style Plain, Sesame)

Baguettes... see Bread

Baking Bars

Baker's - German's Sweet, Semi Sweet Chocolate Chunks

Baking Chips

Baker's - German's Sweet, Semi Sweet Chocolate Chunks

Ener-G▲ - Chocolate Chips

Enjoy Life▲ - Semi Sweet Chocolate Chips●

Nonuttin' Foods ▲ - Dark Chocolate Chunks, Semi Sweet Chocolate Chips

Tropical Source - Semi Sweet Chocolate Chips

Woodstock Farms - Organic Dark Chocolate Chips w/Evaporated Cane Juice

Baking Cocoa

Dagoba - Organic

Hy-Vee

Spartan Brand - Cocoa Baking Chocolate

Baking Decorations & Frostings

B

Betty Crocker -

Cookie Icing (Chocolate, Red, White)

Cupcake Icing (Cloud White)

Decorating Decors (Chocolate Sprinkles, Nonpareils, Rainbow Mix Sprinkles, Red White & Blue Sprinkles, Sugars)

Decorating Gels (All Colors)

Decorating Icing (All Colors)

Easy Squeeze Icing (All Colors *Except Dark Chocolate & Milk Chocolate*)

Select Sugar Decors

Cherrybrook Kitchen - Gluten Free Frosting (Chocolate, Vanilla) *(Box Must Say Gluten-Free)*, Ready To Spread Vanilla Frosting

Duncan Hines -

Frosting

Caramel

Classic (Chocolate, Vanilla)

Coconut Supreme *(Coconut Pecan is NOT Gluten-Free)*

Dark Chocolate Fudge

French Vanilla

Lemon Supreme

White Chocolate Almond

Edward & Sons - Let's Do...Sprinkelz (Carnival, Chocolatey, Confetti)

Food-Tek Fast & Fresh - Dairy Free Chocolate Flavored Icing, Dairy Free Vanilla Flavored Icing

Gluten-Free Creations▲ - Frosting Mix (Chocolate●, White●)

Gluten-Free Essentials▲ - Frosting Mix (Lemon Glaze●, Supreme Chocolate●, Vanilla Royal●)

Kinnikinnick▲ - Icing Sugar

Manischewitz - Dairy Free Rich & Creamy (Chocolate, Vanilla)

Namaste Foods▲ - Chocolate Fudge, Toffee Vanilla

Pamela's Products▲ - Frosting Mix (Confetti, Dark Chocolate, Vanilla)

B Baking Mix... see Bread Mix

Baking Powder

  Barkat

  Bob's Red Mill▲

  Clabber Girl

  Davis

  El Peto▲ - Aluminum & Corn Free, Aluminum Free

  Ener-G▲ - Double Acting, Regular

  Glutino▲

  Hain Pure Foods

  Hannaford Brand

  Hearth Club

  Hy-Vee - Double Acting

  KC

  Kinnikinnick▲ - KinnActive

  Royal

  Rumford

  Spartan Brand

  Wegmans Brand - Double Acting

Baking Soda

  Albertsons

  Arm & Hammer

  Bob's Red Mill▲

  El Peto▲

  Ener-G▲ - Calcium Carbonate (Baking Soda Substitute)

  Hannaford Brand

  Hy-Vee

  Meijer Brand

  Spartan Brand

  Winn Dixie

barbeque sauce

B

Banana Chips
  Brothers All Natural▲ - Crisps (Banana, Strawberry Banana)
  Woodstock Farms - Banana Chips (Regular, Sweetened)
Bananas... *All Fresh Fruits & Vegetables Are Gluten/Casein Free*
  Chiquita
  Dole
  Woodstock Farms - Organic Frozen Bananas
Barbeque Sauce
  Bone Suckin' Sauce - Habanero, Original
  Cattlemen's - Classic, Smokehouse, Sweet
  Daddy Sam's - Bar B Que Sawce (Ginger Jalapeno, Original)
  Fischer & Wieser - Plum Chipotle BBQ
  Hannaford Brand - Honey, Kansas City Style, Original, Sweet & Zesty
  Homestyle Meals - Original, Smoked Chipotle
  Hy-Vee - Hickory, Honey Smoke, Original
  Isaly's - Original, Spicy
  Jack Daniels - Hickory Brown Sugar, Honey Smokehouse, Original No. 7 Recipe
  Kraft - Original Barbecue Sauce
  Midwest Country Fare - Hickory, Honey, Original
  Mr. Spice Organic - Honey BBQ
  Mrs. Renfro's - Barbecue Sauce
  Organicville - Organic BBQ Sauce (Original, Tangy)
  Publix - Deli BBQ, Hickory, Honey, Original
  Safeway Select - Hickory Smoked, Honey (Mustard, Smoked), Original
  San-J - Gluten Free Asian BBQ●
  Saz's - Original, Sassy, Vidalia Onion
  Spartan Brand - Hickory & Brown Sugar, Honey, Original
  Sweet Baby Ray's - Hickory & Brown Sugar, Honey, Honey Chipotle, Hot 'N Spicy, Original, Sweet Vidalia Onion
  Walden Farms - Hickory Smoked, Honey, Original, Thick & Spicy

B **Wegmans Brand** - Memphis Style, Tropical
Wild Thymes - Spicy Island BBQ Sauce
Winn Dixie - Hickory, Honey, Original

Bars... (includes Breakfast, Energy, Fruit, Protein, etc.)

1-2-3 Gluten Free▲ - Sweet Goodness Pan Bars●

Aller Energy Bars - Apple Cinnamon, Cherry Blossom, Chocolate
Swirl, Wild Berry

Alpsnack - Apricots & Cranberries, Coconut/Mango & Pineapple,
Fair Trade (Dark Chocolate, Espresso Chocolate), Plums &
Currants

Arico - Cookie Bars (Almond Cranberry, Lemon Ginger, Peanut Butter)

Bakery On Main - Gluten Free Granola Bars (Cranberry Maple Nut,
Extreme Trail Mix, Peanut Butter Chocolate Chip)

Boomi Bar -
Apricot Cashew
Cashew Almond
Cranberry Apple
Fruit & Nut
Healthy Hazel
Macadamia Paradise
Maple Pecan
Perfect Pumpkin
Pineapple Ginger
Pistachio Pineapple
Walnut Date

Bumble Bar - Awesome Apricot, Chai w/Almonds, Cherry Chocolate,
Chocolate Crisp, Chunky Cherry, Lushus Lemon, Original Flavor,
Original Flavor w/(Almonds, Cashews, Hazelnuts, Mixed Nuts), Tasty
Tropical

Clif Nectar - Organic (Cherry Pomegranate, Cranberry Apricot Almond,
Dark Chocolate Walnut, Lemon Vanilla Cashew)

Crispy Cat - Candy Bars (Chocolate Sundae, Mint Coconut, Toasted
Almond)

B

Dagoba - All Dark Chocolate Bars

Eat Natural -

100% Organic Brazils Hazelnuts & Sultans

Blackcurrants Walnuts Mango & Dark Chocolate

Brazils Sultanas Almonds & Hazelnuts

Cranberry Macadamia & Dark Chocolate

Dates Walnuts & Pumpkin Seeds

Macadamias Brazils & Apricots

Peanuts Almonds & Hazelnuts

Ener-G▲ - Chocolate Chip Snack Bar

Enjoy Life▲ - Boom Choco Boom (Crispy Rice●, Dark Chocolate●, Rice Milk●), Caramel Apple●, Cocoa Loco●, Sunbutter Crunch●, Very Berry●

Frankly Natural Bakers - Apricot, Date Nut, Raisin, Tropical

Glutino▲ - Breakfast Bars (Apple, Blueberry, Chocolate, Cranberry)

Gopal's - Adam & Eve, Apple Delicious, Ayurvedic, Carob Quinoa, Country (All), Happy Herb w/Maca, Pineapple Nut, Pumpkin Agave, Rawmesan, Sesame Mango, Walnut Fig

Goraw - Bar (Banana Bread Flax●, Live Granola●, Live Pumpkin●, Real Live Flax●, Spirulina Energy●)

Jennies - Omega 3 Energy Bar (Coconut, Coconut Almond, Coconut Chocolate)

Larabar - Apple Pie●, Banana Cookie●, Cashew Cookie●, Cherry Pie●, Chocolate Coconut●, Cinnamon Roll●, Cocoa Mole●, Coconut Cream Pie●, Ginger Snap●, Jocalat (Chocolate●, Chocolate Cherry●, Chocolate Hazelnut●, German Chocolate Cake●, Chocolate Coffee●, Chocolate Mint●), Key Lime Pie●, Lemon Bar●, Peanut Butter & Jelly●, Peanut Butter Cookie●, Pecan Pie●, Pistachio●, Tropical Fruit Tart●

Mixes From The Heartland▲ - Coffee Bars (Apple Cinnamon●, Cinnamon●, Cranberry●, Tropical●)

Mrs. May's Naturals - Trio (Bananas & Blueberry Plus, Black Sesame Plus, Cranberry Crunch, Mango & Strawberry Plus)

B

Nature's Path Organic - Crispy Rice Bars (Cheetah Berry, Fruity Burst, Lemur Peanut Choco Drizzle, Peanut Butter)

Nonuttin' Foods▲ - Granola Bars (Apple Cinnamon, Chocolate Chip, Double Chocolate Chunk, Raisin)

NuGO Free - Gluten Free Bars (Carrot Cake●, Dark Chocolate Crunch●, Dark Chocolate Trail Mix●)

Nutiva Bars - Organic (Flax Chocolate, Flax & Raisin, Hempseed Original)

Omega Smart Bars▲ - Banana Chocolate Chip, Organic (Apricot & Almond, Carrot Cake, Chocolate Nut, Cinnamon Apple, Raisin Spice), Pomegranate Strawberry Colada, Pumpkin Spice

Organic Food Bar -

Organic Food Bar (Active Greens, Active Greens Chocolate, Chocolate Chip, Cranberry, Omega 3 Flax, Original, Protein, Vegan, Wild Blueberry)

Organic Food Bar Kids (Oohmega Cherry Pie, Oooatmeal Apple Pie, Keerunch Chocolate Brownie Crunch)

Raw Organic Food Bar (Chocolate Coconut, Chocolatey Chocolate Chip, Cinnamon Raisin, Fiber Chocolate Delite)

Orgran▲ - Fruit Bars (Fruit Medley), Fruit Filled Bar (Apricot, Blueberry)

Oskri Organics -

Coconut Bar (Almond, Cherry, Mango, Original, Pineapple, Strawberry)

Date Fruit

Fig Fruit

Honey Bar (Cashew, Desert Date, Flaxseed, Granola, Mixed Nuts, Muesli, Turkish Delight)

Jalow (Almond Cranberry, Cashew Cranberry, Pecan Raisin)

Sesame Bar (Black Sesame, Date Syrup & (Black Cumin, Fennel, Regular), Molasses & (Black Cumin, Fennel, Regular), Quinoa)

Prana - Apple Pie, Apricot Goji, Apricot Pumpkin, Cashew Almond, Coconut Acai, Pear Ginseng

B

PURE Bar - Organic (Apple Cinnamon, Cherry Cashew, ChocChip Trailmix, Chocolate Brownie, Cranberry Orange, Wild Blueberry)

Ruth's Hemp Power -

Cranberry Trail HempPower

CranNut Flax Power

Ginger Almond MacaPower

Very Berry Flax Power

Vote Hemp Blueberry Bar

Shakti Bar - Organic Blueberry Chai

Taste Of Nature -

Exotics (Caribbean Ginger Island●, Chilean Blueberry Fields●, Himalayan Goji Summit●, Persian Pomegranate Garden●)

Regular (Argentina Peanut Plains●, Brazilian Nut Fiesta●, California Almond Valley●, Niagara Apple Country●, Quebec Cranberry Carnival●)

thinkFruit - Apple Noni Nourish, Cashew Acai Protect, Chocolate Pomegranate Power, Peanut Goji Glow

thinkGreen - Blueberry Noni

thinkOrganic Apricot Coconut, Cashew Pecan, Cherry Nut, Chocolate Coconut

Wegmans Brand - Fruit Flats (Cherry, Grape, Raspberry, Strawberry)

Basmati Rice... see Rice

Bean Dip... see Dip/Dip Mix

Beans... *All **Fresh** Fruits & Vegetables Are **Gluten/Casein Free***

Albertsons - Pork & Beans, Refried Beans (Fat Free, Regular, Spicy, Vegetarian)

Amy's - Light In Sodium (Black, Traditional), Organic Refried Beans (Black, Traditional, w/Green Chiles), Vegetarian Baked

Arrowhead Mills - Adzuki, Anasazi, Garbanzo (Chickpeas), Green Split Peas, Lentils (Green, Red), Pinto, Soybeans

B&M Baked Beans - Baked Beans w/(Bacon & Onion, BBQ Flavored, Country Style, Maple Flavor, Original, Vegetarian), Red Kidney

B **Birds Eye** - All Plain Frozen Vegetables

Bush's Best -

    Baked Beans (Bold & Spicy, Boston Recipe, Country Style, Homestyle w/Bacon & Brown Sugar, Honey, Maple Cured Bacon, Onion, Original, Vegetarian)

    Black

    Butter (Baby, Large, Speckled)

    Cannellini

    Garbanzo

    Great Northern

    Grillin' Beans (Bourbon & Brown Sugar, Smokehouse Tradition, Southern Pit Barbecue, Steakhouse Recipe)

    Kidney (Dark Red, Light Red)

    Microwaveable Cup Original

    Navy

    Pinto (Regular, w/Pork)

    Red

    Refried Beans Traditional

C & W - All Plain Frozen Vegetables

C R Darbell's - Pork & Beans

Cascadian Farms - Organic Frozen (Cut Green Beans, French Cut Green Beans w/Toasted Almonds, Petite Whole Green Beans)

Del Monte - All Plain Canned Beans

Eden -

    Organic (Aduki, Baked w/Sorghum & Mustard, Black, Black Eyed Peas, Black Soybeans, Butter, Cannellini, Caribbean Black, Garbanzo, Great Northern, Kidney, Navy, Pinto, Small Red)

    Organic Dried (Aduki, Black, Black Soybeans, Garbanzo, Green (Lentils, Split Peas), Kidney, Navy, Pinto, Small Red)

    Refried (Black, Blacksoy & Black, Kidney, Pinto, Spicy Black, Spicy Pinto)

    Rice & (Cajun Small Red, Caribbean Black, Garbanzo, Kidney, Lentils, Pinto)

beans

B

Fantastic World Foods - Hummus Original, Instant (Black, Refried)

Food Club Brand - Frozen (Baby Lima, Cut Green, French Style Green, Whole Green)

Freshlike - Frozen Plain Vegetables *(Except Pasta Combos & Seasoned Blends)*

Full Circle - Organic Frozen Cut Beans

Grand Selections - Fancy (Cut Green, Whole Green), Frozen Whole Green

Great Value Brand (Wal-Mart) - Dried Beans (Baby Lima, Black, Garbanzo, Great Northern, Large Lima, Light Red Kidney, Navy, Pinto, Small Red)

Green Giant -

Canned

Cut Green (50% Less Sodium, Regular)

French Style Green

Kitchen Sliced Green

Three Bean Salad

Frozen

Baby Lima

Cut Green

Green Beans & Almonds

Select w/No Sauce Whole Green

Simply Steam (Baby Lima No Sauce, Green Beans & Almonds)

Steamers (Cut Green)

Hannaford Brand - Black, Canned Great Northern, Cannellini, Cut Green, Cut Wax, Dark Red Kidney, French Green, Light Red Kidney, No Salt Cut, No Salt French, Pinto, Whole Green

Heinz - Vegetarian Beans

Home Harvest Brand - Canned Green (Cut, French Cut)

Hy-Vee -

Black (Refried, Regular)

Blue Lake (Cut Green, French Style Green, Whole Green)

B

Butter
Chili Style
Country Style Baked
Dark Red Kidney
Dried (Baby Lima, Large Lima, Lentils, Mixed Soup, Navy)
Fat Free Refried
Frozen (Cut Green, French Cut Green)
Garbanzo Beans Chick Peas
Great Northern (Dried, Regular)
Home Style Baked
Light Red Kidney
Maple Cured Bacon Baked
Onion Baked
Original Baked
Pinto (Dried, Regular)
Pork & Beans
Red (Dried, Kidney, Regular)
Spicy Refried
Steam In A Bag Frozen Beans
Traditional Refried
Vegetarian Refried

Joan Of Arc - Black, Butter, Dark Red Kidney, Garbanzo, Great Northern, Light Red Kidney, Pinto, Red

Kid's Kitchen - Beans & Wieners

Kroger Brand - All Plain Beans (Canned, Frozen)

Laura Lynn -
All Dried Beans
Canned (Kidney, Lima)
Cut Green
French Style Green
No Salt Cut Green

B

Lowes Foods Brand -
  Canned
    Black
    Cut Green No Salt
    French
    Garbanzo
    Great Northern
    Green (Cut, French Style, Whole)
    Lima
    Pinto
    Red Kidney Beans (Dark, Light)
    Whole Green
  Dry (Baby Lima, Black Eyed Peas, Great Northern, Lentil, Lima, Mixed, Navy, Pinto)
  Frozen
    Deluxe Whole Green
    Green (Cut, French Cut, Regular)
    Lima (Baby, Deluxe Tiny, Regular)
    Speckled Butter
Meijer Brand -
  Baked Beans Organic
  Canned Beans
    Black (Organic, Regular)
    Butter
    Garbanzo (Organic, Regular)
    Great Northern
    Lima
    Mexican Style
    Pinto (Organic, Regular)
    Red Kidney (Dark, Dark Organic, Light, Regular)

B

Refried (Fat Free, Regular, Vegetarian)

Refried Organic (Black Bean, Black Bean/Jalapeno, Roasted Chili/Lime, Traditional)

Wax Cut

Canned Green Beans Cut

   Blue Lake

   French Style (Blue Lake, No Salt, Organic, Veri Green)

   No Salt

   Organic

   Veri Green

Canned Green Beans Whole

Dry Beans

   Black

   Blackeye

   Great Northern

   Green Split Beans & Peas

   Lentil

   Lima Large

   Navy

   Pinto

   Red Kidney

Frozen Edamame (Soybeans)

Frozen Green Beans (Cut, French Cut, Italian Cut)

Frozen Lima Beans (Baby, Fordhook)

Pork & Beans

Midwest Country Fare - Chili Style, Cut Green, French Style Green, Pork & Beans

Nielsen-Massey - Whole Vanilla Beans●

O Organics - Canned (Cut Green, Pinto), Frozen Whole Green

Old El Paso - Refried Beans (Fat Free, Spicy Fat Free, Traditional, Vegetarian, w/Green Chiles)

B

Ortega - Refried (Fat Free, Regular)
Pictsweet - All Plain Frozen Beans
Publix -
  Canned
    Baked
    Black Beans (Frijoles Negros, In Seasoned Sauce)
    Garbanzo
    Great Northern
    Green (French Cut, French Style, Italian Cut, Lima, No Salt
      Added, Original, Veggi Green, Whole)
    Kidney (Dark, Light)
    Pinto
    Pork & Bean
  Dry
    Baby Lima
    Black
    Blackeye
    Garbanzo
    Great Northern
    Green Split Peas
    Large Lima
    Lentils
    Light Red Kidney
    Navy
    Pinto
    Small Red
  Frozen
    Butter
    Green (Cut, French Cut, Pole)
    Lima (Baby, Fordhook)

B

Publix GreenWise Market - Organic Canned (Black, Dark Red Kidney, Garbanzo, Green, Pinto, Soy)

S&W - All Plain Canned Beans

Safeway Brand -

Canned

Black (Eyed, Regular)

Chick

Dark Kidney

Green (Cut, Cut No Salt, French Style, Whole)

Light Kidney

Lima

Pinto

Pork & Beans

Dried

Baby Lima

Black (Eyed, Regular)

Great Northern

Green Split

Large Lima

Lentils

Light Red Kidney

Navy

Pink

Pinto

Small (Red, White)

Frozen (Baby Lima, Cut, Fordbook Lima, French Style, Whole)

Refried Beans (Fat Free, Traditional, Vegetarian)

Spartan Brand -

Canned

Baked (Regular, w/Bacon & Maple Flavor, w/Onions)

Black

B

Butter
Chilli Beans
Dark Red Kidney
Garbanzo
Great Northern
Green (Cut, French Cut French Style)
Homestyle Baked
Light Red Kidney
Lima
Pinto
Pork & Beans
Red
Refried (Fat Free, Regular)
Wax
Whole Green
Dried
  Black
  Black Eyed
  Great Northern
  Kidney
  Lentil
  Lima (Baby, Large)
  Navy
  Pinto
Frozen
  Baby Lima
  Cut Green
  French Cut Green
  Whole Green

B   **Stop & Shop Brand** -
   Baby Lima
   Beans
   Black
   Dark Red Kidney
   Fordhook Lima
   Garbanzo
   Green Beans (Cut, French, No Added Salt, Whole)
   Kidney Light
   Lima
   Organic Green
   Pinto
Thrifty Maid - Frozen Green Beans
Trader Joe's -
   Black
   Cuban Style Black
   Garbanzo
   Organic (Baked, Black, Garbanzo, Pinto)
   Red Kidney
   Refried Black w/Jalapeno Peppers
   French Green
Wegmans Brand -
   Baby Lima
   Baked Beans (Homestyle, Original, Vegetarian, w/Brown Sugar & Bacon)
   Black
   Butter
   Canned (Black, Chili Seasoned, Dark Red Kidney, Great Northern, Light Red Kidney, Pinto, Red)
   Cannellini Beans
   Cut Green Beans (No Salt, Regular)

B

Dark Kidney
French Style Green Beans (No Salt, Regular)
Garbanzo Beans Italian Classics
Great Northern
Green (Cut, French Style, Italian Cut, Regular, Whole)
Light Kidney
Lima
Pinto
Pork & Beans In Tomato Sauce
Seasoned Chili
Wax Cut
Winn Dixie -
　Canned
　　Baked
　　Baked w/Bacon & Onion
　　Black
　　Butter
　　Dark Red Kidney
　　Garbanzo
　　Green No Salt Added
　　Green Whole
　　Light Red Kidney
　　Mexican Style Chili
　　Navy
　　Pinto
　　Pork & Beans
　Dried
　　Baby Lima
　　Bean Soup Mix
　　Garbanzo

B

    Great Northern

    Large Lima

    Lentils

    Light Red Kidney

    Navy

    Pinto

Frozen Green Beans (Cut, Organic Cut, Whole)

Frozen Lima Beans (Baby, Fordhook, Petite, Speckled)

Refried Beans (Fat Free, Traditional)

Woodstock Farms - Dried Green Beans, Organic Frozen (Baby French Beans, Cut Green Beans, Lima)

Beef... *All **Fresh** Meat Is **Gluten/Casein Free** (Non-Marinated, Unseasoned)*

Applegate Farms -

    Natural (Beef Hot Dogs, Roast Beef)

    Organic (Frozen Beef Burger, Roast Beef)

Carl Buddig -

    Deli Thin Sliced (Beef, Corned Beef)

    Extra Thin Sliced (Beef, Corned Beef)

Garrett County Farms -

    Beef Franks (4XL Big, Old Fashioned, Premium)

    Corned Beef Brisket (Half, Whole)

Great Value Brand (Wal-Mart) - Frozen 100% Pure Beef Patties

Hillshire Farms - Deli Select Thin Sliced (Corned Beef, Roast Beef), Deli Select Ultra Thin Roast Beef

Homestyle Meals - Shredded Beef In BBQ Sauce

Hormel -

    Corned Beef

    Corned Beef Hash

    Deli Sliced Cooked Corned Beef

    Dried Beef

    Natural Choice Roast Beef

B

Hy-Vee - Quarter Pounders, Thin Sliced (Corned Beef, Regular)

Isaly's - Beef Deli Meat

John Soules Foods - Ready To Cook (Beef For Fajitas)

Lloyd's - Beef Ribs w/Original BBQ Sauce, Shredded Beef In Original BBQ Sauce

Meijer Brand - Ground Beef (Chuck Fine, Fine)

Organic Prairie -

> Fresh Organic
>> Ground Beef 1lb. (85% Lean, 90% Lean)
>> Sliced Roast Beef 6 oz.
> Frozen Organic
>> Beef Liver Steak 12 oz.
>> Ground Beef 12 oz.
>> Ground Beef Patties 10.6 oz.
>> Ribeye Steak 8 oz.
>> New York Strip Steak 8 oz.

Oscar Mayer - Shaved Deli Fresh (French Dip Roast Beef, Slow Roasted Roast Beef)

Primo Taglio - Cooked Corned Beef, Roast Beef (Caramel Color Added, Coated w/Seasonings)

Sol Cuisine - Biologique Ground Beef Alternative

Wellshire Farms - Roast Beef (Sliced Top Round, Whole)

Wellshire Organic - Organic Beef Franks

Winn Dixie - Corned Beef

Beef Jerky... see Jerky/Beef Sticks

Beef Sticks... see Jerky/Beef Sticks

Beer

> AMERICAN
>> **Anheuser-Busch** - Redbridge Beer
>> **Bard's Tale Beer** - Dragon's Gold Gluten Free Lager
>> **Lakefront Brewery** - New Grist Beer

B   Old Hat Brewery - Bees Knees
        Ramapo Valley Brewery - Passover Honey Lager

IMPORTED

Bi-Aglut - Special 76 Lager (Italy)

Brauerei Grieskirchen AG - Beer Up Glutenfrei Pale Ale (Austria)

Carlsberg Brewery - Saxon Premium Lager (Finland)

Fine Ale Club - Against The Grain (England)

Glutaner - Glutenfrei Pils (Belgium)

Green's - Discovery, Explorer, Herald, Pioneer, Trailblazer (England)

Hambleton Ales - GFA, GFL, Pale (England)

Koff - Lager, Taytelainen Kevytolut (Finland)

Laitilan - Kukko Pils III Lager, Kukko Tumma III Dark Lager
    (Finland)

Les Bieres de la Nouvelle France - La Messagere Pale Ale
    (Canada)

Liebhart's Privatbrauerai - Bio Reis Gold, Bio Reis Gold Dunkel
    (Germany)

O'Brien - Brown Ale, Pale Ale, Premium Lager (Australia)

Schnitzer Brau - Glutenfrei Bier (Germany)

Silly Yaks - Aztec Gold (Australia)

St. Peter's Brewery - G Free (England)

Beets... *All Fresh Fruits & Vegetables Are Gluten/Casein Free*

Del Monte - All Plain Canned Beets

Food Club Brand - Canned (Sliced, Whole)

Hannaford Brand - Cut, Sliced, Whole

Hy-Vee - Fancy (Diced, Sliced)

Laura Lynn - Cut, Sliced

Lowes Foods Brand - Cut, Whole

Meijer Brand - Harvard Sweet Sour, Sliced (No Salt, Pickled, Regular),
    Whole (Medium, Pickled)

Publix - Canned

B

S&W - Pickled

Safeway Brand - Canned (Sliced, Whole)

Spartan Brand - Diced, Sliced, Whole

Stop & Shop Brand - Sliced No Salt Added

Wegmans Brand - Harvard, Sliced (No Salt, Pickled, Regular), Whole (Pickled, Regular)

Berries... *All Fresh Fruits & Vegetables Are **Gluten/Casein Free***

Cascadian Farm - Organic Frozen Harvest Berries

Del Monte -

Canned/Jarred Fruit (All Varieties)

Fruit Snack Cups (Metal, Plastic)

Great Value Brand (Wal-Mart) - Frozen

Meijer Brand - Frozen Berry Medley, Frozen Triple Berry Blend

Publix - Frozen Mixed Berries

Spartan Brand - Frozen Berry Medley

Stop & Shop Brand - Frozen Berry Medley

Wegmans Brand - Berry Medley

Woodstock Farms - Organic Frozen Mixed Berries

Beverages... see Drinks/Juice

Biscotti

Ener-G▲ - Chocolate Chip

Foods By George▲ - Currants Nut & Seed

Orgran▲ - Amaretti, Classic Chocolate

Sorella▲ - Biscottines (Chocolate Almond, Chocolate Chip, Cinnamon Swirl, Hazelnut Anise, Vanilla)

Biscuits

1-2-3 Gluten Free▲ - Southern Glory Biscuits●

Bob's Red Mill▲ - Wheat Free Biscuit & Baking Mix

Cause You're Special▲ - Hearty Gluten Free Biscuit Mix

Mixes From The Heartland▲ - Biscuit Mix (Country●, Dilly●, Garlic●, Roasted Pepper●, Sun Dried Tomato●)

B   Namaste Foods▲ - Biscuits Piecrust & More Mix
     Really Great Food▲ - Biscuit Mix (Loaf, Old Time)
     Schar▲ - Cioccolini, Fior Di Sole, Frollini, Savoiardi

Bittermelon... *All **Fresh** Fruits & Vegetables Are **Gluten/Casein Free***

Black Eyed Peas... see Peas

Blackberries... *All **Fresh** Fruits & Vegetables Are **Gluten/Casein Free***
  Albertsons - All Plain Frozen Fruit
  Cascadian Farm - Organic Frozen
  Food Club Brand
  Great Value Brand (Wal-Mart) - Frozen
  Meijer Brand - Frozen
  Publix - Frozen
  Safeway Brand - Frozen
  Spartan Brand - Frozen
  Stop & Shop Brand - Frozen
  Trader Joe's - Plain Frozen
  Wegmans Brand
  Winn Dixie - Frozen
  Woodstock Farms - Organic Frozen

Blueberries... *All **Fresh** Fruits & Vegetables Are **Gluten/Casein Free***
  Albertsons - All Frozen Fruit
  Cascadian Farm - Organic Frozen
  Food Club Brand - Frozen
  Full Circle - Organic Blueberries
  Great Value Brand (Wal-Mart) - Frozen
  Hy-Vee - Frozen
  Kroger Brand - Plain Frozen Fruit
  Meijer Brand - Frozen (Organic, Regular)
  Publix - Frozen
  Safeway Brand - Frozen
  Spartan Brand - Frozen

bouillon/bouillon cubes

B

Trader Joe's - Plain Frozen

Wegmans Brand

Winn Dixie - Frozen

Woodstock Farms - Organic Frozen Wild

Bok Choy... *All Fresh Fruits & Vegetables Are **Gluten/Casein Free***

Bologna

Applegate Farms - Turkey Bologna

Honeysuckle White - Turkey

Hy-Vee - Garlic, German Brand, Regular, Thick, Thin

Midwest Country Fare - Sliced, Thick Sliced

Publix - Deli Pre Pack Sliced Lunch Meat (Beef Bologna, German Bologna)

Shelton's - Uncured Turkey

Wellshire Farms - Sliced Beef Bologna

Bouillon/Bouillon Cubes

Better Than Bouillon - Base (Chili, Ham, Vegetable), Organic (Beef, Chicken, Vegetable), Reduced Sodium Chicken, Vegan No (Beef, Chicken)

Cellfibr Bouillon Cubes (Vegetable Medley, Vegetarian Beef, Vegetarian Chicken), Bouillon Soup Base (French Onion Vegetable Medley, Vegetarian Beef, Vegetarian Chicken)

Edward & Sons - Garden Veggie, Low Sodium Veggie, Not Beef, Not Chick'n

Harvest Sun - Organic Bouillon Cubes (All Flavors)

Herb-Ox - Low Sodium (Beef, Chicken)

Hy-Vee - Bouillon Cubes (Beef, Chicken), Instant Bouillon (Beef, Chicken)

Lee Kum Kee - Chicken Bouillon Powder

Marigold - Swiss Vegetable, Vegan Reduced Salt

Massel - Ultracubes (Beef, Chicken, Vegetable)

Spartan Brand - Soup Beef Bouillon (Cube, Granular), Soup Chicken Bouillon (Cube, Granular)

Winn Dixie - Beef Bouillon Cubes

B Bourbon... *All **Distilled** Alcohol Is **Gluten/Casein Free** [2]*

Bowls

Amy's -

Baked Ziti Bowl

Brown Rice & Vegetable Bowl (Light In Sodium, Regular)

Brown Rice w/Black Eyed Peas & Veggies Bowl

Cream Of Rice Hot Cereal

Teriyaki Bowl

Chi-Chi's - Fiesta Plates Salsa Chicken

Lundberg▲ - Organic Brown Rice Bowls (Country Wild, Long Grain, Short Grain)

Thai Kitchen - Rice Noodle Soup Bowls (Lemongrass & Chili, Mushroom, Roasted Garlic, Spring Onion)

Bratwurst... see Sausage

Bread... (includes Rolls)

Andrea's Fine Foods▲ - Loaf (Casein Free Sandwich), Dairy Free Dinner Rolls

Apple's Bakery▲ - Loaf (Olive Oil)

Aunt Gussie's▲ - Kalamata Garlic Bread, Rosemary Focaccia

Celiac Specialties▲ -

Bread (Cinnamon Raisin, Flat, Flaxseed, Multigrain, Multigrain Flat, Navy Bean, Light White, White)

Buns (Hamburger, Hot Dog, Sub)

Cybros Inc. - 100% Rice Bread & Rolls & Nuggets, Mock Rye & Rolls, Rice & Raisin, Tapioca Almond

El Peto▲ -

Bread

Brown Rice

Flax Seed Loaf

Millet

Multi Grain

Potato

B

      Raisin
      Tapioca
      White Rice
   Rolls
      Brown
      Multi Grain
      White

Ener-G▲ -
   Sliced Breads
      Brown Rice
      Cinnamon Rolls
      Corn
      Egg Free Raisin
      Four Flour
      Hi Fiber
      Light (Brown Rice, Tapioca, White Rice, White Rice Flax)
      Papas
      Raisin Loaf w/Eggs
      Rice Starch
      Seattle Brown
      Tapioca Loaf (Dinner Rolls, Regular Sliced, Thin Sliced)
      White (Regular, Rice Flax)
      Yeast Free (Brown Rice, Sweet, White Rice)
   Specialty Breads
      Bread Crumbs
      Broken Melba Toast
      Communion Wafers
      Plain Croutons

Food For Life -
   Almond Rice
   Bhutanese Red Rice

B

Brown Rice

Multi Seed Rice

Raisin Pecan

Rice Pecan

White Rice

French Meadow Bakery - Gluten Free (Cinnamon Raisin Bread●, Italian Rolls●, Sandwich Bread●)

Gillian's Foods▲ - Caramelized Onion Rolls, Cinnamon Raisin (Loaf, Rolls), Crostini, English Muffins, Everything Dinner Rolls, French (Bread, Rolls), Garlic Bread, Poppyseed Rolls, Rye No Rye Loaf, Sandwich Loaf, Sesame Seed Rolls, Sundried Tomato & Roasted Garlic Loaf

Glutano▲ - Multi Grain, Three Grain, White

Gluten Free Life▲ - Country Brown Pure, Multi Grain Pure, Pumpernickel

Gluten-Free Creations▲ - Almond Flax●, Herb Baguettes●, Herb Loaf Bread●, Herb Rolls●, Honey Oat●, Hot Dog Buns●, Rye Bread w/Caraway Seeds●, Seeded Multigrain●, White●, Whole Grain●, Wild Rice●

Glutino▲ -

Premium

Cinnamon & Raisin Bread

Corn Bread

Fiber Bread

Flax Seed Bread

Good Juju Bakery▲ -

Dinner Rolls

Exceptional English Muffins

Katz Gluten Free▲ -

Bread (Sliced Challah, White, Whole Grain)

Chocolate (Rugelech, Strip)

Cinnamon (Rugelech, Strip)

Farfel

Honey Loaf

Kiska Kugel

Marble Cake

Rolls (Large Callah, Sandwich, Small Challah)

Kinnikinnick▲ -

Brown Sandwich

Candida Yeast Free Multigrain Rice

Festive

Many Wonder Multigrain Rice

Robins Honey Brown Rice

Sunflower Flax Rice

Tapioca Rice (Italian, Raisin, Regular, Yeast Free)

Tru Fibre Multigrain Rice

White Sandwich

Namaste Foods▲ - Bread Mix

Nu-World Foods - Flatbread Amaranth (Buckwheat●, Garbanzo●, Sorghum●)

O'Doughs▲ - Buns (Breakfast, Flax, White), Loaf (Flax, Flax Half, White, White Half)

Orgran▲ - Crisp Bites (Balsamic Herb, Corn, Onion & Chives), Crisp Bread (Corn, Rice, Rice & Cracked Pepper, Rice & Garden Herb, Salsa)

Rose's Bakery▲ -

French (Bread●, Rolls●)

Millet●

Sandwich●

Seeded Sandwich●

Teff●

Schar▲ - Bread (Classic White, Multi Grain), Rolls (Classic White)

Bread Mix... (includes Baking Mix, Roll Mix)

1-2-3 Gluten Free▲ - Aaron's Favorite Rolls●

Arrowhead Mills - All Purpose Baking Mix

B

Authentic Foods▲ -

Cinnamon Bread Mix

Wholesome Bread Mix

Bob's Red Mill▲ - Bread Mix (Cinnamon Raisin, Hearty Whole Grain, Homemade Wonderful)

Breads From Anna▲ - Bread Mix (All Purpose, Banana, Classic Herb, Original Dairy Free, Pumpkin)

Cause You're Special▲ - Bread Mix (Homestyle White, Traditional French)

Chebe▲ -

Bread Mix (All Purpose, Cinnamon Rolls, Focaccia Italian Flatbread, Pizza Crust)

Garlic Onion Breadsticks Mix

El Peto▲ - Bread Mix (Brown, Potato, White)

Ener-G▲ - Mix (Corn, Potato, Rice)

Fearn - Baking Mix (Brown Rice, Rice)

Gifts Of Nature▲ -

Basic/Muffin/Quick Bread Mix●

French Bread/Pizza Crust Mix●

Sandwich White Bread & Roll Mix●

Gillian's Foods▲ - All Purpose Baking Mix, French Bread Mix

Gluten-Free Creations▲ - Break Mix (Almond Flax●, Cinnamon Raisin●, Honey Oat●, Seeded Multigrain●)

Gluten-Free Essentials▲ - All Purpose Baking Mix●, Holiday Gingerbread●, Lemon Poppy Seed●, Multi Grain (Cinnamon Spice●, Meatloaf Starter●, Original●, Zesty Italian●)

Gluten-Free Pantry▲ - French Bread & Pizza Mix, Toms Light Gluten Free Bread, Whole Grain Bread Mix, Yankee Cornbread Mix

Hodgson Mill▲ - Gluten Free Bread Mix, Multi Purpose Baking Mix

Kinnikinnick▲ -

All Purpose Mix

Candida Yeast Free Rice

Cornbread & Muffin Mix

B

    Kinni Kwik Bread & Bun Mix

    Kinni Kwik Sunflower Flax Bread & Bun Mix

    Tapioca Rice

    White Rice

Mixes From The Heartland▲ - Bread Machine Mix (Garden Veggie●, Garlic Roasted Pepper●, Plain●), Corn Bread Mix●, Sweet Bread Mix (Banana●, Blueberry●, Cranberry●, Zuchini●)

Namaste Foods▲ - Bread Mix

Orgran▲ - Bread Mix (Alternative Grain Wholemeal, Easy Bake)

Pamela's Products▲ - Amazing Bread Mix

Really Great Food▲ - Bread Mix (Brown Rice, Dark European, French/Country Farm, Home Style Cornbread, Irish Soda, Old Fashioned Cinnamon, Original White, Rye Style)

Schar▲ - Classic White Bread Mix

Simply Organic - Banana●, Chai Spice Scone Mix●

Sylvan Border Farm - Bread Mix (Non Dairy)

Breadcrumbs... see Coating

Breadsticks

    Chebe▲ - Garlic & Onion Breadsticks Mix

    Glutino▲ -

        Pizza Breadsticks

        Sesame Breadsticks

    Schar▲ - Italian Breadsticks

Breakfast

    Amy's - Tofu Scramble

    Dietz & Watson - Breakfast Ham Slices w/Water Added

    Honeysuckle White - Breakfast Turkey Sausage (Links, Patties)

    Ian's -

        Wheat Free Gluten Free Recipe French Toast Sticks

        Wheat Free Gluten Free Wafflewiches Maple Sausage & Egg

B **Jennie-O Turkey Store** - Fresh Breakfast Sausage (Mild Links, Mild Patties)

Jimmy Dean -
Breakfast Skillets
Bacon
Ham
Sausage
Smoked Sausage
Heat N' Serve Sausage Links (Hot, Maple, Regular)
Heat N' Serve Sausage Patties

Johnsonville -
Original Breakfast (Links, Patties)
Vermont Maple Syrup (Links, Patties)

Jones Dairy Farm -
All Natural
Hearty Pork Sausage Links●
Light Pork Sausage and Rice Links●
Little Link Pork Sausage●
Maple Sausage Patties●
Original Pork Roll Sausage●
Pork Sausage Patties●
All Natural Golden Brown Cooked & Browned Sausage Patties (Maple Fully●, Mild Fully●)
All Natural Golden Brown Fully Cooked & Browned Turkey●
All Natural Golden Brown Light Fully Cooked & Browned Sausage & Rice Links●
All Natural Golden Fully Cooked & Browned Sausage Links (Made From Beef●, Maple●, Mild●, Spicy●)

Only Oats - Breakfast Blend (Apple & Cinnamon●, Maple & Roasted Flax●)

Sunshine Burger - Organic Breakfast Patty

Van's - Wheat Free French Toast Sticks

B

Broccoli... *All Fresh Fruits & Vegetables Are Gluten/Casein Free*

Albertsons - Canned & Frozen

Birds Eye - All Plain Frozen Vegetables

C & W - All Plain Frozen Vegetables

Cascadian Farm -

Organic Frozen (Broccoli Cuts, Broccoli Florets)

Purely Steam Organic Frozen Broccoli & Carrots

Food Club Brand - Frozen (Chopped, Cut)

Freshlike - All Plain Frozen Vegetables *(Except Pasta Combos & Seasoned Blends)*

Green Giant - Frozen Chopped

Home Harvest Brand - Cuts

Hy-Vee - Frozen (Chopped, Cuts, Florets)

Kroger Brand - All Plain Vegetables (Canned, Frozen)

Lowes Foods Brand - Frozen (Chopped, Cuts, Deluxe Baby Florets, Deluxe Florets, Spears)

Meijer Brand - Frozen (Chopped, Cuts, Spears)

Midwest Country Fare - Frozen (Chopped, Cuts)

Nature's Promise - Organic Broccoli Mini Spears

Pictsweet - All Plain Frozen Vegetables

Publix - Frozen (Chopped, Cuts, Florets, Spears)

Safeway Brand - Frozen (Cuts, Florets, Stem In Bag)

Spartan Brand - Cuts, Florets

Stop & Shop Brand - Broccoli (Chopped, Cuts, Spears), Broccoli & Cauliflower

Trader Joe's - All Plain Frozen Vegetables

Wegmans Brand - Broccoli (Chopped, Cuts), Broccoli Cuts & Cauliflower Florets, Spears

Winn Dixie - Frozen (Chopped, Cuts, Florets, Spears), Steamable Broccoli Cut

Woodstock Farms - Organic Frozen Broccoli Florets

B Broth

Baxters - Chicken

College Inn - Garden Vegetable, White Wine & Herb Culinary Chicken

El Peto▲ - Broth Concentrate (Beef, Chicken)

Health Valley -

Fat Free (Beef Flavored (No Salt Added, Regular), Chicken, Vegetable)

Low Fat Chicken (No Salt Added, Regular)

Imagine - Organic Beef (Low Sodium, Regular), Organic Free Range Chicken (Low Sodium, Regular), Organic No Chicken, Organic Vegetable (Low Sodium, Regular)

Lipton - Recipe Secrets Onion Soup & Dip Mix

Meijer Brand -

Naturals Broth

Carton (Beef, Chicken, Vegetable)

Concentrate (Beef, Chicken, Turkey)

Midwest Country Fare - Chicken

Pacific Natural Foods - Beef Broth, Free Range Chicken, Organic (Beef, Free Range Chicken, Low Sodium Chicken, Low Sodium Vegetable, Mushroom, Vegetable Broth)

Safeway Brand - Beef, Chicken (99% Fat Free, Fat Free Reduced Sodium, Regular)

Shelton's -

Chicken (Fat Free Low Sodium, Regular)

Organic (Chicken, Chicken Fat Free Low Sodium)

Spartan Brand - Beef, Chicken

Swanson -

Chicken Broth (Canned, Carton)

Natural Goodness Chicken Broth (Canned, Carton)

Vegetarian Broth (Canned)

Trader Joe's - Organic (Hearty Vegetable)

brownies/brownie mix

Winn Dixie -

B

Resealable Boxes

Chicken (Fat Free, Organic Fat Free, Reduced Sodium, Regular)

Fat Free Beef

Vegetable (Organic Fat Free)

Brown Sugar... see Sugar

Brownies/Brownie Mix

1-2-3 Gluten Free▲ - Devilishly Decadent Brownies●, Divinely Decadent Brownies●

Arrowhead Mills - Gluten Free Brownie Mix

Betty Crocker▲ - Gluten Free Chocolate Brownie Mix

Bob's Red Mill▲ - Gluten Free Brownie Mix

Celiac Specialties▲ - Gluten Free Brownie (Round, Tray)

Cherrybrook Kitchen - Gluten Free Fudge Brownie Mix *(Box Must Say Gluten-Free)*

Crave Bakery▲ - Brownies (Dark Chocolate, Toasted Pecan)

El Peto▲ - Brownie Mix

Ener-G▲ - Brownies

Foods By George▲ - Brownies

Frankly Natural Bakers - Carob Almondine, Cherry Berry, Java Jive, Misty Mint, Wacky Walnut

French Meadow Bakery - Gluten Free (Frozen Fudge Brownies●, Fudge Brownie Bites●, Fudge Brownies●)

Gillian's Foods▲ - Brownie Mix, Brownies

Gluten Free Life▲ - The Ultimate Gluten Free Cake Muffin & Brownie Mix

Gluten-Free Creations▲ - Rich Brownie Mix●

Gluten-Free Essentials▲ - Brownie Mix (Chocolate Mint Fudge●, Decadent Chocolate Fudge●, Speedy Bake Fudge●

Hol Grain - Chocolate Brownie Mix

Kinnikinnick▲ - JB Brownie Squares

B Mixes From The Heartland▲ - Sweet Potato Brownie Mix●

Namaste Foods▲ - Brownie Mix

Really Great Food▲ - Aunt Tootsie's Brownie Mix

Rose's Bakery▲ - Chocolate Brownies●

The Cravings Place▲ - Ooey Gooey Chocolatey Chewy Brownie Mix

Bruschetta

Classico - Basil & Tomato, Extra Garlic

Santa Barbara

Tassos - Mediterranean

Brussel Sprouts... *All Fresh Fruits & Vegetables Are Gluten/Casein Free*

Birds Eye - All Plain Frozen Vegetables

C & W - All Plain Frozen Vegetables

Food Club Brand - Frozen

Hy-Vee - Frozen

Lowes Brands Foods - Frozen (Deluxe Baby, Regular)

Meijer Brand - Frozen

Midwest Country Fare - Frozen

Pictsweet - All Plain Frozen Vegetables

Publix - Frozen

Stop & Shop Brand

Spartan Brand - Frozen

Trader Joe's - All Plain Frozen Vegetables

Wegmans Brand - Frozen

Winn Dixie - Frozen

Buckwheat

Arrowhead Mills

Bob's Red Mill▲ - Organic Buckwheat (Groats, Kasha)

Buckwheat Bread... see Bread

Buckwheat Groats

Arrowhead Mills

Bob's Red Mill▲ - Organic Buckwheat Groats

B

Buffalo Wings... see Wings

Buns

   Celiac Specialties▲ - Buns (Hamburger, Hot Dog, Sub)

   Cybro's - Gluten Free Rice Rolls

   El Peto▲ -

   Hamburger Buns (Brown Rice, Millet, Multigrain, Potato, Tapioca, White)

   Hot Dog Buns (Millet, Potato, White Rice)

   Ener-G▲ -

   Hamburger Buns (Brown Rice, Seattle Brown, Tapioca, White Rice)

   Hot Dog Buns (Seattle Brown, Tapioca)

   Gluten-Free Creations▲ - Hamburger Buns (Regular●, White●), Hot Dog Buns●

   Kinnikinnick▲ -

   Tapioca Rice Buns

      Cinnamon

      Hamburger Buns

      Hot Cross

      Hot Dog, Multigrain Seed & Fibre

      Tray

   Quejos - Buns (Dairy Free Quejos, Soya Quejos)

   Schar▲ - Classic White Rolls

Burgers... *All Fresh Ground Meat Is Gluten/Casein Free (Non-Marinated, Unseasoned)*

   Amy's - Bistro Burger

   Applegate Farms - Organic (Beef, Turkey)

   Butterball - Turkey Burgers (All Natural, Seasoned)

   Great Value Brand (Wal-Mart) - 100% Frozen Beef Patties

   Henry & Lisa's - White Alaskan Salmon Gluten Free Burgers

   Honeysuckle White - Fresh Ground Turkey Patties, Frozen Turkey Burgers

B   **Jennie-O Turkey Store** - Fresh Lean Turkey Burger Patties (Regular, Seasoned), Frozen All Natural Turkey Burgers

Organic Prairie - Frozen Organic Ground Beef Patties 10.6 oz.

Shelton's - Turkey

Sol Cuisine - Organic Falafel Burger, Original Burger, Spicy Bean Burger, Vegetable Burger

Sunshine Burgers - Organic (Barbecue, Breakfast, Falafel, Garden Herb, Original, South West)

Wellshire Farms - All Natural Frozen (Beef Hamburgers, Turkey Burgers)

Wild Wood Organics - Tofu Veggie Burgers (Original, Shiitake, Southwest)

Winn Dixie - Frozen Angus Beef Patties (Original, w/Grill Seasoning, w/Sweet Onion)

Burrito Seasoning Mix

Old El Paso

Burritos

Glutenfreeda▲ - Vegetarian & Dairy Free

Butter... see also Spread

Earth Balance -

Natural Buttery Spread

Olive Oil

Original

Soy Free

Soy Garden

Natural Shortening

Organic Buttery Spread (Original Whipped)

Vegan Buttery Sticks

Eden Organic - Apple, Apple Cherry, Montmorency Tart Cherry

Ian's - Soy Butter 4 ME

Manischewitz - Apple Butter

Natucol - Natural Buttery Spread

Odell's - Clarified Butter, Popcorn Butter, Seafood Butter
Purity Farms - Organic Ghee (Clarified Butter)
Smart Balance - Organic
Spectrum - Essential Omega 3 Naturals

B
C

C

Cabbage... *All **Fresh** Fruits & Vegetables Are **Gluten/Casein Free***

Cake/Cake Mix

1-2-3 Gluten Free▲ - Delightfully Gratifying Bundt Poundcake●, Peri's Perfect Chocolate Bundt Poundcake●, Yummy Yellow Cake Mix●

Authentic Foods▲ - Cake Mix (Chocolate, Devil's Food Chocolate, Lemon, Vanilla)

Betty Crocker▲ - Gluten Free Cake Mix (Devil's Food, Yellow)

Bob's Red Mill▲ - Chocolate Cake Mix

Cause You're Special▲ - Golden Pound, Moist (Lemon, Yellow), Rich Chocolate

Celiac Specialties▲ - Angel Food Cake

Cherrybrook Kitchen - Gluten Free Chocolate Cake Mix *(Box Must Say Gluten-Free)*

Crave Bakery▲ - Chocolate Cupcake, Mama Z's Chocolate Cake

Ener-G▲ - Poundcake

Food-Tek Fast & Fresh - Cake Mix Dairy Free Minute (Chocolate, Cinnamon Coffee, White Cake, Yellow Cake)

Gifts Of Nature▲ - Yellow Cake Mix●

Glutino▲ - Cake Mix (Chocolate, White)

Gluten Free Life▲ - The Ultimate Gluten Free Cake Muffin & Brownie Mix

Gluten-Free Creations▲ - Yellow Cake●, Yellow Cupcakes●, Winkies●

C

Gluten-Free Essentials▲ -

Mix (Extreme Chocolate Cake●, Holiday Gingerbread●, Spice Cake & Muffin●, Yellow Velvet Cake●)

Speedy Bake Mix (Chocolate Mud●, Spice Is Nice●, Yella Vanilla●)

Gluten-Free Pantry▲ -

Chocolate Chip Cookie & Cake Mix

Coffee Cake Mix

Decadent Chocolate Cake Mix

Old Fashioned Cake & Cookie Mix

Spice Cake & Gingerbread Mix

Hodgson Mill▲ - Gluten Free Chocolate Cake Mix, Gluten Free Yellow Cake Mix, Multi Purpose Baking Mix

Jo-Sef▲ - Brownie Roll●, Jelly Roll●

Katz Gluten Free▲ -

Cup Cakes (Chocolate, Vanilla)

Kinnikinnick▲ - Angel Food, Chocolate, Fruit, Sponge, White

Laurel's Sweet Treats▲ - Cake Mix (Cinnamon Spice, Morris Chocolate, Vanilla)

Madwoman Foods▲ - Tea Cakes (Banana Chocolate, Banana Cinnamon, Blueberry Chocolate Cherry, Cocoa Mocha, Lemon Blueberry, Lemon Poppyseed, Orange Chocolate, Orange Cranberry, Pecan Cocoa Mocha)

Maggie's Gluten Free Goodies▲ - Scrumptious Chocolate Cake Mix

Mixes From The Heartland▲ - Cake Mix (Chocolate Angel Food●, Chocolate Poundcake●, Cinnamon Orange●, Lime Poundcake●, Raspberry Poundcake●, Strawberry Angel Food●, Strawberry Poundcake●, Upside Down●, Vanilla Angel Food●, Vanilla Poundcake●)

Namaste Foods▲ - Cake Mix (Chocolate, Spice, Vanilla)

O'Doughs▲ - Cake (Banana, Carrot, Chocolate)

Orgran▲ - Cake Mix (Chocolate, Vanilla)

Pamela's Products▲ - Cake Mix (Chocolate, Classic Vanilla)

Really Great Food▲

Cake Mix

Angel Food

Banana Bread

Chocolate (Cupcake, Regular)

Colonial Spice

Devil's Food

Gingerbread

Golden

Grandma's Pound

Lemon Poppy

Orange

Pineapple

Pumpkin (Bread, Spice)

White

Yellow

Ruby Range - Gluten Free Baking Mix (Chocolate Truffle Cake & Cupcakes●, Spice Cake & Cupcakes●)

Simply Organic -

Banana Bread Mix●

Carrot Cake Mix●

Cocoa Cayenne Mix●

Honeypot Ginger●

Sof'ella▲ - Gluten Free Chocolate Cake Mix & Frosting Mix●

Sylvan Border Farm - Cake Mix (Chocolate, Lemon)

The Cravings Place▲ - Cinnamon Crumble Coffeecake Mix, Dutch Chocolate Cake Mix, Raisin Spice Cookie & Cake Mix

Calamari... *All Fresh Seafood Is Gluten/Casein Free*

Candy/Candy Bars

Altoids - Large Tins (Peppermint, Wintergreen)

Amanda's Own - All Varieties

C

C **Candy Tree** -
   Licorice
      Black Licorice (Bites, Laces, Vines)
      Cherry (Bites, Laces, Vines)
      Raspberry (Bites, Laces, Vines)
      Strawberry (Bites, Laces, Vines)
   Lollipops
      Cherry
      Lemon
      Orange
      Raspberry
      Strawberry
Cherry Mash - Cherry Flavored Candy Bar
Cry Baby - Candy, Gumballs, Twist Gum
Dots -
   Crows
   Fruit Flavors
   Regular
   Tropical
Fluff Stuff - Cotton Candy, Tear Jerkers
Gimbal's Fine Candies▲ - All Varieties
Great Value Brand (Wal-Mart) -
   Butterscotch Discs
   Cinnamon Discs
   Fruit Slices
   Gummy (Bears, Worms)
   Orange Slices
   Peppermints Starlight Mints
   Spearmint Starlight Mints
   Spice Drops

C

Hannaford Brand - Butterscotch, Canada Mints, Candy Corn, Canola Wintergreen, Circus Peanuts, Gummy Bears, Gummy Worms, Jelly Beans, Jumbo Gum Drops, Licorice Bears, Orange Slices, Peppermint Starlites, Red Fish, Soft Peppermint, Sour Neon Crawlers, Spearmint Leaves, Spice Drops, Sugar Free (Cinnamon Buttons, Peppermint Starlights, Rootbeer Barrels)

Haribo -

Alphabet Letters

Centipedes

Clown Fish

Fizzy Cola

Frogs

Fruit Salad

Gold Bears

Gummi Apples

Happy Cola

Mini Rainbow Frogs

Peaches

Pink Grapefruit

Raspberries

Rattle Snakes

Sour Cherries

Strawberries Regular

Super Cola

Techno Bears

Twin Cherries

Hershey's -

Jolly Ranchers (Gummies, Hard Candy)

Hy-Vee -

Assorted Gum Balls

Butterscotch Buttons

Cinnamon Imperials

C

Circus Peanuts
Dubble Bubble Gum
Dum Dum Suckers
Gummi (Bears, Peach Rings, Worms)
Lemon Drops
Orange Slices
Smarties
Spice Drops
Starlight Mints
Wax Bottles

Jelly Belly - Jelly Beans (All Varieties)
Let's Do...Organic - All Gummi Bears
Lifesavers - Original
Maple Grove Farms Of Vermont - Blended Maple, Pure Maple
Mars -

Skittles (All Varieties)
Starburst (All Varieties)

Nestle - Spree
Nik-L-Nip - Wax Bottles
Orgran▲ - Molasses Licorice
Publix -

Candy Corn
Circus Peanuts
Fruit Slices
Gummi (Bears, Worms)
Jelly Beans
Orange Slices
Pastel Mints
Smarties Candy
Spearmint Starlight Mints

C

    Spice Drops

    Starlight Mints Candy

    Sweet Stripes

Razzles - Gum (Regular, Sour, Tropical)

Safeway Brand - Candy Corn, Dessert Mints, Gummi Bears, Gummi Lemon Drops, Orange Slices, Spice Drops, Regular Worms, Star Light Mints

Sharkies▲ - Energy Sports Chews (Berry Blast, Citrus Squeeze, Fruit Splash, Peach Tea Breeze, Watermelon Scream)

Skittles - All Varieties

Sour Patch Kids - All Varieties

Spangler - Candy Canes, Dum Dum Pops

St. Claire's Organics - All Candy, Mints, Sour Tarts

Starburst - All Varieties

Swedish Fish

The Ginger People - Ginger Chews

Trader Joe's -

    Black Licorice Scottie Dogs

    Brown Rice Marshmallow Treats

    Organic Pops

Wack-O-Wax - Wax Fangs, Wax Lips

Winn Dixie -

    Butterscotch Buttons

    Candy Corn

    Circus Peanuts

    Gummi (Bears, Worms)

    Jelly Beans

    Orange Slices

    Peach Rings

    Sour Worms

    Spice Drops

    Starlight Mints

C

Wonka -
  Bottlecaps
  Gobstoppers (Original)
  Laffy Taffy
  Nerds (Regular)
  Lik M Aid Fun Dip
  Mix Ups
  Pixy Stix
  Runts (Original)
  Sweet Tarts
Woodstock Farms -
  Vegetarian
    Jelly Pebbles
    Gummy Cubs
Canned Chicken
  Hormel - Chunk Meats (Breast Of Chicken)
  Meijer Brand - Chicken Chunk White
  Member's Mark - Premium Chunk
  Sweet Sue - Boned Chicken Breast
  Winn Dixie - Chicken Breast In Water
Canned Ham
  Black Label - Canned Hams
  Hormel - Chunk Ham Meat
  SPAM -
    Classic
    Less Sodium
    Lite
    Oven Roasted Turkey
    Smoke Flavored
  Underwood - Deviled Ham

Canned Salmon... see Salmon

Canned Tuna... see Tuna

Canned Turkey

   Hormel - Chunk Turkey Meat

   SPAM - Oven Roasted Turkey

Canola Oil... see Oil

Capers

   B&G - Spanish Style Capote

   Wegmans Brand - Italian Classics (Capote, Nonpareil)

Cappuccino... see Coffee

Carbonated Beverages... see Soda Pop/Carbonated Beverages

Carrots... *All **Fresh** Fruits & Vegetables Are **Gluten/Casein Free***

   Albertsons - Canned, Frozen

   Birds Eye - All Plain Frozen Vegetables

   C & W - All Plain Frozen Vegetables

   Del Monte - All Plain Frozen Vegetables

   Food Club Brand - Canned Sliced, Crinkle Cut, Whole Baby

   Freshlike - All Frozen Plain Carrots *(Except Pasta Combos & Seasoned Blends)*

   Grand Selections - Frozen Whole Carrots

   Great Value Brand (Wal-Mart) - Canned Sliced Carrots

   Hannaford Brand - Sliced, Whole Baby

   Hy-Vee - California, Classic Cut & Peeled Baby, Frozen Crinkle Cut, Sliced

   Kroger Brand - All Plain Vegetables (Canned, Frozen)

   Laura Lynn - Sliced Carrots, Whole Baby Carrots

   Lowes Foods Brand - Deluxe Whole Baby, Peas & Carrots, Sliced

   Meijer Brand - Canned Sliced (No Salt, Regular), Frozen Carrots (Crinkle Cut, Whole Baby)

   Midwest Country Fare - Sliced Carrots

C

Pictsweet - All Plain Frozen Carrots

Publix - Canned Carrots, Frozen (Crinkle Cut, Peas & Carrots, Whole Baby)

Publix GreenWise Market - Organic (Baby, Carrots, Chips, Juicing, Shreds, Snack)

S&W - All Plain Canned Carrots

Safeway Brand - Sliced

Spartan Brand - Canned (Peas & Sliced Carrots, Sliced), Frozen (Crinkle Cut, Peas & Carrots, Whole Baby)

Stop & Shop Brand - Carrots

Trader Joe's - All Plain Frozen Carrots

Wegmans Brand - Baby Cut, Carrots/Potatoes/Celery & Onions, Crinkle Cut, Organic, Sliced Carrots (No Salt Added, Regular), Whole Style

Winn Dixie - Frozen (Crinkle Cut, Whole Baby)

Cashews... see Nuts

Cauliflower... *All Fresh Fruits & Vegetables Are Gluten/Casein Free*

Albertsons - Canned & Frozen

Birds Eye - All Plain Frozen Vegetables

C & W - All Plain Frozen Vegetables

Freshlike - Frozen Plain Vegetables *(Except Pasta Combos & Seasoned Blends)*

Hy-Vee - Frozen Cauliflower Florets

Kroger Brand - All Plain Vegetables (Canned, Frozen)

Lowes Foods Brand - Frozen Cauliflower

Meijer Brand - Frozen Cauliflower Florets

Midwest Country Fare - Frozen Cauliflower

Pictsweet - All Plain Frozen Vegetables

Publix - Frozen

Safeway Brand - Frozen

Spartan Brand - Frozen Florets

Trader Joe's - All Plain Frozen Vegetables

Wegmans Brand - Florets

Winn Dixie - Frozen

Caviar

Romanoff - Black Lumpfish, Black Whitefish, Red Lumpfish, Red Salmon

Celery... *All Fresh Fruits & Vegetables Are Gluten/Casein Free*

Celery Salt... see Seasonings

Cereal

Amy's - Cream Of Rice Hot Cereal Bowl

Ancient Harvest Quinoa - Quinoa Flakes

B & G - Cream Of Rice Hot Cereal

Bakery On Main - Gluten Free Granola (Apple Raisin Walnut, Cranberry Orange Cashew, Extreme Fruit & Nut, Nutty Maple Cranberry, Rainforest)

Barbara's Bakery - Honey Rice Puffins, Multigrain Puffins, Organic Brown Rice Crisps, Organic Corn Flakes

Bob's Red Mill▲ - Creamy Rice Hot Cereal (Organic, Regular), Flaxseed Meal, Gluten Free Mighty Tasty Hot, Organic Creamy Buckwheat

Earth's Best Organic Baby Food - Whole Grain Rice Cereal

Eat Natural - For Breakfast (Gluten Free Toasted Buckwheat Pumpkin Seeds Raisins & Mango, Gluten Free Raisins Almonds Mixed Seeds & Crispy Rice)

Eco-Planet - 7 Whole Grains Hot Cereal (Apples & Cinnamon●, Maple & Brown Sugar, Original●)

El Peto▲ - Apple Cinnamon Cream Of Rice, Cream Of Brown Rice, Cream Of White Rice, Sweetened Corn Flakes, Unsweetened Corn Flakes

Ener-G▲ - Rice Bran

Enjoy Life▲ -

Granola Crunch

Cinnamon●

Cranapple●

Very Berry●

C **Erewhon** -
Aztec Crunchy Corn & Amaranth
Brown Rice Cream
Corn Flakes
Crispy Brown Rice (Cocoa, Gluten Free Regular, w/Mixed Berries)
Rice Twice
Strawberry Crisp
General Mills▲ - Chex (Corn, Honey Nut, Rice)
Gerber - Rice Single Grain Cereal
Gerber Organic - Brown Rice Whole Grain Cereal
Glutano▲ - Cornflakes, Pops
Gluten Free Sensations - Cream Of Brown Rice, Granola (Cherry Vanilla Almond, Cranberry Pecan, French Vanilla Almond)
Glutenfreeda▲ - Instant Oatmeal (Apple, Banana Maple, Cinnamon, Maple Raisin)
Health Valley - Blue Corn Flakes, Corn Crunch Ems, Rice Crunch Ems
Kinnikinnick▲ - Kinni Crisp Rice Cereal, Rice Bran
Lundberg▲ - Hot 'N Creamy Purely Organic Rice
Meijer Brand - Grits (Quick)
Montana Monster Munchies - Whole Grain Oat Bran●
Nature's Path -
Envirokidz Organic
Amazon Frosted Flakes
Gorilla Munch
Koala Crisp
Leapin Lemurs
Peanut Butter Panda Puffs
Nature's Path Organic
Corn Flakes
Crispy Rice
Crunchy Maple

C

    Crunchy Vanilla
    Honey'd Corn Flakes
    Mesa Sunrise
    Whole O's

New Morning - Cocoa Crispy Rice

Nu-World Foods -
    Amaranth Berry Delicious●
    Amaranth O's (Original●, Peach●)
    Cereal Snaps (Cinnamon●, Cocoa●, Original●)
    Puffed Amaranth Cereal●

Orgran▲ - Multigrain O w/Quinoa

Perky's - Apple Cinnamon O's●, Frosted O's●, Nutty Flax●, Nutty Rice●, Original O's●

Pocono - Cream Of Buckwheat

Seitenbacher - Whole Grain Cornflakes, Musli #7

Wegmans Brand - Fruity Rice Crisps

Chamomile Tea... see Tea

Champagne... *All Champagne **Made In USA** Is Gluten/Casein Free.* [2]

Cheese
    Eat In The Raw - Parma Vegan Parmesan (Chipotle Cayenne, Original)
    Follow Your Heart - Vegan Gourmet (Cheddar, Monterey Jack, Mozzarella, Nacho)
    Galaxy Nutritional Foods -
        Rice Vegan (Slices) *(Must Say 'Vegan')*
        Vegan (Blocks, Slices, Grated Topping) *(Must Say 'Vegan')*
    Gopal's - Rawmesan
    Road's End Organics - Organic (GF Alfredo Chreese Mix, GF Cheddar Chreese Mix)
    The Vegetarian Express - Parma Zaan Sprinkles

C Cherries... *All **Fresh** Fruits & Vegetables Are **Gluten/Casein Free***

 Cascadian Farm - Organic Frozen Sweet Cherries

 Food Club Brand - Frozen Dark Sweet Cherries

 Great Value Brand (Wal-Mart) - Maraschino

 Hy-Vee - Frozen Cherry Berry Blend, Red Maraschino Cherries (Regular, w/Stems)

 Lucky Leaf - Red Tart Pitted Cherries

 Meijer Brand - Frozen (Dark Sweet, Tart), Maraschino Cherry (Red, Red w/Stems)

 Midwest Country Fare - Maraschino Cherries

 Musselman's - Red Tart Pitted Cherries

 Publix - Frozen (Cherries, Dark Sweet), Maraschino

 S&W - All Canned/Jarred Fruits

 Safeway Brand - Frozen Dark Sweet Cherries, Maraschino Cherries

 Spartan Brand - Frozen Dark Sweet Cherries, Maraschino Cherries (Green, Red, Red w/Stems, Salad)

 Stop & Shop Brand - Dark Sweet Cherries

 Thrifty Maid - Maraschino Cherries

 Traverse Bay Fruit Co. - Premium Dried Cherries

 Wegmans Brand - Maraschino (Jumbo w/out Stems, w/Stems, w/out Stems), Sweet, Triple Cherry Fruit Mix In Light Syrup

 Winn Dixie - Dark Sweet Cherries, Maraschino Cherries

 Woodstock Farms - Organic Frozen Dark Sweet Cherries

Cherries Jubilee

 Lucky Leaf

 Musselman's

Chewing Gum

 5

 B Fresh - All Varieties

 Bazooka

 Big Red

C

Bubblicious - All Varieties
Dentyne Ice - All Varieties
Doublemint
Dubble Bubble
Eclipse
Extra
Freedent
Hubba Bubba - All Varieties
Juicy Fruit
Nicorette - Fresh Mint, Fruit Chill, White Ice Mint
Orbit
Orbit White
Stride - All Varieties
Trident -
 Bubblegum
 Minty Sweet Twist
 Original
 Spearmint
 Splash (Strawberry Lime)
 Tropical Twist
 Watermelon Twist
 Wild Blueberry Twist
Winterfresh
Wrigley's - Spearmint
Chick Peas... see Beans
Chicken... *All Fresh Chicken Is Gluten/Casein Free (Non-Marinated, Unseasoned)*
 Applegate Farms - Gluten Free Chicken Nuggets, Organic (Roasted Chicken Breast, Smoked Chicken Breast)
 Bakers & Chefs - Canned All Natural Chicken Breast

C **Bell & Evans** - Gluten Free Breaded Boneless Skinless Chicken
Breasts (Regular), Gluten Free Chicken Nuggets, Gluten Free
Chicken Patties, Gluten Free Grilled Chicken Breasts (Regular)

Butterball - Thin Sliced Oven Roasted Chicken Breast

Carl Buddig - Deli Thin Sliced Chicken

Chi-Chi's - Fiesta Plates (Chicken Salsa)

Dinty Moore - Microwave Meal (Rice w/Chicken)

Empire Kosher - Chicken Bologna Slices, Organic (Breasts,
Drumsticks), Rendered Chicken Fat

Farmer John - California Natural Chicken Sausage (Apple Chicken
Smoked, Cajun Style Smoked, Chicken Brat Smoked, Lemon
Cracked Pepper Chicken Smoked, Mango & Habanero Smoked)

Garrett County Farms - Chicken Franks, Dino Shaped Chicken
Bites, Frozen Chicken Apple Breakfast Links

Gillian's Foods▲ - Chicken Cutlets

GF Naturals - 1oz. Boneless Wing●, 2oz. Tender●, 4oz. All Natural
Filet●, 4oz. Whole Muscle Filet●

Great Value Brand (Wal-Mart) - Canned Chunk Chicken Breast

Hannaford Brand - Chicken Breast Chunk In Water

Hillshire Farms - Deli Select Thin Sliced Oven Roasted Chicken
Breast

Homestyle Meals - Shredded Chicken In BBQ Sauce

Honeysuckle White - Chicken Breast Deli Meat (BBQ, Buffalo Style,
Oil Browned)

Hormel - Chunk Meats (Breast Of Chicken, Chicken), Natural
Choice (Grilled Carved Chicken Breast, Oven Roasted Carved
Chicken)

Hy-Vee - Thin Sliced Chicken

Ian's - Wheat Free Gluten Free Recipe (Chicken Finger Kids Meal,
Chicken Nuggets, Chicken Patties)

Jennie-O - Deli Chicken Breast (Mesquite Smoked)

John Soules Foods -
Ready To Cook (Chicken Breast For Fajitas, Chicken Thigh For
Fajitas)

C

Lloyd's - Shredded Chicken In Original BBQ Sauce
Member's Mark - Canned Premium Chunk Chicken Breast
Organic Prairie -
  Fresh Organic
    Sliced Roast Chicken Breast 6 oz.
  Frozen Organic
    Boneless Skinless Chicken Breasts
    Chicken Italian Sausage 12 oz.
    Ground Chicken 12 oz.
    Whole Young Chicken
Oscar Mayer -
  Chicken Breast Strips (Honey Roasted, Oven Roasted)
  Deli Fresh Oven Roasted Chicken Breast
  Shaved Deli Fresh (Cajun Seasoned Chicken Breast, Rotisserie
    Style Chicken Breast)
  Thin Sliced Deli Fresh Oven Roasted Chicken Breast
Perdue - Rotisserie Oven Stuffer Roaster Breast
Saz's - Barbecue Chicken Meat Tub
S'Better Farms▲ -
  Ballontine
  Fingers
  Party Wings
  Siciliano
  Szechwan
Shelton's - Capon, Free Range (Breasts, Thighs, Whole), Organic
  (Boneless/Skinless Breast, Breast, Cut Up, Whole Chicken,
  Whole Legs)
Smart Chicken - All Varieties
Smart Ones - Frozen Entrees Chicken (Lemon Herb Piccata, Santa Fe)
Spartan Brand - Chicken Breast Chunk, Frozen Boneless Skinless
  (Breasts, Tenders)

C **Sweet Sue** - Premium Chicken Breast Pouch
Trader Joe's -
  Grilled Chicken Strips
  Just Chicken (Plain)
Tyson Simply Perfect -
  100% All Natural Fresh Chicken
    Boneless
    Chicken Breast Tenders
    Skinless (Chicken Breasts, Split Chicken Breasts)
    Thin & Fancy Chicken Breast
Valley Fresh - 100% Natural (Premium White Chicken, White & Dark Chicken)
Wellshire Farms -
  Chicken Franks
  Sliced Oven Roasted Chicken Breast
Wellshire Kids - Dino Shaped Chicken Bites Refrigerated
Wellshire Organic - Organic Chicken Franks
Chicken Broth... see Broth
Chicken Noodle Soup... see Soup
Chicken Nuggets... see Chicken
Chicken Wings... see Wings
Chiles
  Chi-Chi's - Green Chiles
  Food Club Brand - Diced Green
  La Victoria - Green Chiles (Diced, Whole)
  Meijer Brand - Diced Mild Mexican Style
  Old El Paso - Green Chiles (Chopped, Whole)
  Ortega
  Safeway Brand - Diced Green
  Spartan Brand - Green Chiles

C

Chili

Amy's - Organic Chili (Black Bean, Light In Sodium, Medium, Medium w/Vegetables, Spicy), Southwestern Black Bean

Health Valley -

Organic Chunky Chili -

Mild Vegetarian (Black Bean, Three Bean)

No Salt Added (Mild Vegetarian, Spicy Vegetarian)

Spicy Vegetarian (Black Bean, Regular)

Hormel - Chili Master (Chipotle Chicken No Bean, Chipotle Chicken w/Beans), Chili w/Beans (Chunky, Hot, Regular)

Hy-Vee - Hot Chili w/Beans, Mild w/Beans

Kettle Cuisine - Angus Beef Steak Chili w/Beans●, Three Bean Chili●

Meijer Brand - Chili (No Beans Regular, w/Beans Regular)

Mimi's Gourmet - Black Bean & Corn, Spicy White Bean & Jalapeno, Three Bean w/Rice

Shelton's - Mild Chicken, Mild Turkey, Spicy Chicken, Spicy Turkey

Spartan Brand - Bean Soup Mix

Stagg -

Chunkero

Classic

Dynamite Hot

Ranch House Chicken

Silverado Beef

Steak House

Winn Dixie - Chili w/Beans

Chili Powder

Chugwater Chili

Dr. McDougall's -Crowd Pleasing Chili Mix

Durkee

McCormick

C   Spartan Brand
Spice Islands
Tone's

Chili Sauce
A Taste Of Thai - Garlic Chili Pepper Sauce, Sweet Red Chili Sauce
Frank's RedHot - Chile 'N Lime
Hannaford Brand
Heinz
La Victoria - Red
Las Palmas - Red Chile
Lee Kum Kee - Sriracha Chili
Meijer Brand - Hot Dog Chili
Safeway Brand
Thai Kitchen - Spicy Thai, Sweet Red
Wegmans Brand
Winn Dixie - Sweet

Chips
Arico - Cassava Chips (Barbeque Bliss, Ginger On Fire, Original, Sea Salt Mist)
Baked! Lay's - Original
Baked! Ruffles - Original
Baked! Tostitos - Scoops! Tortilla Chips
Boulder Canyon Natural Foods -
Canyon Cut Potato Chips
Salt & Cracked Pepper
Totally Natural
Kettle Cooked Potato Chips
50% Reduced Salt
Balsamic Vinegar & Rosemary
Hickory Barbeque
Limon

Sea Salt & Cracked Pepper

Tomato & Basil

Totally Natural

Rice & Adzuki Bean Snack Chips

Natural Salt

Brothers All Natural▲ - Potato Crisps (Black Pepper & Sea Salt, Fresh Onion & Garlic, Original w/Sea Salt, Szechwan Pepper & Fresh Chives)

Cape Cod -

Potato

40% Reduced Fat

Classic

Robust Russet

Sea Salt & Vinegar

Sweet Mesquite Barbeque

Chi-Chi's - White Corn Tortilla (Authentic, Rounds)

Deep River Snacks -

Asian Sweet & Spicy

Mesquite BBQ

Original Salted

Reduced Fat Original Salted

Salt & Cracked Pepper

Sweet Maui Onion

Zesty Jalapeno

Doritos -

Diablo

Salsa Verde

Toasted Corn

Eat Smart - Veggie Crisps (Regular)

Eden - Brown Rice

C

Food Should Taste Good - Tortilla Chips (Buffalo●, Chocolate●, Cinnamon●, Jalapeno●, Lime●, Multigrain●, Olive●, Potato & Chive●, Sweet Potato●, The Works!●, Yellow Corn●)

Fritos -

Corn Chips (Original, Scoops)

Honey BBQ Flavor Twists

Frontera - Tortilla Chips (Blue Corn, Lime w/Sea Salt, Restaurant Style, Yellow Corn)

Glenny's - Spud Delites Natural Potato Crisps (Sea Salt, Texas BBQ)

Goraw - Super Chips (Pumpkin●, Spirulina●)

Hannaford Brand -

Potato Chips (Kettle Cooked Original, No Salt Added, Original, Ripple, Wavy)

Tortilla Chips (White Bite Size, Yellow Rounds)

Health Market Organic - Tortilla Corn (Blue, White, Yellow)

Herr's -

Potato Chips

Crisp 'N Tasty

Honey BBQ

Ketchup

Lightly Salted

Mesquite BBQ Kettle

No Salt

Old (Bay, Fashioned)

Red Hot

Ripple

Tortilla/Corn Chips

Bite Size Dippers

Regular Corn Chips

Restaurant Style

Hy-Vee - Baked Chips (Barbecue, Original), Potato Chips (No Salt, Original)

Kettle Brand -

Baked Potato Chips
Hickory Honey Barbeque
Lightly Salted
Salt & Fresh Ground Pepper
Sea Salt & Vinegar
Krinkle Cut Potato Chips
Classic Barbeque
Lightly Salted
Salt & Fresh Ground Pepper
Organic Potato Chips
Chipotle Chili Barbeque
Lightly Salted
Sea Salt & Black Pepper
Potato Chips
Backyard Barbeque
Death Valley Chipotle
Honey Dijon
Jalapeno
Lightly Salted
Salt & Fresh Ground Pepper
Sea Salt & Vinegar
Spicy Thai
Unsalted
Tortilla Chips
Black Bean
Blue Corn
Chili Lime
Yellow Corn

C   Lay's -
   Potato Chips
      Classic
      Deli Style Original
      Kettle Cooked (Mequite BBQ Extra Crunchy, Original,
         Reduced Fat Original)
      Light Original
      Lightly Salted
      Limon Tangy Lime
      Natural Sea Salt Thick Cut
   Wavy Potato Chips
      Original
Lay's Stax - Original Potato Crisps
Lundberg▲ -
   Rice Chips
      Honey Dijon
      Pico de Gallo
      Santa Fe Barbecue
      Sea Salt
      Wasabi
Maui Style - Potato Chips (Regular)
Michael Season's -
   Baked Multigrain Chips (Honey Chipotle, Original)
   Baked Thin Potato Crisps (Original, Sweet Barbecue)
   Thin & Crispy (Honey Barbecue, Lightly Salted, Ripple, Salt &
      Pepper, Unsalted)
Miguel's -
   Organic Tortilla Dippers (Everything●, Three Pepper●, Vegetable
      & Seed●)
   Tortilla Chips (Blue Corn●, White Corn●)

Miss Vickie's -
  Kettle Cooked Potato Chips
    Simply Sea Salt
    Smokehouse BBQ

Mr. Krispers -
  Baked Rice Krisps (Barbecue●, Sea Salt & Pepper●)
  Multi Seed Chips (Original●)

Munchos - Regular Potato Crisps

O Organics Tortilla Chips (Blue w/Flax Seed, Blue w/Sesame, White, Yellow)

Old Dutch -
  Potato Chips (Ketchup, Original)

Pan De Oro - Tortilla Chips (Red White & Blue●)

Pinnacle Gold - Natural Baked Potato Chips Original, Natural Baked Veggie Chips

Pringles - Fat Free (Original)

Publix -
  Potato Chips (Dip Style, Original Thins, Wavy Style)
  Tortilla Chips (White Corn, White Corn Restaurant Style, Yellow Corn Round Style)

Publix GreenWise Market - Tortilla Chips (Blue, Yellow)

RiceWorks - Rice Crisps (Salsa Fresca, Sea Salt, Sweet Chili, Wasabi)

Ruffles -
  Potato Chips
    Natural Reduced Fat Sea Salted
    Original (Light, Reduced Fat, Regular)

Sabritas - Chile Piquin Flavored, Habanero Limon

Santitas - Tortilla Chips (White Corn Restaurant Style, Yellow Corn)

Snyder's Of Hanover -
  Corn Tortilla Chips (Restaurant Style, White, Yellow)
  Potato Chips (Barbeque, Jalapeno, Original, Ripple Potato)

C

Solea -
Olive Oil Chips
Cracked Pepper
Rosemary
Sea Salt
Polenta Chips
Sea Salt
Spartan Brand - Potato (Regular, Ripple)
Tostitos -
Tortilla Chips
100% White Corn Restaurant Style
Bite Size (Gold, Rounds)
Crispy Rounds
Light Restaurant Style
Natural Corn Restaurant Style (Blue, Yellow)
Scoops (Hint Of Jalapeno, Regular)
Trader Joe's -
Regular Chips
Blue Corn Tortilla
Hemp Tortilla w/Black Sesame Seeds
Soy & Flaxseed Tortilla (Regular)
Vegetable Root
Veggie
Veggie & Flaxseed Tortilla
Organic Chips
Baked Blue Corn Tortilla
Tortilla Longboard
White Corn Tortilla
UTZ -
All Natural Kettle Cooked
Dark Russet

Gourmet Medley
Lightly Salted
Grandma UTZ Kettle Cooked
Barbeque
Plain
Home Style Kettle Cooked Plain
Kettle Classics
Dark Russet
Plain
Sweet Potato
Mystic Kettle Cooked Chips
Dark Russet
Plain
Sea Salt & Vinegar
Regular Chips
Barbeque
Carolina BBQ
Crab
Honey BBQ
No Salt Regular
Plain (Flat, Ripple, Wavy Cut)
Red Hot
Reduced Fat
Tortilla Chips
Baked
Wegmans Brand -
Corn
Kettle (Memphis Style BBQ Flavor, Original)
Lime
Original Potato

C

Thai BBQ

Tortilla 100% White Corn (Blue Corn, Bite Size Round, Yellow Corn)

Wavy

Winn Dixie -

Corn Chips (BBQ, Big Dipper, Original)

Potato Chips

Classic

No Salt

Salt & Vinegar

Wavy

Tortilla Chips

Bite Size Rounds

Restaurant Style White

Wise -

Corn Chips (BBQ Flavored Dipsy Doodles, Dipsy Doodles Rippled)

New York Deli (Jalapeno Flavored, Kettle Cooked)

Onion & Garlic

Potato Chips (Flat Cut, Lightly Salted, Unsalted, Wise Wavy)

Ridgies

Tortilla Chips Bravos! (Restaurant Style, White Round)

Woodstock Farms - Veggie Chips

Chocolate

Earth Source Organics - Organic Raw Chocolate Bar (Acai●, Caramel●, Goji●, Maca●)

Newman's Own Organics - Bars (Dark Chocolate, Espresso Dark, Orange Dark, Super Dark)

Safeway Select - Extra Dark

Sjaaks▲ -

Organic Fair Trade Chocolate

Acai Small Bites

Caramel Small Bites

Ginger Small Bites

Mint (Mills, Small Bites)

Orange Small Bites

Vegan Almond Butter Bites

Vegan Extra Dark Bites

Vegan Peanut Butter Bites

Vegan Solid Dark Chocolate Hearts

Tropical Source - Mint Crunch Dark Chocolate, Raspberry Dark Chocolate, Rice Crisp Dark Chocolate, Rich Dark Chocolate, Semi Sweet Chocolate Chips, Toasted Almond Dark Chocolate

Woodstock Farms - Chocolate (Almonds, Ginger, Raisins) w/Evaporated Cane Juice, Organic Chocolate (Dark, Milk) Almonds w/Evaporated Cane Juice, Organic Dark Chocolate Chips w/Evaporated Cane Juice

Chocolate Bars... see also Candy Bars and/or Chocolate

Enjoy Life▲ - Boom Choco Boom (Crispy Rice●, Dark Chocolate●, Rice Milk●)

Chocolate Chips... see Baking Chips

Chocolate Syrup... see Syrup

Chole

Tamarind Tree - Alu Chole

Chutney

Baxters -

Albert's Victorian

Crushed Pineapple & Sweet Pepper

Spiced Fruit

Spicy Mango

Tomato

Hannaford Brand - Mango Chutney

Native Forest - Chutney (All Varieties)

Patak's - Chutney (Hot Mango, Major Grey, Sweet Mango)

Sharwood's - Green Label (Mango, Mango Chilli, Smooth)

C **Trader Joe's** - Apple Cranberry

Wild Thymes - Apricot Cranberry Walnut, Caribbean Peach Lime, Mango Papaya, Plum Currant Ginger

Cider

Doc's Draft - Apple, Pear, Raspberry *(Alcoholic)*

Safeway Brand - Apple Cider

Sonoma Sparkler - Natural (Peach, Pear, Raspberry), Organic (Apple, Lemonade)

Woodchuck▲ - Draft Ciders (All Styles) *(Alcoholic)*

Wyder's - All Styles *(Alcoholic)*

Cinnamon

Durkee

McCormick

Spice Islands

Tone's

Cinnamon Rolls

Chebe▲ - Cinnamon Roll Mix

Kinnikinnick▲ - Tapioca Rice Cinnamon Buns

Clams... *All Fresh Seafood Is **Gluten/Casein Free (Non-Marinated, Unseasoned)***

Bumble Bee - Chopped, Fancy Smoked, Fancy Whole Baby, Minced

Chicken Of The Sea - Minced, Whole Baby Clams

Crown Prince -

Natural (Boiled Baby Clams, Clam Juice, Smoked Baby Clams In Olive Oil)

Regular (Baby Clams Smoked In Oil, Baby Boiled, Chopped, Clam Juice, Minced)

Ocean Prince - Chopped

Club Soda... see Soda Pop/Carbonated Beverages

Coating

A Taste Of Thai - Peanut Bake

Dakota Lakes▲ - Gourmet Coating●

C

El Peto▲ - Bread Crumbs

Ener-G▲ - Breadcrumbs

Gillian's Foods▲ - Breadcrumbs (Cajun Style, Italian Style, Plain)

Gluten-Free Essentials▲ - Breading & Batter Mix (Seasoned●, Unseasoned●)

Gluten-Free Pantry▲ - Crisp & Crumble Topping

Hol Grain - Brown Rice Bread Crumbs, Crispy Chicken Coating Mix

Katz Gluten Free▲ - Bread Crumbs

Kinnikinnick▲ - Chocolate Cookie Crumbs, Coating Mix (Crispy Chicken, General), Graham Style Cracker Crumbs

Nu-World Foods - Amaranth Bread Crumbs●

Orgran▲ - All Purpose Crumbs, Corn Crispy Crumbs

Schar▲ - Bread Crumbs

Southern Homestyle - Corn Flake Crumbs, Tortilla Crumbs

Cocktail Mix

Clamato - Original

Holland House -

Daiquiri Drink

Manhattan

Pina Colada

Strawberry Daiquiri Margarita Mix

Sweet & Sour Mix

Margaritville - Margarita Mix

Mr. & Mrs. T's -

Mai Tai

Margarita

Pina Colada

Strawberry Daiquiri Margarita

Sweet & Sour

Whiskey Sour

C Rose's -

    Grenadine, Infusions (Blue Raspberry, Cranberry Twist, Sour Apple)

    Mojito (Mango, Passion Fruit, Traditional)

    Sweetened Lime Juice

Cocktail Sauce... see also Seafood Sauce

    Frontera - Cocktail & Ceviche Sauce (Cilantro Lime, Tomato Chipotle)

    Hannaford Brand - Cocktail Sauce

    Heinz - Cocktail Sauce (Original)

    Hy-Vee - Cocktail Sauce For Seafood

    Lee Kum Kee - Shrimp Sauce

    Lou's Famous - Cocktail Sauce

    McCormick - Extra Hot, Gold Dipt (Regular), Original, Seafood Sauce (Cajun Style, Lemon Herb, Mediterranean, Santa Fe Style)

    Old Bay

    Publix - Seafood Cocktail Sauce

    Safeway Brand

    Spartan Brand

    Texas Pete - Seafood Cocktail

    Walden Farms

Cocoa Mix/Powder

    Dagoba - Authentic Hot Chocolate, Chocolate Syrup, Organic Cacao Powder, Unsweetened Hot Chocolate, Xocolatl Hot Chocolate

    Ghirardelli -

        Double Chocolate

        Hazelnut

        Mocha

        Sweet Ground Chocolate & Cocoa

        White Mocha

    Hershey's - Chocolate Syrup (Lite, Regular, Special Dark), Cocoa (Special Dark, Unsweetened Regular)

    Safeway Brand - Instant Chocolate Drink Mix

    Shiloh Farms - Cocoa Powder

Coconut

    Baker's - Coconut (Bags, Cans)

    Food Club - Sweetened Coconut

    Great Value Brand (Wal-Mart) - Sweetened Flaked Coconut

    Hy-Vee - Flake Coconut

    Kroger Brand - Regular, Sweetened

    Laura Lynn

    Let's Do...Organic - Creamed, Flakes, Shredded (Reduced Fat, Regular, Unsweetened)

    Lowes Foods Brand - Flakes

    Publix - Coconut Flakes

    Safeway Brand - Coconut (Sweetened)

    Spartan Brand - Coconut Flakes

    Wegmans Brand - Sweetened Flakes

    Winn Dixie - Coconut

    Woodstock Farms - Coconut Medium Shred

Coconut Milk

    A Taste Of Thai - Coconut Milk (Lite, Regular)

    Native Forest - Organic Coconut Milk (Light, Regular)

    So Delicious - Original●, Unsweetened●, Vanilla●

    Thai Kitchen - Thailand (Lite, Lite Organic, Premium, Premium Organic)

    Trader Joe's - Light

Cod... see Fish

    All Fresh Fish Is Gluten/Casein Free (Non-Marinated, Unseasoned)

Coffee

    Brown Gold - All Varieties

    Folger's - Classic (Decaf, Regular)

C

Food Club Brand - Ground Coffee (Classic Roast, Columbian, Decaf, French Roast, Lite Classic Roast)

Full Circle - Organic (Espresso Blend Ground, French Roast, Ground, Guatamalan Reserve Ground, Morning Blend Ground, Morning Blend Whole Bean, Signature Blend Ground)

Great Value Brand (Wal-Mart) -

100% Arabica Premium (Ground Coffee, Instant Coffee)

100% Colombian Premium Ground Coffee (Naturally Decaf, Regular)

French Roast - 100% Arabica Premium Ground Coffee

Naturally Decaf Premium Instant Coffee

Hannaford Brand - Columbian, Decaf Premium, House Blend, Light Columbian Instant, Premium Blend

Hy-Vee -

100% Colombian

Breakfast Blend

Classic Blend

Classic Decaf

Coffee (Instant, Regular)

Decaf (Instant, Regular)

French Roast

Kroger Brand - Unflavored (Ground, Instant, Whole)

Lowes Foods Brand -

Bag (100% Colombian (Decaf, Regular), French Roast, Signature Blend)

Brick (100% Colombian, Decaf, French Roast, Lite, Regular)

Can (Regular)

Instant (Decaf, Regular)

Singles (Microwaveable)

Maxwell House -

Coffee Bags (Decaf, Master Blend, Regular)

Ground (Breakfast Blend, Dark Roast, Hazelnut, Original, Slow Roast, Vanilla)

C

Filter Packs & Singles (Decaf, Original)

Instant (Decaf, Reduced Caffeine/Lite, Original)

Meijer Brand - Decaf, French Roast, Ground (Colombian, French Roast, Lite 50% Decaf), Regular

Midwest Country Fare - Classic Blend

Millstone - All Coffee Beans, All Ground Coffee

Nescafe - Classic Instant, Taster's Choice Instant (Original)

O Organics - All Coffee Beans

Prestige - 100% Colombian Whole Bean

Publix - All Varieties

Safeway Brand - Decaf Classic Roast, Espresso Coffee Beans

Safeway Select - Whole Bean (Flavored)

Sanka - Decaf Coffee

Spartan Brand -

Coffee (French Roast, Instant, Instant Decaf, Regular)

Coffee Ground (Colombian, Decaf, Light, Regular)

Starbucks - All Coffee Beans, All Ground Coffee

Taster's Choice - Instant (Original)

Wegmans Brand -

Ground (100% Colombian, 100% Colombian Medium Roast, Breakfast Blend Light Roast, Breakfast Blend Light Roast Decaf, Caffeine Lite, Decaf, Espresso Dark Roast, French Roast, Traditional)

Instant

Pure Origin Coffee (Day Break Roast, Ground Jamaican Mid Day, Kona Evening, Smooth Morning, Sumatra Night)

Traditional Coffee Singles

Whole Bean Coffee (100% Colombian Medium Roast, Breakfast Blend Light Roast, Espresso Dark Roast, Espresso Dark Roast Decaf)

Winn Dixie - Colombian, Classic, Classic Decaf, Special Blend

C

Yuban -
Instant (Decaf, Reduced Caffeine/Lite, Regular)
Roast & Ground (Decaf, Reduced Caffeine/Lite, Regular)

Coffee Beans... see Coffee

Coffee Creamer... see Creamer

Coffee Syrup -
Nescafe - Ice Java Coffee Syrup (Cappuccino Fat Free, Chocolate Mocha, French Vanilla Café Fat Free)

Cold Cuts... see Deli Meat

Cole Slaw Dressing... see Salad Dressing

Collards... see Greens

Communion Wafers
Ener-G▲ - Communion Wafers

Concentrate... see Drinks/Juice

Cones
Barkat - Ice Cream Cones, Waffle Cones
Cerrone Cone - Waffle Cones
Goldbaum's - Gluten Free Ice Cream Cones (Regular, Sugar)
Let's Do...Organic - Gluten Free Ice Cream Cones

Cookie Mix... see also Cookies/Cookie Dough
1-2-3 Gluten Free▲ - Chewy Chipless Scrumdelicious Cookies●, Lindsay's Lipsmackin' Roll Our & Cut Sugar Cookies●, Sweet Goodness Pan Bars●
Arrowhead Mills - Gluten Free Chocolate Chip Mix
Bob's Red Mill▲ - Chocolate Chip
Cause You're Special▲ - Chocolate Chip, Classic Sugar
Cherrybrook Kitchen - Gluten Free Chocolate Chip Cookie Mix, Gluten Free Sugar Cookie Mix *(Box Must Say Gluten-Free)*
El Peto▲ - Old Fashion Sugar Cookie Mix
Gifts Of Nature▲ - Fancy Cookie●, Triple Treat●
Gluten Free Life▲ - The Ultimate Gluten Free Cookie Mix

cookies/cookie dough

C

Gluten Free Sensations - Chocolate Chip Cookie Mix

Gluten-Free Essentials▲ - Chocolate Chip Cookie Mix●, Cocoa Mudslide●, Speedy Bake Mix (Chocolate Chip●, Make Mine Chocolate●)

Gluten-Free Pantry▲ - Cookie & Cake Mix (Chocolate Chip, Old Fashioned)

Hodgson Mill▲ - Gluten Free Cookie Mix

InclusiLife▲ - Cookie Dough (Chocolate Chip, Fudge Brownie, Sugar)

Jules Gluten Free▲ - Graham Cracker/Gingersnap Mix●

Kinnikinnick▲ - Cookie Mix

Maggie's Gluten Free Goodies▲ - Super Duper Sugar Cookie Mix

Namaste Foods▲ - Blondies, Cookie

Really Great Food▲ - Biscotti (Anise, Lemon Poppy), Butter, Chocolate Crinkle, Coconut Macaroon, Versatile

Ruby Range - Old Fashioned Cookies Gluten Free Baking Mix●

Simply Organic▲ - Biscotti Mix●

The Cravings Place▲ - Peanut Butter, Raisin Spice

Cookies/Cookie Dough

Apple's Bakery▲ - Gluten Free Cookies (Lemon Drop)

Crave Bakery▲ - Monster Cookie

Cybros Inc. - Lemon Almond, Peanut Butter, Sugar

El Peto▲ - Almond Shortbread, Carob Chip, Chocolate (Chip, Coconut Macaroons), Cinnamon/Hazelnut, Coconut Macaroons, Gingersnaps, Hazelnut/Raspberry

Ener-G▲ -

Chocolate (Chip Biscotti, Chip Potato, Regular)

Cinnamon

Ginger

Sunflower Cookies

Vanilla

White Chocolate Chip

C **Enjoy Life**▲ - Chewy Chocolate Chip●, Double Chocolate Brownie●, Gingerbread Spice●, Happy Apple●, Lively Lemon●, No Oats "Oatmeal"●, Snickerdoodle●

French Meadow Bakery - Gluten Free (Chocolate Chip Cookie Dough●, Chocolate Chip Cookies●)

Glow Gluten Free ▲ - Chocolate Chip, Double Chocolate Chip, Gingersnap, Snickerdoodle

Glutafin - Chocolate Chip

Gluten Free Life▲ - Deluxe Sugar

Gluten-Free Creations▲ - Nutty Trail Mix●, Oatmeal Raisin●, Pecan Wedding●

Gluten-Free Essentials▲ - Vanilla Sugar Cookies●

Glutino▲ - Wafers (Lemon, Strawberry)

Gopal's - Nature's Gift Cookies (Almond Raisin, Goldenberry Brazil, Hazelnut Cherry, Macadamia Goji, Pineapple Flax)

Goraw - Super Cookies (Chocolate●, Original●)

Jennies - Zero Carb Macaroons (Carob, Coconut)

Jo-Sef▲ - Chocolate Chip (Pecan●, Regular●), Cinnamon●, Crème Filled (Chocolate●, Cinnamon●, Coffee●, Double Chocolate●), Egg Free Chocolate Chip●, Fancy Sandwich w/Chocolate●, Lemon●, Linzer●, Orange●, Sugar●, Vanilla●

Katz Gluten Free▲ - Cookies (Chocolate Chip, Chocolate Dipped, Colored Sprinkle, Sugar Free Vanilla, Vanilla)

Kinnikinnick▲ -

Almond (Biscotti, Regular)

Chocolate Cookie Crumbs

Double Chocolate Almond

Ginger Snap

KinniKritters Animal Cookies

KinniToos Sandwich (Chocolate Vanilla, Vanilla Crème)

Lemon Cranberry

Montana's Chocolate Chip

Kookie Karma - All Varieties●

Manischewitz - Coconut Tenders, Macaroons (Chocolate Chip, Chocolate ChunkCherry, Rocky Road), Peppermint Patties

Mi-Del - *(Packages Must Say Gluten-Free)* Cinnamon Snaps, Ginger Snaps, Sandwich (Chocolate, Royal Vanilla)

Namaste Foods▲ - Blondies Mix, Cookie Mix

Nana's -

Cookie Bars (Berry Vanilla, Chocolate Munch, Nana Banana)

Cookie Bites (Ginger, Fudge, Lemon Dreams, Spice)

No Gluten Cookie (Chocolate, Chocolate Crunch, Ginger, Lemon)

Nature's Path Organic - Animal Cookies (Vanilla)

Orgran▲ -

Amaretti Biscotti

Classic Chocolate Biscotti

Classic Chocolate Cookie

Itsy Bitsy Bears

Mini Outback Animals (Chocolate, Vanilla)

Outback Animals (Chocolate, Vanilla)

Wild Raspberry Fruit Flavored Biscuits

Pamela's Products▲ -

Extreme Chocolate Mini Cookies

Ginger (Mini Snapz, w/Sliced Almonds)

Organic (Old Fashion Raisin Walnut, Spicy Ginger w/Crystallized Ginger)

Peanut Butter

Rose's Bakery▲ - Gingersnaps●, Macaroons●

Schar▲ - Cocoa Wafers, Ladyfingers, Shortbread Cookies

Cooking Spray

Albertsons - Canola Oil

Crisco - Butter, Olive Oil, Original

Hy-Vee - Canola, Olive Oil, Vegetable Oil

Mazola - All Cooking Sprays

C

Meijer Brand - Butter, Olive Oil Extra Virgin, Vegetable Oil

Pam - Olive Oil, Original

Publix - Butter Flavored, Grill, Olive Oil, Original Canola

Safeway Brand - Canola, Grill, Olive Oil, Vegetable

Spartan Brand - Extra Virgin Olive Oil, Regular

Trader Joe's - Canola Oil Spray (All)

Wegmans Brand - Canola Oil, Corn Oil, Olive Oil

Winn Dixie - Canola, Corn, Grilling, Olive

Cooking Wine

Eden - Rice Mirin

Holland House -

Marsala

Red

Sherry

White

Vermouth

White w/Lemon Flavor

Publix

Corn... *All **Fresh** Fruits & Vegetables Are **Gluten/Casein Free***

Albertsons - Canned (Creamed Style, Regular), Frozen

Birds Eye - All Plain Frozen Vegetables

C & W - All Plain Frozen Vegetables

Cascadian Farm - Organic Frozen (Super Sweet Corn, Sweet Corn)

Del Monte - All Plain Canned Vegetables

Food Club Brand -

Canned (Golden, White, w/Peppers)

Frozen (Golden, White)

Freshlike - Frozen Plain Vegetables *(Except Pasta Combos & Seasoned Blends)*

Full Circle - Organic Frozen Whole Kernel Corn, Organic Gold Corn

C

Grand Selections - Frozen (Super Sweet Cut, White Shoepeg)

Great Value Brand (Wal-Mart) - Canned (Cream Style Corn, Golden Sweet Whole Kernel Corn, No Salt Added Golden Sweet Whole Kernel Corn)

Green Giant -

Canned

Cream Style Sweet Corn

Mexicorn

Niblets (Extra Sweet, No Salt Added, Whole Kernel Extra Sweet Corn, Whole Kernel Sweet Corn)

Southwestern Style

Super Sweet Yellow & White Corn

White Shoepeg Corn

Frozen

Cream Style Corn

Nibblers (12 Count, 24 Count)

Steamers Niblets Corn

Haggen - Whole Kernel Corn

Hannaford Brand - Cream Style, Crisp & Sweet, Mexican Style, Whole Kernel

Health Market - Organic Whole Kernel

Home Harvest Brand - Canned, Frozen Whole Kernel Gold

Hy-Vee - Corn On The Cob, Cream Style (Golden Corn), Frozen Cut Golden Corn, Steam In A Bag Frozen Corn, Whole Kernel (Corn, Gold Corn, White Sweet Corn)

Kroger Brand - All Plain Vegetables (Canned, Frozen)

Laura Lynn - Corn (Cream Style, Gold 'N White, No Salt Whole Kernel, Vacuum Packed, Whole Kernel)

Lowes Foods Brand -

Canned (White)

Frozen (Corn Cob Full Ear, Corn Cob Mini Ear, Cut)

C

Meijer Brand -

Canned (Cream Style, Golden Sweet Organic, Whole Kernel (Crisp & Sweet, Golden, Golden No Salt, White))

Frozen (Corn Cob Mini Ear, Corn On Cob, Whole Kernel, Whole Kernel Golden)

Midwest Country Fare - Cream Style, Frozen Cut, Whole Kernel

Native Forest - Organic Cut Baby Corn

Nature's Promise - Organic Corn (Cut, On The Cob)

O Organics - Canned Whole Kernel, Frozen Golden Cut

Pictsweet - All Plain Vegetables (Frozen)

Publix -

Canned (Cream Style Golden, Golden Sweet, Whole Kernel Crispy, Whole Kernel Crispy 50% Less Salt)

Frozen (Corn On Cob, Cut)

Publix GreenWise Market - Organic Canned Whole Kernel

S&W - All Plain Canned Vegetables

Safeway Brand - Cream Style, Frozen Corn On The Cob, No Salt Whole Kernel, Steam In Bag (Petite, White)

Spartan Brand -

Canned Corn

Frozen (Baby Corn Blend, Corn On The Cob, Mini Ear Corn On The Cob, Plain, White Super Sweet)

Stop & Shop Brand - Corn (& Peas, Cut, Mexican Style, On The Cob, Super Sweet Corn On The Cob), Whole Kernel Corn

Trader Joe's - All Plain Frozen Vegetables

Wegmans Brand -

Canned (Bread & Butter, Cream Style Golden Sweet, Crisp 'N Sweet Whole Kernel, Whole Kernel, Whole Kernel No Salt)

Frozen (Baby Corn Cleaned And Cut, Bread & Butter Sweet Whole Kernel, Super Sweet Steamable)

Winn Dixie -

Canned (Creamed Style, Mexican Style, White Whole Kernel, Yellow Whole Kernel, Yellow Whole Kernel No Salt)

Frozen Corn (Organic Yellow Cut, Steamable Yellow Cut, White Cut, Yellow Cut)

Frozen Corn On The Cob (Mini, Regular)

Woodstock Farms - Organic Frozen Cut Corn (Regular, Supersweet (Regular, White)), Toasted Corn

Corn Dog

Ian's - Wheat Free Gluten Free Recipe Popcorn Turkey Corn Dogs

S'Better Farms▲ - Beef Corn Dogs

Corn Oil... see Oil

Corn Starch... see Starch

Corn Syrup... see Syrup

Cornbread/Cornbread Mix

Chi-Chi's - Fiesta Sweet Corn Cake Mix

Bob's Red Mill▲ - Gluten Free Cornbread Mix

Food-Tek Fast & Fresh - Dairy Free Minute Cornbread Mix

Gluten-Free Pantry▲ - Yankee Cornbread

Glutino▲ - Premium Cornbread

Kinnikinnick▲ - Cornbread & Muffin Mix

Mixes From The Heartland▲ - Corn Bread Mix●

Orgran▲ - Cornbread & Muffin Mix

Really Great Food▲ - Cornbread Muffin Mix

Corned Beef... see also Beef

Armour - Corned Beef Hash

Carl Buddig -

Deli Thin Sliced Corned Beef

Extra Thin Sliced Corned Beef

Dietz & Watson - Corned Beef Brisket, Corned Beef Flat (Extra Lean)

Great Value Brand (Wal-Mart)

Hormel - Corned Beef, Corned Beef Hash, Deli Sliced Cooked Corned Beef

Meijer Brand - Hash

C

Safeway Brand - Hash

Wellshire Farms - Corned Beef Brisket (Regular, Whole), Round Corned Beef, Sliced Round Corned Beef

Cornflake Crumbs... see Coating

Cornish Hens... *All **Fresh** Poultry Is **Gluten/Casein Free (Non-Marinated, Unseasoned)***

Shelton's - Game Hens

Cornmeal

Arrowhead Mills - Organic Blue, Organic Yellow

El Peto▲ - Cornmeal

Hodgson Mill▲ - Organic Yellow, Plain White, Plain Yellow

Kinnikinnick▲

Safeway Brand - Yellow Corn Meal

Shiloh Farms - Corn Meal

Couscous

Lundberg▲ - Brown Rice Couscous (Mediterranean Curry, Plain, Savory Herb)

Crabmeat... *All **Fresh** Seafood Is **Gluten/Casein Free (Non-Marinated, Unseasoned)***

Chicken Of The Sea - Jumbo Lump, Lump Crab, Original, White Crab

Crown Prince - Natural (Fancy White Lump), Regular (Fancy Pink, Fancy White, Lump White)

Great Value Brand (Wal-Mart) - Crab Meat

Ocean Prince - Pink

Crackers

Blue Diamond Natural - Nut Thins (Smokehouse)

Crunchmaster - Multi Grain●, Multi Seed (Original●), Rice Crackers (Toasted Sesame●)

Eden - Brown Rice, Nori Maki Rice

Edward & Sons - Brown Rice Snaps (Black Sesame, Onion Garlic, Salsa, Tamari (Seaweed, Sesame), Exotic Rice Toast (Brown Jasmine Rice & Spring Onion, Purple Rice & Black Sesame, Thai Red Rice & Flaxseeds), Toasted Onion, Unsalted Plain, Unsalted Sesame, Vegetable)

C

Ener-G▲ - Cinnamon, Gourmet, Gourmet Onion, Seattle

Glutano▲ - Crackers

Healthy Valley - Rice Bran Crackers

Jo-Sef▲ - Graham Crackers (Chocolate●, Cinnamon●, Coffee●, Vanilla●)

Kinnikinnick▲ - Graham Style Cracker Crumbs

Kookie Karma - All Varieties●

Mary's Gone Crackers▲ - Black Pepper, Caraway, Herb, Onion, Original

Mr. Krispers - Tasty Snack Crackers (Original Sesame●)

Orgran▲ - Crispbreads (Corn, Rice, Rice & Cracked Pepper, Rice & Garden Herb, Salsa Corn), Crispibites (Balsamic Herb, Corn, Onion & Chive), Crackers (Premium Deli)

Real Foods - Corn Thins (Cracked Pepper & Lemon, Multigrain, Original, Sesame, Soy & Linseed), Rice Thins (Wholegrain)

Roland - Rice Crackers (Nori Seaweed, Original, Wasabi)

San-J - Rice Crackers (Black Sesame, Sesame, Tamari)

Schar▲ - Snack Crackers, Table Crackers

Trader Joe's - Savory Thins (Multiseed w/Soy Sauce, Original)

Cranberries... *All Fresh Fruits & Vegetables Are Gluten/Casein Free*

Publix - Frozen Cranberries

Oceanspray - Dried Cranberries (Original)

Cranberry Sauce

  Baxters

  Great Value Brand (Wal-Mart)

  Hannaford Brand - Jellied

  Hy-Vee - Jellied, Whole Berry

  Ocean Spray - Jellied, Whole Berry

  S&W - Jellied, Whole Berry

  Safeway Brand - Jellied, Whole

  Spartan Brand - Jellied, Whole

  Wegmans Brand - Jellied, Whole Berry

C **Wild Thymes** - Cranberry Apple Walnut, Cranberry Fig, Cranberry Raspberry, Original

Winn Dixie - Jellied

Cream... see Milk Alternative and/or Creamer

Cream Cheese

Follow Your Heart

Tofutti - Better Than Cream Cheese (All Varieties)

Creamer

Alpro Soya - Alternative Soy Cream

MimicCreme -

Sugar Free Sweetened

Sweetened

Unsweetened

Silk Soymilk - French Vanilla, Hazelnut, Original

Crisps

Baked Lay's - Potato Crisps (Original)

Baked Ruffles - Potato Crisps (Original)

Brothers All Natural▲ -

Fruit Crisps (Asian Pear, Banana, Fuji Apple, Pineapple, Strawberry, Strawberry Banana, White & Yellow Peach)

Potato Crisps (Black Pepper & Sea Salt, Fresh Onion & Garlic, Original w/Sea Salt, Szechwan Pepper & Fresh Chives)

Eat Smart -

Veggie Crisps

Regular

Sun Dried Tomato & Pesto

Herr's - Veggie Crisps

Lay's Stax - Potato Crisps (Original)

Michael Season's - Baked Thin Potato Crisps (Original, Sweet Barbecue)

C

Mr. Krispers -
Baked Rice Krisps (Barbecue●, Sea Salt & Pepper●)
Multi Seed Chips (Original●)
Tasty Snack Crackers (Original Sesame●)
Orgran▲ - Crispibites (Balsamic Herb, Onion & Chive, Original Corn)
Trader Joe's - Sea Salt & Pepper Crisps, Soy Crisps BBQ
Croutons
Ener-G▲ - Plain Croutons
Gillian's Foods▲ - Garlic Croutons
Gluten-Free Pantry▲ - Olive Oil & Garlic Croutons
Cucumbers... *All Fresh Fruits & Vegetables Are Gluten/Casein Free*
Cupcakes... see Cake/Cake Mix
Curry Paste
A Taste Of Thai - Curry Paste (Green, Red, Yellow)
Patak's -
Biryani
Madras
Tandoori
Tikka
Vindaloo
Sharwood's - Green, Red
Thai Kitchen - Curry Paste (Green, Red)
Curry Powder
Durkee
McCormick
Spice Island
Tones
Custard
Orgran▲ - Custard Mix

D D

Deli Meat

Applegate Farms -

Natural (Black Forest Ham, Coppa, Genoa Salami, Herb Turkey, Honey & Maple Turkey Breast, Honey Ham, Hot Genoa Salami, Hot Soppressata, Pancetta, Pepperoni, Roast Beef, Roasted Turkey, Slow Cooked Ham, Smoked Turkey Breast, Soppressata, Turkey Bologna, Turkey Salami)

Organic (Genoa Salami, Herb Turkey Breast, Roast Beef, Roasted Chicken, Smoked Chicken, Smoked Turkey Breast, Uncured Ham)

Butterball -

Extra Thin Sliced Deep Fried Turkey Breast (Cajun Style, Original, Thanksgiving Style)

Extra Thin Turkey Breast (Honey Roasted, Oven Roasted, Smoked)

Family Size (Honey Roasted Turkey Breast, Oven Roasted Turkey Breast, Smoked Turkey Breast, Turkey Bologna, Turkey Ham)

Thick Sliced Deep Fried Turkey Breast (Cajun Style, Original, Thanksgiving Style)

Thick Sliced Turkey Breast (Honey Roasted, Oven Roasted, Smoked)

Thin Sliced Oven Roasted Chicken Breast

Thin Sliced Turkey Breast (Honey Roasted, Oven Roasted, Smoked)

Carl Buddig -

Deli Thin Sliced

Beef

Chicken

Corned Beef

Ham

Honey Ham

Honey Turkey

Oven Roasted Turkey

Pastrami

Turkey

Extra Thin Sliced
  Beef
  Corned Beef
  Ham
  Honey Ham
  Honey Turkey
  Turkey

Dietz & Watson -
  Black Forest Knockwurst
  German Brand Bologna

Farmer John - Lunch Meats (Black Forest Ham, Bologna, Brown Sugar & Honey Ham, Cotto Salami, Headcheese, Premium Oven Roasted Turkey Breast)

Great Value Brand (Wal-Mart) -
  Deli Meat
    97% Fat Free (Baked Ham Water Added, Honey Ham Water Added)
    Thinly Sliced Smoked (Ham, Honey Ham)

Hannaford Brand -
  Sliced (Cooked Ham, Danish Brand Ham, Honey Ham, Oven Roasted Turkey)
  Thin Sliced (Black Forest Turkey, Honey Cured Turkey, Honey Ham, Oven Roasted Turkey, Roast Beef)

Hebrew National -
  From The Deli Counter (Beef Bologna, Beef Salami, Corned Beef, Pastrami)
  Sliced Lunchmeats (Beef Bologna, Beef Salami, Lean Beef Bologna, Lean Beef Salami)

Hillshire Farms -
  Deli Select
    Baked Ham
    Honey (Ham, Roasted Turkey Breast)

D

Deli Select Premium Hearty Slices
  Honey (Ham, Roasted Turkey)
  Oven Roasted Turkey Breast
  Virginia Brand Baked Ham
Deli Select Thin Sliced
  Brown Sugar Baked Ham
  Corned Beef
  Honey Roasted Turkey Breast
  Mesquite Smoked Turkey Breast
  Oven Roasted (Chicken Breast, Turkey Breast)
  Roast Beef
  Smoked (Chicken Breast, Ham, Turkey Breast)
Deli Select Ultra Thin
  Brown Sugar Baked Ham
  Honey (Ham, Roasted Turkey Breast)
  Mesquite Smoked Turkey
  Oven Roasted Turkey Breast
  Pastrami
  Roast Beef
  Smoked Ham
Homeland - Hard Salami
Honeysuckle White -
  Chicken Breast Deli Meats (BBQ, Buffalo Style, Oil Browned)
  Hickory Smoked Cooked Turkey Salami
  Hickory Smoked Turkey Ham
  Hickory Smoked Turkey Pastrami
  Lunch Meats Deli Sliced
    Hickory Smoked Honey Turkey Breast
    Hickory Smoked Turkey Breast
    Oven Roasted Turkey Breast
    Turkey Pastrami

D

Turkey Bologna
Turkey Breast Deli Meats
    Cajun Style Hickory Smoked
    Golden Roasted
    Hickory Smoked (Peppered , Regular)
    Honey Mesquite Smoked
    Oil Browned
    Oven Prepared
Turkey Breast Estate Recipe
    Buffalo Style
    Canadian Brand Maple
    Dry Roasted
    Hickory Smoked (Honey Pepper, Original)
    Honey Smoked
    Mesquite Smoked
Hormel -
Deli Sliced
    Black Forest Ham
    Cooked (Corned Beef, Ham, Pastrami)
    Honey Ham
    Oven Roasted Turkey Breast
    Prosciutto Ham
Diced Ham
Natural Choice
    Cooked Deli Ham
    Honey Deli (Ham, Turkey)
    Oven Roasted Deli Turkey
    Roast Beef
    Smoked Deli (Ham, Turkey)
    Uncured Hard Salami

D Hy-Vee -
Loaf
Old Fashioned
Pickle
Spiced Luncheon
Jennie-O -
Grand Champion Turkey Breast
Hickory Smoked
Honey Cured
Mesquite Smoked
Oven Roasted
Pan Roasted
Tender Browned
Natural Choice Deli Counter Turkey Breast
Applewood Smoked
Honey Roasted
Peppered
Tender Browned
Premium Fresh Deli Counter Turkey Breast
Golden Classic Herb Roasted
Hickory Smoked Honey Roasted
Honey Cured
Mesquite Smoked
Oven Roasted
Premium Seasoned Deli Counter Turkey Breast
Bourbon Maple
Cajun Style
Cracked Pepper
Cranberry Sage
Italian Style Roasted Garlic
Sun Dried Tomato
Sweet Maple

Norwestern Deli Turkey - Oven Roasted

D

Oscar Mayer -

Deli Fresh Meats

Cooked Ham (96% Fat Free, Regular)

Honey Ham

Oven Roasted (98% Fat Free Turkey, Chicken Breast, Turkey Breast)

Smoked (Ham, Turkey Breast)

Shaved Deli Fresh Meats

Black Forest Ham

Brown Sugar Ham

Cajun Seasoned Chicken Breast

Cracked Black Peppered Turkey Breast

French Dip Roast Beef

Honey Ham

Honey Smoked Turkey Breast

Mesquite Turkey Breast

Oven Roasted Turkey Breast

Rotisserie Style Chicken Breast

Slow Roasted Roast Beef

Smoked Ham

Smoked Turkey Breast

Virginia Brand Ham

Thin Sliced Deli Fresh

97% Fat Free Smoked Ham

Brown Sugar Ham

Honey Smoked Turkey Breast

Mesquite Turkey Breast

Oven Roasted Chicken Breast

Oven Roasted Turkey Breast

Smoked Turkey Breast

D   Primo Taglio -
Old Fashioned Maple Ham w/Natural Juices
Prosciutto Dry Cured Ham
Roast Beef Coated w/Seasonings (Caramel Color Added)
Salami Coated w/Gelatin & Black Pepper

Publix -
Deli Pre Pack Sliced Lunch Meat
Beef
Bologna
Bottom Round Roast
Cooked Ham
Corned Beef
Extra Thin Sliced (Honey Ham, Oven Roasted Turkey Breast, Smoked Turkey Breast)
German Bologna
Low Salt Ham
Pickle & Pimento Loaf
Smoked Turkey
Spanish Style Pork
Sweet Ham
Tavern Ham
Turkey Breast
Virginia Brand Ham

Wegmans - Chicken Breast Cutlets (Honey Mustard, Italian, Rosemary Balsamic Tangy), Corned Beef w/ Juices, Pork Tenderloin Honey Mustard, Roast Beef Organic, Turkey Breast No Salt, Turkey Oven Browned

Winn Dixie - Thin Sliced (Cooked Ham, Honey Ham, Roast Beef, Oven Roasted Turkey, Smoked Honey Turkey, Smoked Turkey)

Dill Pickles... see Pickles

Dinner Meals... see Meals

Dip/Dip Mix **D**

   Eat Smart - Tres Bean Dip

   Fantastic World Foods - Original Hummus

   Fritos -

   Bean

   Hot Bean

   Lipton - Recipe Secrets Onion Soup & Dip Mix

   Road's End Organics - Non Dairy Nacho Chreese Dip (Mild, Spicy)

   Safeway Select - Balsamic Garlic Dipping Sauce

   Salpica - Dip (Chipotle Black Bean, Mexican Red Bean)

   Scarpetta - Spicy Red Pepper Spread

   Sharwood's - Green Label Mango Chutney & Chilli

   T. Marzetti -

   Hummus

   Original

   Red Pepper

   Roasted Garlic

   Veggie

   UTZ -

   Mt. Misery Mike's Salsa Dip

   Sweet Salsa Dip

   Walden Farms - Fruit Dip (Caramel, Chocolate, Marshmallow),
   Veggie & Chip Dip (Bacon, Blue Cheese, French Onion, Ranch)

Donuts/Doughnuts

   Celiac Specialties▲ -

   Gluten Free/Casein Free Donut Holes

   Cinnamon Sugar

   Glazed

   Plain

   Powder Sugar

   Ener-G▲ - Plain Doughnut (Holes, Regular)

D   Gluten-Free Creations▲ -
   Chocolate●
   Cinnamon & Sugar●
   Insane Chocolate●
   Plain Jane●
   Superb Sprinkles●
Kinnikinnick▲ -
   Chocolate Dipped
   Cinnamon Sugar
   Glazed Chocolate
   Maple Dipped
   Vanilla Dipped
Dressing... see Salad Dressing
Dried Fruit
   Brothers All Natural▲ - Fruit Crisps (Asian Pear, Banana, Fuji Apple, Pineapple, Strawberry, Strawberry Banana, White & Yellow Peach)
   Eden Organic - Cranberries, Montmorency Dried Tart Cherries, Wild Blueberries
   Hy-Vee - Apples, Apricots, Banana Chips, Blueberries, Cherries, Cranberries, Mixed (Berries, Fruit), Pineapple
   Member's Mark - 7 Fruit Blend, Mediterranean Dried Apricots
   Nonuttin' Foods▲ - Fruit Snacks
   Oceanspray - Dried Cranberries (Original)
   Publix - Dried Plums, Fruit Snacks (Curious George, Dinosaurs, Sharks, Snoopy, Veggie Tales)
   Safeway Brand - Berries & Cherries, Cranberries, Island Inspirations, Philippine Mango, Prunes, Raisins, Tropical Treasures
   Spartan Brand - Cranberries, Raisins
   Sun-Maid -
      Raisins (Baking, Golden, Natural California, Regular)
      Zante Currants
   Trader Joe's - Dried (Apricots, Baby Sweet Pineapple, Berry Medley, Bing Cherries, Blueberries, Pineapple Rings, Pitted Tart

D

Montmorency, White Peaches, Wild Blueberries), Freeze Dried Bananas, Freeze Dried Mango, Organic Dried Cranberries, Unsulphured & Sweetened Dried Mango

Traverse Bay Fruit Co. - Certified Organic Dried Tart Cherries, Dried Natural Cherries, Dried Tart Cherries

Wegmans Brand - Seedless Raisins

Woodstock Farms -

Apple Rings (Regular, Unsulphured)

Apricots Turkish

Banana Chips (Regular, Sweetened)

Black Mission Figs

Blueberries

Calmyrna Figs

Cherries Unsulphured

Cranberries Sweetened

Dates Deglet w/Pit

Flame Raisins

Ginger (Crystallized, Slices Unsulphured)

Goji Berries

Kiwi Slices

Mango (Diced, Slices (Regular, Unsulphured))

Medjool Dates w/Pit

Papaya Spears Lo Sugar Unsulphered

Pineapple Slices Unsulphered

Prunes Pitted

Thompson Raisins

Winn Dixie -

Apricots

Banana Chips

Blueberries

Cherries

D
    Cranberries
    Plums
    Raisins (Golden, Organic, Regular)

Drink Mix

  Country Time - Lemonade, Pink Lemonade, Raspberry Lemonade

  Crystal Light -

    Decaf Iced Tea (Lemon, Regular)

    Fruit Punch

    Green Tea Raspberry

    Iced Tea (Peach, Raspberry, Regular)

    Immunity Natural Cherry Pomegranate

    Lemonade

    Pineapple Orange

    Raspberry (Lemonade, Peach)

    Strawberry Kiwi

    Sunrise (Berry Tangerine Morning, Classic Orange, Orange Wake Up, Ruby Red Grapefruit, Tangerine Strawberry, Tropical Morning)

    White Grape

  Flavor Aid -

    Powdered Soft Drinks

      Berry Punch

      Cherry

      Grape

      Kiwi Watermelon

      Lemon Lime

      Lemonade

      Orange

      Raspberry

      Strawberry

      Tropical Punch

D

Hannaford Brand - Regular (Cherry, Fruit Punch, Lemonade, Orange, Strawberry) Sugar Free (Fruit Punch, Iced Tea, Lemon Lime, Lemonade, Raspberry Lemonade)

Hawaiian Punch - All Varieties

Hy-Vee -

Splash Drink Mix (Cherry, Grape, Lemonade, Orange, Strawberry, Tropical, Tropical Fruit Punch)

Sugar Free Splash Drink Mix (Fruit Punch, Iced Tea, Lemonade, Pink Lemonade, Raspberry)

Kool-Aid -

Soft Drink Mix Sugar Sweetened (Cherry, Grape, Lemonade, Strawberry)

Soft Drink Mix Unsweetened (Cherry, Grape, Lemonade, Strawberry, Tropical Punch)

Langers Juices - All Juices

Meijer Brand -

Breakfast Orange

Cherry

Chocolate Flavor

Grape

Ice Tea

Lemon Sugar Free

Lemonade

Lemonade Stix

Orange (Free & Lite, Regular)

Pink Lemonade (Regular, Sugar Free)

Punch

Raspberry Stix

Raspberry Sugar Free

Strawberry (Flavor, Regular)

Strawberry/Orange/Banana

Nestea - Iced Tea Mix Unsweetened (Decaf, Regular)

D

Safeway Brand - Cherry (Light, Regular), Instant Chocolate, Peach (Light, Regular), Pink Lemonade (Light, Regular), Strawberry (Light, Regular), Spiced Apple Cider, Sugar Free Raspberry & Lemonade

Snapple - All Diet Drink Mixes

Tang - Grape, Orange, Orange Kiwi, Tropical Passionfruit, Wild Berry

Wegmans Brand - Powdered Drink Mix (Lemonade Flavor, Pink Lemonade)

Winn Dixie -

Regular (Cherry, Fruit Punch, Grape, Lemonade, Orange, Pink Lemonade, Raspberry, Strawberry Kiwi)

Sugar Free (Fruit Punch, Lemon Iced Tea, Lemonade, Peach Iced Tea, Pink Lemonade)

Wyler's - All Powdered Soft Drinks (Light, Regular, Sugar Free)

Drinks/Juice (Non-Carbonated)... (Carbonated Drinks... see Soda Pop)

Apple & Eve - All Vegetable & Fruit Juices *(Except Tribal Tonic Peach Mango Energy Green Tea)*

Arizona -

50% Juice & Decaf Tea (Apple Green, Pomegranate Green)

Arnold Palmers Lite (Green Tea Lemonade, Half & Half Iced Tea Lemonade)

Blueberry Tea (Green, White)

Decaf Diet w/Ginseng

Diet

Peach Iced Tea

Iced Tea w/(Raspberry Flavor, White Cranberry Apple Green)

Energy Drinks Green Tea (Diet, Regular)

Ginseng & Honey Original Blend Green Tea

Green Tea (Diet, Regular, w/Ginger, w/Ginseng)

Half & Half (Iced Tea/Lemonade, Lite Green Tea/Lemonade)

Iced Teas

Sun Brewed, w/(Ginseng Extract, Lemon Flavor)

No Caffeine Herbal

D

Mandarin Orange

Peach Green Tea

Plum Green Tea

Pomegranate & Acai Green Tea

White Cranberry/Apple Green Tea (Diet, Regular)

Campbell's - Tomato Juice (Low Sodium, Organic, Original)

Capri Sun -

Coastal Cooler Strawberry Banana Blend

Grape

Mountain Cooler

Orange

Pacific Cooler Mixed Fruit

Splash Cooler Mixed Fruit

Strawberry

Strawberry Raspberry Blend

Sunrise Berry Strawberry Tangerine

Sunrise Orange Wake Up

Sunrise Tropical Morning

Surfer Cooler Mixed Fruit Blend

Tropical Punch

Wild Cherry Blend

Cascadian Farms - Organic Frozen Juice Concentrate (Apple, Cranberry, Grape, Lemonade, Orange, Raspberry)

Ceres - All Varieties

Country Time - Lemonade

Dei Fratelli - Juice (Tomato (Regular, Tasty Tom Spicy), Vegetable)

Dole - All Fruit Juice

Eden Organic - Apple Juice, Cherry Concentrate, Montmorency Tart Cherry Juice

Enviga - Sparkling Green Tea (Berry, Regular)

D

Food Club Brand -
    Cranberry (Apple, Grape, Light Grape, Light Raspberry, Raspberry,
      White Cranberry Strawberry)
    Frozen (Apple, Lemonade, OJ Original, OJ Pulp Free, Pink Lemonade)
    Juices (Apple, Cranberry, Grapefruit & Tangerine, Lemon, Lime,
      Pineapple, Pomegranate, Pomegranate Blueberry, Prune, Ruby
      Red Grapefruit, Tomato, Vegetable, White Grape, White Grapefruit)
    Refrigerated (OJ Groves Best, OJ Premium, OJ (w/Calcium,
      w/Omega 3))

Fruit2O - All Varieties

Full Circle - Organic (Apple Natural, Blueberry 100% Juice,
    Cranberry Cocktail, Cranberry Raspberry, Grape 100% Juice,
    Tomato Juice, Vegetable Juice)

Fuze - All Varieties *(Except 'Refresh' Drinks)*

Gardner Groves - 100% Grapefruit Juice

Gold Peak - Iced Tea (Diet, Green Sweetened, Lemon, Sweetened,
    Unsweetened)

Great Value Brand (Wal-Mart) -

    From Concentrate

        100% Juice Apple Juice Punch Blend

        100% Juice Unsweetened Apple Juice

        Fruit Punch

        Natural Strength Lemon Juice

        Tomato Juice

        Vegetable Juice

    Frozen Juice Concentrate

        Country Style Orange Juice Pure Unsweetened

        Florida Grapefruit Juice Pure Unsweetened

        Fruit Punch

        Grape Juice Drink

        Limeade

        Orange Juice w/Calcium

        Pink Lemonade

D

Juice

  100% Juice Apple Juice (Juice Boxes)

  100% Juice Fruit Punch (Juice Boxes)

  Prune Juice

Refrigerated Drinks

  Country Style Orange Juice

  Fruit Punch

  Grape Drink

  Orange Juice (Regular, w/Calcium)

Hannaford Brand -

  From Concentrate (Apple, Apple & Grape Blend, Berry Blend, Blueberry Cranberry, Cherry Blend, Cranberry Juice Cocktail, Fruit Punch, Grape Blend, Grapefruit, Light Cranberry, Light Grape Cranberry, Light Raspberry Cranberry, Low Sodium Vegetable Juice, Orange Juice, Raspberry Cranberry, Ruby Red Grapefruit, Tomato Juice, Vegetable Juice, White Cranberry Peach)

  Premium Juice Blend (Cranberry Flavored, Cranberry Raspberry, Grape Cranberry)

Hansen's - All (Bottled Juices, Diet Green Tea Sodas, Diet Soda, Junior Juices, Juice Slams, Natural Green Tea Sodas, Natural Soda, Natural Soda Mixers, Organic Juice Slams, Organic Junior Water, Smoothies, Sparking Green Tea Sleek, Sparkling Sleek)

Hawaiian Punch - Light, Original

Home Harvest Brand - Apple Juice, Cranberry Juice Cocktail, Original Orange Juice, Tomato Juice, Vegetable Juice Cocktail

Honest Ade - Cranberry Lemonade, Limeade, Orange Mango w/Mangosteen, Pomegranate Blue, Super Fruitpunch

Honest Kids - Berry Berry Good Lemonade, Goodness Greatness, Tropical Tangopunch

Honest Mate - Agave Mate, Sublime Mate, Tropical Mate

Hood - All Juices

D Hy-Vee -

100% Juice Blend (Cranberry, Cranberry Apple, Cranberry Raspberry)

Concord Grape Juice

Frozen Concentrate (Apple (Light, Regular), Fruit Punch, Grape Juice Cocktail, Grapefruit Juice, Lemonade, Limeade, Orange (Regular, w/Calcium), Pineapple, Pink Lemonade)

Juice Cocktail From Concentrate (Cranberry, Cranberry Apple, Cranberry Grape, Cranberry Raspberry, Grapefruit, Lemon, Light Cranberry Raspberry, Ruby Red Grapefruit)

Juice From Concentrate (100% Apple, 100% Unsweetened Prune, 100% White Grape, Apple, Apple Kiwi, Country Style Orange, Lemonade, Light Apple Raspberry, Light Grape Cranberry, Orange Juice, Orange Juice w/Calcium, Pineapple, Pomegranate, Prune Juice, Tomato, Unsweetened Apple Cider, Vegetable)

Izze -

Sparkling Juice Beverages

Blackberry

Blueberry

Clementine

Grapefruit

Peach

Pomegranate

Lakewood - All Juices (Organic)

Lowes Foods Brand -

Juice

Apple (Natural, Regular)

Concord Grape

Cranberry Apple

Cranberry Cocktail (Light, Regular)

Cranberry Grape (Light, Regular)

Cranberry Raspberry

Grape Cocktail Light

Lemon (Regular, Squeeze)

Orange (Regular, Unsweetened)

Pink Grapefruit

Premium Cranberry Cocktail 100% Juice

Prune

Ruby Red Grapefruit Tangerine

Tomato

Vegetable Cocktail

White (Grape, Grapefruit)

Lucky Leaf - Apple (Cider, Juice, Premium Juice)

Manischewitz - Grape Juice

Marsh Brand - Orange Juice (Refrigerated)

Meijer Brand -

100% Juice (Berry, Cherry, Cranberry/Raspberry, Grape, Punch)

Cranberry Juice Drink (Grape, Raspberry, Strawberry, White)

Drink Thirst Quencher (Fruit Punch, Lemon Lime, Orange)

Frozen Concentrate Juice (Apple, Fruit Punch, Grape, Grapefruit, Lemonade, Limeade, Orange, Pink Lemonade, White Grape)

Frozen Concentrate Orange Juice (High Pulp, Pulp Free, w/Calcium)

Fruit Punch (Genuine, Light, Regular)

Juice (Apple, Apple Natural, Cherry, Grape, Grapefruit, Fruit Mix, Lemon, Lime, Pineapple, Pink Grapefruit, Prune, Ruby Red Grapefruit, Tangerine & Ruby Red, White Grape, White Grapefruit)

Juice Blend (Acai & Blueberry, Acai & Grape, Pomegranate & Blueberry, Pomegranate & Cranberry, White Cranberry, White Grape & Peach, White Grape & Raspberry)

Juice Cocktail (Cranapple, Cranberry (Light, Regular), Cranberry Grape (Light, Regular), Cranberry Raspberry (Light, Regular), Cranberry Strawberry, Cranberry White Peach, Light Grape Splenda, Ruby Red Grapefruit (Light, Light 22%, Regular), White Cranberry, White Cranberry Peach, White Cranberry Strawberry, White Grape, White Grapefruit)

D

Juice Refrigerated Orange (Original, Reconstituted)

Juice Refrigerated Orange Premium (Calcium Carafe, Carafe, Hi Pulp Carafe, Original, Pulp, w/Calcium)

Lemon Juice Squeeze Bottle

Organic Juice (Apple, Concord Grape, Cranberry, Lemonade)

Orange Reconstituted (Original, Pulp, w/Calcium)

Splash (Berry Blend, Strawberry Kiwi, Tropical Blend)

Midwest Country Fare - 100 % Unsweetened From Concentrate (Apple Cider, Apple Juice), Cranberry, Cranberry Apple, Cranberry Raspberry, Grape

Minute Maid -

Lemonade (Light, Original, Pink)

Limonada/Limeade

Orange Juice (Country Style, Heart Wise, Home Squeezed Style, Kids +, Low Acid, Original, Original + Calcium, Pulp Free)

Orange Tangerine

Pomegranate Blueberry

Punch (Berry, Citrus, Fruit, Grape, Tropical)

Mondo - All Fruit Squeezers

Mott's - All Varieties

Musselman's - Apple (Cider, Fresh Pressed Apple Cider, Juice, Premium Juice, Sparkling Cider)

Nantucket Nectars - All Varieties

Nestea - Citrus Green Tea (Diet, Regular), Lemon (Diet, Sweetened), Red Tea, White Tea Berry Honey (Diet, Regular)

Nestle - Juicy Juice (All Flavors), Juicy Juice Harvest Surprise (All Flavors)

Newman's Own -

Grape Juice

Green Tea w/Honey

Lemon Aided Iced Tea

Lemonade (Lightly Sweetened, Old Fashioned, Organic, Pink)

Limeade

Orange Mango

Organic Virgin Lemonade

Razz Ma Tazz Raspberry

O Organics - Bottled Juices (Apple, Berry Blend, Blueberry Blend, Cranberry Cocktail, Grape, Lemonade, Unfiltered Apple), Orange Juice (Refrigerated)

Ocean Spray - All Varieties

Odwalla -

All Natural Carrot Juice

All Natural Lemonade

All Natural Orange Juice

All Natural Smoothie (Mango Tango, Strawberry Banana)

B Monster (Blueberry B)

C Monster (Citrus C, Strawberry C)

Mo' Beta

Mojito Mambo

Pomegranate Strawberry

Serious Energy (Tropical Energy)

Serious Focus (Apple Raspberry)

Wholly Grain (Tropical Medley)

Organic Valley - Orange Juice (Pulp Added, Pulp Free, w/Calcium)

Powerade - Grape, Ion 4 Mountain Berry Blast, Lemon Lime

Publix -

From Concentrate

Orange Juice (Regular, w/Calcium)

Ruby Red Grapefruit Juice

Refrigerated

Premium Orange Juice (Calcium Plus, Grove Pure, Old Fashioned, Original)

Premium Ruby Red Grapefruit Juice

D

Shelf Stable

Apple

Cranberry (Apple Juice Cocktail, Juice Cocktail, Reduced Calorie Cocktail, w/Calcium)

Grape

Grape Cranberry Juice Cocktail

Lemonade (Deli Old Fashion)

Pineapple

Raspberry Cranberry Juice Cocktail

Ruby Red Grapefruit (Regular, w/Tangerine)

Tomato

White Grape

Publix GreenWise Market - Organic (Apple, Cranberry, Grape, Lemonade, Tomato)

R.W. Knudsen -

Juice

Black (Cherry, Currant)

Blueberry

Blueberry Pomegranate

Cranberry

Cranberry Pomegranate

Lemon Ginger Echinacea

Morning Blend

Organic (Acai Berry, Cranberry Blueberry, Pomegranate, Prune, Tomato)

Pomegranate

ReaLemon - 100% Lemon Juice

ReaLime - 100% Lime Juice

Safeway Brand -

Frozen (Apple, Berry Punch, Cranberry, Grape, Lemonade, Limeade, Orange, Orange Country Style, Orange w/Calcium, Pink Lemonade, Raspberry Lemonade)

Juice

D

Apple (Cider, Regular)

Cranberry (Apple, Cocktail, Light Cocktail, Light Raspberry, Raspberry)

Grape (Light, Regular)

Grapefruit (Cocktail, Pink, Regular, Ruby Red Cocktail, White)

Lemon

Orange

Prune

Tomato

Vegetable

White Grape

Shelby's Grove - Apple Juice 100% Juice

Simply Apple

Simply Grapefruit

Simply Lemonade - Original, w/Raspberry

Simply Limeade

Simply Orange - Calcium Pulp Free, Country Stand Medium Pulp w/Calcium, High Pulp, Pulp Free, w/Pineapple, w/Mango

Snapple - All (100% Juices, Diet Drinks, Flavored Waters, Juice Drinks, Teas) *(Except Go Bananas Juice Drink)*

SoBe -

Elixir (Orange Carrot)

Energy (Berry, Citrus, Tropical)

Green Tea

Lean Diet (Mango Melon)

Nirvana (Mango Melon)

Power (Fruit Punch)

Sonoma Sparkler - Natural (Peach, Pear, Raspberry), Organic (Apple, Lemonade)

D **Spartan Brand -**

Apple Juice (Natural, Regular)

Cranberry Juice Cocktail (Low Calorie, Regular)

Cranberry Juice Drink (Apple, Grape, Raspberry, Strawberry)

Frozen Concentrate (Apple Juice, Grape Juice Cocktail, Fruit Punch, Grapefruit Juice, Lemonade, Orange Juice (Country Style, Pulp Free, Regular, w/Calcium), Pink Lemonade)

Grape Juice (Regular, White)

Grapefruit Juice

Lemon Juice

Premium Orange Juice (Country Style Pulp, Regular, w/Calcium)

Premium Ruby Red Grapefruit

Prune Juice

Reconstituted Orange Juice (Country Style Pulp, Regular, w/Calcium)

Ruby Red Grapefruit Juice

Tomato Juice

Vegetable Juice Cocktail

SunnyD - All Varieties

Tipton Grove - Apple Juice 100% Juice

Tropicana - All 100% Juices

V8 -

Diet Splash (Berry Blend, Tropical Blend)

Splash (Berry Blend, Fruit Medley, Mango Peach, Strawberry Kiwi Blend, Tropical Blend)

Splash Smoothies (Strawberry Banana, Tropical Colada)

V-Fusion (Acai Berry, Goji Raspberry, Passionfruit Tangerine, Peach Mango, Pomegranate Blueberry, Strawberry Banana, Tropical Orange)

V-Fusion Light (Peach Mango, Pomegranate Blueberry, Strawberry Banana)

Vegetable Juice (Calcium Enriched, Fiber, Low Sodium, Organic, Original, Spicy Hot)

Vruit - Apple Carrot, Berry Veggie, Orange Veggie, Tropical

D

Wegmans Brand -

  100% Juice

    Cranberry (Blend, Raspberry)

    Ruby Red Grapefruit Blend

  Frozen Juice Concentrate

    Apple

    Fruit Punch

    Lemonade

    Limeade

    Pink Lemonade

  Juice

    Apple (Natural, Regular)

    Cranberry (Peach, Raspberry, Regular)

    Grape (Juice Cocktail, Regular, White)

    Grapefruit

    Juice Blends (Berry, Cherry, Concord Grape Cranberry, Cranberry Apple, Orange Peach Mango, Ruby Red Grapefruit, Sparkling Cranberry, White Grape Cranberry, White Grape Peach)

    Lemon Juice Reconstituted

    Orange (Regular, Unsweetened)

    Prune

    White Grape (Peach Blend, Raspberry Blend, Regular)

  Juice From Concentrate

    100% Juice (Orange, Tomato, Vegetable (No Salt Added, Regular))

    Blueberry Flavor Juice Blend

    Lemon

    Lemonade

    Limeade

    Orange Juice (Calcium Enriched, Regular, w/Calcium)

    Pomegranate Flavor Juice Blend

    Prune

D

Organic Juice From Concentrate
  Apple
  Apricot Nectar
  Cranberry
  Mango Nectar
  Orange
Punch (Berry, Fruit, Pineapple Orange)
Premium 100% Juice
  Orange (Extra Pulp, No Pulp, Some Pulp, w/Calcium,
    w/Calcium & Vitamins)
  Ruby Red Grapefruit
Premium Orange Juice (No Pulp, Some Pulp)
Sparkling Beverage
  Calorie Free (Lemon Mandarin Orange, Mixed Berry, Tangerine
    Lime, Raspberry)
  Diet (Black Cherry, Cranberry Raspberry, Key Lime, Kiwi
    Strawberry, Mixed Berry, Peach, Peach Grapefruit, Tangerine
    Lime, White Grape)
  Lime, Grape Juice Alcohol Free, Lemonade
Sparkling Grape Juice Alcohol Free (Pink, Red, White)

Welch's - All Varieties

Winn & Lovett - Juice (Black Cherry, Cranberry, Pomegranate)

Winn Dixie -

Juice (Cranberry, Cranberry Apple, Cranberry Raspberry,
  Premium Apple, Reconstituted Lemon, Light Cranberry, Light
  Cranberry Grape, Light Grape, Pomegranate Blend,
  Pomegranate Blueberry Blend, Pomegranate Cranberry Blend,
  Ruby Red Grapefruit, Ruby Red Grapefruit Cocktail,
  Vegetable)
Juice From Concentrate (Apple Cider, Apple, Grape, Grapefruit,
  Orange, Orange w/Calcium, Pink Lemonade, Prune, Prune w/Pulp,
  White Grape)
Nectar Drinks (Guava, Mango, Mango Pineapple Guava, Peach,
  Pear)

egg replacer/substitute

Orange Juice (From Concentrate, From Concentrate w/Calcium, Premium Not From Concentrate)   **D**

Organic Juice (Apple, Cranberry, Grape, Lemonade, Mango Acai Berry Blend, Orange Mango Blend, Tomato)   **E**

Woodstock Farms - Non Organic Juices (All Varieties), Organic Juices (All Varieties)

Zola - Original, w/Blueberry, w/Pineapple

Duck... *All Fresh Poultry Is Gluten/Casein Free (Non-Marinated, Unseasoned)*

Shelton's - Duckling

Wellshire Farms - Smoked Duck Breast

Dumplings

Mixes From The Heartland▲ - Country Dumpling Mix●

E

Edamame

Cascadian Farm - Organic Frozen (Edamame, Shelled Edamame)

Imperial - All Natural Edamame

Meijer Brand - Edamame (Soybeans)

Melissa's - In Shell

O Organics - Frozen

Safeway Brand - Edamame

Stop & Shop Brand - In Pod

Sunrich Naturals - In The Shell, Organic, Shelled

Trader Joe's - Dry Roasted

Woodstock Farms - Organic Frozen Edamame (Shelled, Whole Pods)

Egg Replacer/Substitute

Albertsons - Egg Substitute (Amazing Eggs, Amazing Egg Whites)

All Whites - All Varieties

Better'n Eggs - All Varieties

E

Eggbeaters - Garden Vegetable, Original, Southwestern Style

Ener-G▲ - Egg Replacer

Hy-Vee - Refrigerated Egg Substitute

Lucerne - Best Of The Egg

Meijer Brand - Refrigerated Egg Substitute

Orgran▲ - No Egg Egg Replacer

Publix - Egg Stirs

Spartan Brand - Eggmates

Wegmans Brand - Egg Busters, Liquid Egg Whites

Eggnog

Vitasoy - Holly Nog

Eggplant... *All Fresh Fruits & Vegetables Are Gluten/Casein Free*

Tasty Bite - Punjab Eggplant

Eggs... *All Fresh Eggs Are Gluten/Casein Free*

Enchilada Sauce

Frontera - Chipotle Garlic, Classic Red Chile

La Victoria - Green Mild, Red (Hot, Mild)

Las Palmas - Red

Safeway Select - Mild

Enchiladas

Amy's - Black Bean Vegetable (Light In Sodium, Regular, Whole Meal)

Trader Joe's - Black Bean & Corn

Energy Bars... see Bars

Energy Drinks

AMP - Elevate, Lightning, Overdrive, ReLaunch, Sugar Free, Traction, w/Black Tea, w/Green Tea

Hansen's - All Varieties

Inko's - White Tea Energy

Monster - Assault, Hitman (Lobo, Original, Sniper), Import, Khaos, Lo-Carb, M-80, MIXXD, Regular (Green)

NOS - Energy Drink

No Fear - Bloodshot, Motherload, Super Energy

Red Bull -
    Cola
    Energy Shots
    Regular
    Sugar Free
Red Rain - Diet, Regular
Rehab

English Muffins
    Ener-G▲ - Brown Rice English Muffins w/(Flax, Tofu), English Muffins
    Foods By George▲ -
        English Muffins
            Cinnamon Currant
            No Rye Rye
            Plain
    Kinnikinnick▲ - Tapioca Rice

Espresso... see Coffee

Extract
    Albertsons - Imitation Vanilla, Pure Vanilla
    Durkee - Vanilla (Imitation, Pure)
    Flavorganics - Almond, Anise, Chocolate, Coconut, Hazelnut, Lemon, Orange, Peppermint, Rum, Vanilla
    Hannaford Brand -
        Imitation (Almond, Vanilla)
        Pure (Lemon, Vanilla)
    Hy-Vee - Pure Vanilla
    Marcin - Pure Vanilla
    Marcum - Pure Vanilla
    McCormick - Pure Lemon, Pure Vanilla
    Meijer Brand - Imitation Vanilla, Vanilla
    Nielsen-Massey - Madagascar Bourbon Pure Vanilla●
    Publix - Almond, Lemon, Vanilla

E

Spartan Brand - Imitation Vanilla, Vanilla
Spice Island - Vanilla (Imitation, Pure)

F

Tones - Vanilla (Imitation, Pure)
Trader Joe's - Pure Vanilla
Wegmans Brand - Vanilla Extract

F

Fajita Seasoning Mix... see also Seasonings
McCormick - Seasoning Packet
Old El Paso - Seasoning Mix
Safeway Brand
Falafel Mix
Authentic Foods ▲
Orgran ▲
Fettuccini... see Pasta
Fiber
Kinnikinnick ▲ - Easy White Fiber Mix, Pea Hull Fibre
Fish... *All Fresh Fish Is Gluten/Casein Free (Non-Marinated, Unseasoned)*
Chicken Of The Sea -
Canned
Chunk Light Tuna
Chunk Light Tuna In Canola Oil
Chunk Light Tuna In Oil
Jack Mackerel
Low Sodium Chunk Light Tuna In Water
Pink Salmon Chunk Style In Water
Pink Salmon Traditional Style
Sardines In Mustard Sauce
Sardines In Oil Lightly Smoked

Sardines In Water
Solid White Albacore Tuna
Solid White Albacore Tuna In Oil
Solid White Albacore Tuna In Water
Solid White Longline Albacore In Water
Pouch
Premium Albacore Tuna In Water
Premium Light Tuna In Water
Skinless & Boneless Pink Salmon
Smoked Pacific Salmon

Crown Prince -
Crosspacked Brisling Sardines In Olive Oil
Fillets of Mackerel In Soy Bean Oil
Fish Steaks (w/Green Chilies, In Louisiana Hot Sauce)
Jack Mackerel In Water
One Layer Brisling Sardines In (Mustard, Oil No Salt Added, Soy Bean Oil, Tomato)
Sardines In (Hot Tomato Sauce, Louisiana Hot Sauce, Mustard, Oil, Tomato Sauce, Water)
Sardines w/Green Chilies
Two Layer Brisling Sardines In (Olive Oil, Soy Bean Oil)

Crown Prince Natural -
Alaskan Pink Salmon
One Layer Brisling Sardines In (Mustard, Spring Water)
Skinless & Boneless Pacific Pink Salmon
Skinless & Boneless Sardines In (Olive Oil, Water)
Smoked Alaskan Coho Salmon
Two Layer Brisling Sardines In Olive Oil

Dr. Praeger's - All Natural Potato Crusted Gluten Free (Fish Fillets, Fish Sticks, Fishies)

F

Full Circle - All Natural (Alaskan Cod Fillets, Alaskan Halibut Steaks, Alaskan Sockeye Salmon Fillets, Skinless Mahi Mahi Fillets, Swordfish Steaks, Yellowfin Tuna Steaks)

Hy-Vee - Canned Alaskan Pink Salmon, Frozen (Salmon, Tilapia), Red Salmon

Ian's -

Wheat Free Gluten Free Recipe

Fish Sticks

Lightly Battered Fish

Meijer Brand - Canned Salmon (Pink, Sock Eye Red)

Morey's - Wild Alaskan Salmon

Publix - Bass Fillets, Cod Fillets, Flounder Fillets, Haddock Fillets, Halibut Fillets, Mahi Mahi Fillets, Orange Roughy Fillets, Snapper Fillets, Swordfish Fillets, Whiting Fillets

Wegmans Brand -

Alaskan Halibut

Atlantic Salmon Fillets (Farm Raised)

Chilean Sea Bass

Lobster Tail

Orange Roughy

Pacific Cod

Smoked Salmon (Nova, Scottish Style)

Sockeye Salmon

Swordfish

Tilapia Fillets (Farm Raised)

Yellowfin Tuna (Sashimi Grade)

Winn Dixie - Frozen (Grouper, Tilapia)

Fish Sauce

A Taste Of Thai - Regular

Thai Kitchen - Regular

Fish Steaks

Crown Prince - In Louisiana Hot Sauce, In Mustard, w/Green Chilies

Ocean Prince - In Louisiana Hot Sauce, In Oil, w/Green Chilies

Fish Sticks

Dr. Praeger's - All Natural Potato Crusted Gluten Free (Fish Sticks, Fishies)

Ian's - Wheat Free Gluten Free Recipe Fish Sticks

Flax Seed

Arrowhead Mills - Flax Seed Meal, Flax Seeds (Golden, Regular)

Bob's Red Mill▲ - Flaxseed Meal (Golden, Original), Organic Flaxseed (Golden, Original)

El Peto▲ - Whole

Hodgson Mill▲ - Organic Golden Milled, Travel Flax All Natural Milled, Travel Flax Organic Golden Milled

Nature's Path - Organic FlaxPlus (Meal, Flaxseeds)

Shiloh Farms - Brown Flax Seed, Golden Flax Seeds, Real Cold Milled Flax Meal

Spectrum - Organic Ground Essential Flax Seed

Trader Joe's - Golden Roasted (Flax Seed w/Blueberries, Whole)

Flax Seed Oil... see Oil

Flour

Amazing Grains - Montina (All Purpose Flour Blend●, Pure Baking Supplement●)

Andrea's Fine Foods▲ - Gluten Free Flour Blend, Super Fine Grind Rice (Brown, Sweet)

Arrowhead Mills - All Purpose Baking Mix, Brown Rice, Organic (Buckwheat, Millet, Soy, White Rice)

Authentic Foods▲ -

Almond Meal

Arrowroot

Bette's Flour Blend

Brown Rice Flour Superfine

Garbanzo

Garfava

Gluten Free Classical Blend

F

    Multi Blend Gluten Free
    Potato (Flour, Starch)
    Sorghum
    Sweet Rice Flour Superfine
    Tapioca
    White (Corn, Rice Flour Superfine)

Bob's Red Mill▲ -

    Almond Meal/Flour
    Black Bean
    Brown Rice
    Fava Bean
    Garbanzo Bean
    Garbanzo & Fava
    Gluten Free (All Purpose Baking, Sweet White Sorghum)
    Green Pea
    Hazelnut Meal/Flour
    Millet
    Organic (Amaranth, Brown Rice, Coconut, Quinoa, White Rice)
    Potato
    Sweet White Rice
    Tapioca
    Teff
    White (Bean, Rice)

Celiac Specialties▲ - Flour Blend

Chateau Cream Hill Estates - Lara's Whole Grain Oat Flour●

ConAgra Mills -

    5 Grain Whole Grain Blend●

    Conventional (Amaranth Seed●, Millet Seed●, Quinoa Seed●, Sorghum Seed●, Teff Seed●, Whole Amaranth Flour●, Whole Millet Flour●, Whole Quinoa Flour●, Whole Sorghum Flour●, Whole Teff Flour●)

flour

F

Organic (Amaranth Seed●, Millet Seed●, Quinoa Seed●, Whole Amaranth Flour●, Whole Millet Flour●, Whole Quinoa Flour●)

Deerfields Bakery▲ - Quick Mix For Sugar Buttons

Domata - Gluten Free All Purpose Flour●

Dowd & Rogers▲ - California Almond, Italian Chestnut

El Peto▲ - All Purpose Flour Mix, Arrowroot, Bean, Brown Rice, Corn, Flax Seed, Garbanzo Fava Bean, Millet, Organic Amaranth, Potato, Quinoa, Sorghum, Soya, Sweet Rice, Tapioca Starch, White Rice

Ener-G▲ -
  Brown Rice
  Gluten Free Gourmet Blend
  Potato (Flour, Starch)
  Sweet Rice
  Tapioca
  White Rice

Expandex▲ - Modified Tapioca Starch●

Flour Nut - Almond Flour

Gifts Of Nature▲ - All Purpose●, Baby Lima Bean, Brown Rice, Tapioca, Sweet Rice, White Rice

Gillian's Foods▲ -
  Brown Rice
  Chick Pea
  Imported Tapioca
  Potato (Regular, Starch)
  Rice

Glutano▲ - Flour Mix It!

Gluten-Free Creations▲ - Baking Flours (Basic●, Enriched●, Sweet●)

Gluten-Free Pantry▲ - Beth's All Purpose Gluten Free Baking Flour

Hodgson Mill▲ - Soy Flour (Organic, Regular), Brown Rice, Buckwheat

Jules Gluten Free▲ - All Purpose Flour●

F **Kinnikinnick▲ -**
    All Purpose Celiac
    Brown Rice
    Corn
    Soya
    Sweet Rice
    White Rice

Laurel's Sweet Treats▲ - Baking Flour Mix

Lotus Foods - Bhutanese Red Rice Flour

Lundberg▲ - Brown Rice Flour (California Nutra Farmed, Organic California)

Meister's Gluten Free Mixtures▲ - All Purpose Gluten Free Flour●

Montana Monster Munchies - Whole Grain Oat Flour●

Montina - All Purpose Baking Flour Blend, Pure Baking Supplement

Namaste Foods▲ - Perfect Flour Blend

Nu-World Foods - Amaranth (Flour●, Puffed●, Toasted Bran Flour●)

Only Oats - Oat Flour●

Orgran▲ - All Purpose Pastry Mix, Gluten Substitute, Plain All Purpose, Self Raising

Pocono - Buckwheat

Ruby Range - Mesquite

Shiloh Farms - Almond, Brown Rice, Corn, Mesquite, Potato, Quinoa, Tapioca, Teff

Sylvan Border Farm - General Purpose Flour

Food Coloring
    Durkee - Blue, Caramel, Egg Shade, Green, Red, Yellow
    Hy-Vee - Assorted
    McCormick - All Varieties
    Spice Islands - Blue, Caramel, Egg Shade, Green, Red, Yellow
    Tones - Blue, Caramel, Egg Shade, Green, Red, Yellow

Frankfurters... see Sausage

French Fries

F

Alexia Foods -

Crispy Potatoes w/Seasoned Salt Waffle Fries

Julienne Fries Spicy Sweet Potato

Julienne Fries Sweet Potato

Julienne Fries w/Sea Salt Yukon Gold

Olive Oil & Sea Salt Oven Fries

Olive Oil Rosemary & Garlic Oven Fries

Olive Oil Sun Dried Tomatoes & Pesto Oven Reds

Organic (Oven Crinkles Classic, Oven Crinkles Onion & Garlic, Oven Crinkles Salt & Pepper, Yukon Gold Julienne Fries w/Sea Salt)

Yukon Gold Potatoes w/Seasoned Salt Potato Nuggets

Cascadian Farm - Organic Frozen (Country Style Potatoes, Crinkle Cut French Fries, Shoe String Fries, Spud Puppies, Straight Cut French Fries, Wedge Cut Oven Fries)

Funster - Natural Potato Letters

Ian's - Alphatots

Ore-Ida -

Frozen

Cottage Fries

Country Style Steak Fries

Crispers

Extra Crispy Fast Food Fries

Golden (Crinkles, Fries)

Pixie Crinkles

Shoestrings

Steak Fries

Publix - Frozen (Crinkle Cut Fries, Extra Crispy Fries, Golden Fries (Fast Food Style, Regular), Original Cut Fries, Shoestring Fries, Southern Style Hash Browns, Steak Fries, Tater Bites)

F **Spartan Brand** - Frozen Fries (Crinkle Cut, Extra Crispy Fast, French, Steak)

Woodstock Farms - Organic Frozen (Crinkle Cut Oven Fries, Shredded Hash Browns, Tastee Taters)

French Toast

  Ian's - Wheat Free Gluten Free Recipe French Toast Sticks

  Van's - Wheat Free Cinnamon French Toast Sticks

Frosting... see Baking Decorations & Frostings

Frozen Desserts... see Ice Cream

Frozen Dinners... see Meals

Frozen Vegetables... see Mixed Vegetables

Frozen Yogurt... see Ice Cream

Fruit Bars... see Bars

Fruit Cocktail

  Albertsons - Heavy Syrup, Light

  Del Monte -

    Canned/Jarred Fruit (All Varieties)

    Fruit Snack Cups (Metal, Plastic)

  Food Club Brand - In Heavy Syrup, Lite

  Great Value Brand (Wal-Mart) -

    Fruit Cocktail In Heavy Syrup

    Fruit Cocktail Sweetened With Splenda

  Hannaford Brand - Extra Light Syrup, Heavy Syrup, No Sugar Added

  Hy-Vee - Lite, Regular

  Meijer Brand - Heavy Syrup, In Juice, In Pear Juice Lite

  Midwest Country Fare

  Laura Lynn - Canned

  Lowes Foods Brand - In Heavy Syrup, In Juice

  Publix - Canned (In Heavy Syrup, Lite In Pear Syrup)

  Safeway Brand - Canned (Lite, Regular)

  Spartan Brand - Heavy Syrup, Light Juice

Stop & Shop Brand - Heavy Syrup, Pear Juice

Wegmans Brand - In Heavy Syrup, In Pear Juice

Winn Dixie - Fruit Cocktail (Heavy Syrup, Light Syrup)

Fruit Drinks... see Drinks/Juice

Fruit Leather... see also Fruit Snacks

Stretch Island Fruit Co. - All Varieties

Fruit Salad

Meijer Brand - Tropical

Native Forest - Organic Tropical

Safeway Brand - Tropical Fruit

Fruit Snacks

Albertsons - Fruit Snacks

Annie's - Organic Bunny Fruit Snacks (Berry Patch, Sunny Citrus, Summer Strawberry, Tropical Treat)

Brothers All Natural▲ - Fruit Crisps (Asian Pear, Banana, Fuji Apple, Pineapple, Strawberry, Strawberry Banana, White & Yellow Peach)

Fruit By The Foot -

Berry Berry Twist

Berry Tie Dye

Color By The Foot

Flavor Kickers (Berry Blast, Tropical Twist)

Mini Feet (Berry Wave)

Razzle Blue Blitz

Strawberry

Variety Pack (Berry Tie Dye, Color By The Foot, Strawberry)

Watermelon

Fruit Flavored Snacks -

Barbie

Fairies Tinkerbell

High School Musical

John Deere

F

Mickey Mouse Clubhouse
Nickelodeon Sponge Bob Square Pants
Operation
Pixar Finding Nemo
Pixar Toy Story
Power Rangers Super Legends
Princess
Strawberry Shortcake

Fruit Gushers -

Punch Berry
Rockin' Blue Raspberry
Strawberry Splash
Triple Berry Shock
Tropical Flavors
Watermelon Blast

Fruit Roll-Ups -

Berry Berry Cool
Blastin' Berry Hot Colors
Crazy Pix (Cool Chix Berry Wave, Wild Ones Blastin' Berry)
Electric Blue Raspberry
Flavor Wave
Stickerz (Berry Cool Punch, Stars Mixed Berry, Twisters Tropical
Berry)
Strawberry (Kiwi Kick, Regular)
Tropical Tie Dye
Variety Pack (Cherry Orange Wildfire, Strawberry, Tropical Tie Dye)

Great Value Brand (Wal-Mart) - Fruit Smiles

Nonuttin' Foods▲ - Fruit Snacks

Publix - Fruit Snacks (Curious George, Dinosaurs, Sharks, Snoopy,
Veggie-Tales)

Safeway Brand - Creatures, Fruity Shapes

Spartan Brand - Build A Bear, Curious George, Dinosaurs, Fruit Rolls (Strawberry, Wild Berry), Maya Miquel, Veggie Tales

Welch's -

Berries N' Cherries

Concord Grape

Fruit Punch

Grape Peach

Mixed Fruit

Strawberry

White Grape Raspberry

Winn Dixie - Fruit Snacks (Dinosaurs, Sharks, Veggie Tales)

Fruit Spread... see Jam/Jelly... see also Spread

F

G

G

Gai Lan... *All Fresh Fruits & Vegetables Are Gluten/Casein Free*

Garbanzo Beans... see Beans

Garlic... *All Fresh Garlic Is Gluten/Casein Free*

Earthbound Farm - Organic Chopped Garlic

Trader Joe's - Crushed

Garlic Powder... see Seasonings

Garlic Salt... see Seasonings

Gelatin

Hannaford Brand - Gelatin Fat Free (Cherry, Orange, Raspberry)

Hy-Vee -

Gelatin (Berry Blue, Cherry, Cranberry, Lemon, Lime, Orange, Raspberry, Strawberry, Strawberry Banana)

Sugar Free (Cherry, Cranberry, Lime, Orange, Raspberry, Strawberry)

G Jell-O -

> Gelatin Snack Cups (Strawberry, Strawberry/Orange, Strawberry/Raspberry, Watermelon/Green Apple)
>
> Regular Instant (Apricot, Berry Blue, Black Cherry, Blackberry Fusion, Cherry, Cranberry, Grape, Island Pineapple, Lemon, Lime, Margarita, Melon Fusion, Mixed Fruit, Orange, Peach, Pina Colada, Raspberry, Strawberry (Banana, Daiquiri, Kiwi, Regular), Tropical Fusion, Watermelon, Wild Strawberry)
>
> Sugar Free Low Calorie (Black Cherry, Cherry, Cranberry, Lemon, Lime, Mixed Fruit, Orange, Peach, Raspberry, Strawberry (Banana, Kiwi, Regular))
>
> Sugar Free Low Calorie Snack Cups (Cherry/Black Cherry, Orange/Lime, Peach/Watermelon, Raspberry/Orange, Strawberry, Strawberry Kiwi/Tropical Berry)

Meijer Brand -

> Gelatin Dessert (Berry Blue, Cherry, Cranberry, Grape, Lime, Orange, Raspberry, Strawberry, Unflavored, Wild Strawberry)
>
> Sugar Free Gelatin Dessert (Cherry, Cranberry, Lime, Orange, Raspberry, Strawberry)

Royal -

> Regular (Blackberry, Cherry, Lime, Orange, Pineapple, Raspberry, Strawberry, Strawberry Banana)
>
> Sugar Free (Cherry, Lime, Orange, Raspberry, Strawberry, Strawberry Banana)

Spartan Brand - Berry Blue, Cherry (Regular, Sugar Free), Lemon, Lime (Regular, Sugar Free), Orange (Regular, Sugar Free), Raspberry (Regular, Sugar Free), Strawberry (Regular, Sugar Free), Unflavored

Wegmans Brand - Sugar Free (Cherry & Black Cherry, Lemon Lime & Orange, Orange & Raspberry, Strawberry)

Gin... *All **Distilled** Alcohol Is **Gluten/Casein Free** [2]*

Ginger

> **Lee Kum Kee -** Minced Ginger
>
> **Wel-Pac -** Sushi Ginger

G

Ginger Ale... see Soda Pop/Carbonated Beverages

Glaze

    Daddy Sam's - Salmon Glaze

    San-J - Gluten Free Sweet & Tangy Polynesian Glazing & Dipping Sauce●

    T. Marzetti - Fruit Glaze (Blueberry, Cranberry, Peach, Strawberry, Sugar Free Strawberry)

Graham Crackers

    Jo-Sef - Graham Crackers (Chocolate, Cinnamon, Vanilla)

    Jules Gluten Free▲ - Graham Cracker/Gingersnap Mix●

    Kinnikinnick▲ - Graham Style Cracker Crumbs

Grains

    Arrowhead Mills - Amaranth, Hulled Millet, Quinoa

    Bob's Red Mill▲ - Organic Amaranth, Quinoa Organic, Teff Whole

    Eden Organic - Brown Rice Flakes, Buckwheat, Millet, Quinoa, Red Quinoa, Wild Rice)

    Shiloh Farms - Millet Grain, Quinoa, Red Quinoa, Sorghum Grain

Granola

    Bakery On Main - Gluten Free Granola (Apple Raisin Walnut, Cranberry Orange Cashew, Extreme Fruit & Nut, Nutty Maple Cranberry, Rainforest)

    Enjoy Life▲ - Granola Crunch (Cinnamon●, Cranapple●, Very Berry●)

    Gluten Free Sensations -

        Cherry Vanilla Almond

        Cranberry Pecan

        French Vanilla Almond

    Goraw - Granola (Apple Cinnamon●, Live●, Live Chocolate●, Simple●)

    Kookie Karma - All Varieties●

    Nonuttin' Foods▲ - Granola Clusters (Vanilla Caramel, Vanilla Cinnamon)

    Rose's Bakery▲ - All Varieties●

G Grapefruit... *All *Fresh* Fruits & Vegetables Are *Gluten/Casein Free*
   Del Monte -
      Canned/Jarred Fruit (All Varieties)
      Fruit Snack Cups (Metal, Plastic)
   Meijer Brand - Sections (In Juice, In Syrup)
   Winn Dixie - Canned
Grapes... *All *Fresh* Fruits & Vegetables Are *Gluten/Casein Free*
Gravy/Gravy Mix
   Barkat - Vegetable Gravy
   Full Flavor Foods▲ - Gravy (Beef●, Chicken●, Pork●, Turkey●)
   Massel - Gravy Mix (Chicken Style, Supreme)
   Maxwell's Kitchen - Gravy Mix (Brown, Chicken, Pork, Turkey)
   Orgran▲ - Gravy Mix
   Road's End Organics - Organic Gravy Mix (Golden, Savory Herb,
      Shiitake Mushroom)
Green Beans... see Beans
Green Peppers... *All *Fresh* Fruits & Vegetables Are *Gluten/Casein Free*
Green Tea... see Tea
Greens... *All *Fresh* Fruits & Vegetables Are *Gluten/Casein Free*
   Albertsons - Canned & Frozen Turnip Greens
   Birds Eye - All Plain Frozen Vegetables
   Bush's Best - Chopped (Collard, Kale, Mixed, Mustard, Turnip, Turnip
      w/Diced Turnips)
   C & W - All Plain Frozen Vegetables
   Laura Lynn - Canned (Chopped Collard Greens, Chopped Mustard
      Greens, Turnip Greens, Turnip Greens w/Diced Turnips), Mustard
      Greens
   Lowes Foods Brand - Frozen (Chopped Collard, Turnip Greens)
   Meijer Brand - Canned Chopped (Kale, Mustard, Turnip), Chopped
      (Collards, Kale, Mustard, Turnip)
   Pictsweet - All Plain Vegetables (Frozen)

G

Publix - Frozen (Collard Chopped, Turnip Chopped, Turnip w/Diced Turnips)

Spartan Brand - Chopped (Collard, Mustard)

Stop & Shop Brand - Collard Greens, Mustard Greens

Trader Joe's - All Plain Frozen Vegetables

Winn Dixie -

Canned (Collard No Salt, Mustard, Turnip)

Frozen (Collard Greens Chopped, Mustard Greens, Steamable Mixed Vegetables)

Grits

Bob's Red Mill▲ - Gluten Free Corn Grits/Polenta, Soy Grits

Meijer Brand - Quick

Winn Dixie - Instant Grits

Groats

Arrowhead Mills - Buckwheat

Chateau Cream Hill Estates - Lara's Oat Groats●

Montana Monster Munchies - Raw & Sproutable Oat Groats●

Pocono - Whole Buckwheat

Ground Beef... see Beef

*All Fresh Meat Is Gluten/Casein Free (Non-Marinated, Unseasoned)

Ground Turkey... see Turkey

*All Fresh Meat Is Gluten/Casein Free (Non-Marinated, Unseasoned)

Guacamole... see also Dip/Dip Mix

Calavo

Fischer & Wieser - Just Add Avocados Guacamole Starter

Guar Gum

Bob's Red Mill▲

El Peto▲

Gluten-Free Essentials▲

Kinnikinnick▲

Gum... see Chewing Gum

H H

Halibut... see Fish

Ham

    Applegate Farms - Natural (Black Forest, Honey, Slow Cooked), Organic Uncured Ham

    Bar S -

        Classic Chopped

        Deli Shaved (Black Forest, Honey, Smoked)

        Deli Style (Honey, Low Fat, Smoked)

        Deli Thin Cut (Honey, Smoked)

        Extra Lean Cooked

        Steaks (Honey, Smoked)

        Premium Deli (Honey, Smoked)

    Black Label - Canned Ham, Chopped Ham

    Boar's Head - 42% Lower Sodium, Sweet Slice Boneless, Virginia

    Carl Buddig - All Ham *(Except Sandwich Kits)*

    Celebrity - Boneless Cooked w/Natural Juices, Regular Ham

    Cure 81 - Boneless Ham Natural Juices

    Dietz & Watson -

        Black Forest Smoked w/Natural Juices

        Capocolla

        Chef Carved Pre Sliced Honey Cured & Glazed

        Classic Trimmed & Tied w/Natural Juices

        Gourmet Lite (Tavern, Virginia Baked)

        Ham Steak w/Natural Juices

        Honey (Cured Dinner w/Natural Juices, Cured Tavern w/Natural Juices, Cured w/Natural Juices)

        Imported (Prosciuttini Italian Style, w/Water Added)

        Rosemary

        Semi Boneless Smoked w/Natural Juices

H

Spiral Sliced

Tavern w/Water Added

Tomato & Basil

Tiffany Boneless w/Natural Juices

Virginia Baked w/Water Added

Garrett County Farms -

Black Forest Boneless Nugget

Deli (Black Forest, Virginia)

Sliced (Black Forest, Breakfast Virgina Brand (Boneless Ham Steak, Deli Ham), Turkey Ham (Ham Steak, Original))

Great Value Brand (Wal-Mart) -

Deli Meat

97% Fat Free (Baked Ham Water Added, Honey Ham Water Added)

Thinly Sliced Smoked (Ham, Honey Ham)

Healthy Choice - Honey

Hillshire Farms -

Deli Select Thin Sliced (Brown Sugar Baked Ham, Smoked Ham)

Deli Select Ultra Thin (Brown Sugar Baked Ham, Honey Ham)

Hormel -

Black Label (Canned, Chopped)

Chunk Meats Ham

Deli Sliced (Black Forest, Cooked, Honey, Prosciutto)

Diced

Natural Choice Ham (Cooked Deli, Honey Deli, Smoked Deli)

Hy-Vee -

Deli Thin Slices (Honey, Smoked)

Thin Sliced (Ham w/Natural Juices, Honey Ham w/Natural Juices)

Isaly's - Chip Chopped, Old Fashioned Baked Deli, Smoked Honey Cured

Jennie-O - Refrigerated Turkey Ham (Extra Lean, Regular)

H Jones Dairy Farm -

    Deli Style Ham Slices (Honey & Brown Sugar●, Old Fashioned Cured●)

    Family Ham (Half●, Whole●)

    Old Fashioned Whole Hickory Smoked Ham●

    Whole Fully Cooked Hickory Smoked●

Kayem - Deli Ham (Amber Honey Cured, Black Forest, Carving, Peppercrust)

Krakus - Imported Polish Ham

Oscar Mayer -

    Deli Fresh Meats (Cooked Ham (96% Fat Free, Regular), Honey Ham, Smoked Ham)

    Shaved Deli Fresh Meats (Black Forest Ham, Brown Sugar Ham, Honey Ham, Smoked Ham, Virginia Brand Ham)

    Thin Sliced Deli Fresh (97% Fat Free Smoked Ham, Brown Sugar Ham)

Primo Taglio - Prosciutto Dry Cured Ham

Publix -

    Deli Pre Pack Lunch Meat (Cooked Ham, Extra Thin Sliced Honey Ham, Low Salt Ham, Sweet Ham, Tavern Ham, Virginia Brand Ham)

    Hickory Smoked Ham (Fully Cooked, Semi Boneless)

    Honey Cured Ham w/Brown Sugar Glaze (Bone In Ham, Boneless Ham)

Russer - Reduced Sodium Cooked, Virginia

Safeway Brand - Boneless Honey

Smithfield -

    Black Forest

    Boneless (Hickory, Honey, Maple Flavored)

    Cooked

    Deli Thin (Cooked, Honey)

    Virginia

H

SPAM - Classic, Less Sodium, Lite, Oven Roasted Turkey, Smoke Flavored

Spartan Brand - Frozen Ham Loaf, Whole Boneless

Underwood Spreads - Deviled

Wegmans Brand - Diced Ham, Thin Shaved (Ham, Honey Maple Flavored Ham)

Wellshire Farms -

Black Forest (Boneless Nugget, Deli, Sliced)

Buffet Half

Glazed Boneless (Half, Spiral Sliced Half, Spiral Sliced Whole)

Old Fashioned Boneless (Half, Whole)

Semi Boneless (Half, Whole)

Sliced (Breakfast, Tavern)

Smoked Ham (Hocks, Shanks)

Top Round Ham Boneless

Turkey Half Ham

Virginia Brand (Boneless Steak, Buffet, Deli, Nugget Honey, Quarter, Sliced)

Winn Dixie - Thin Sliced (Cooked Ham, Honey Ham)

Hamburger Buns... see Buns

Hamburgers... see Burgers... *All Fresh Meat Is Gluten/Casein Free (Non-Marinated, Unseasoned)*

Hash Browns... see Potatoes

Hearts Of Palm... *All Fresh Fruits & Vegetables Are Gluten/Casein Free*

Del Monte - All Plain Canned Vegetables

Native Forest - Organic Hearts Of Palm

Herbal Tea... see Tea

Hoisin Sauce

Premier Japan - Wheat Free

Wok Mei

H Hominy

   Bush's Best - Golden, White
   Great Value Brand (Wal-Mart) - Canned White
   Hy-Vee - Golden, White
   Lowes Foods Brand - White
   Meijer Brand - White
   Safeway Brand - Golden, White
   Spartan Brand - Gold, White
   Winn Dixie - Golden, White

Honey

   Albertsons
   Bramley's - Golden
   Full Circle - Organic 100% Pure Honey
   Great Value Brand (Wal-Mart) - Clover Honey
   Hannaford Brand - Pure Clover
   Home Harvest Brand - Pure Clover, Squeeze Bear
   Hy-Vee - Honey, Honey Squeeze Bear
   Lowes Foods Brand
   Meijer Brand - Honey, Honey Squeeze Bear
   Publix - Clover, Orange Blossom
   Publix GreenWise Market - Organic Honey
   Safeway Brand - Pure
   Spartan Brand
   Trader Joe's
   Virginia Brand - 100% All Natural
   Wegmans Brand - 100% Pure Clover, Clover, Orange Blossom, Squeezable Bear
   Winn Dixie - Clover, Dark, Orange Blossom

Honey Mustard Sauce... see Mustard

Horseradish Sauce

   Baxters
   Di Lusso

Dietz & Watson -
Cranberry
Hot & Chunky
Smokey
Heinz - Horseradish Sauce
Hy-Vee - Prepared Horseradish
Lou's Famous - Horseradish (Creamy, Regular)
Manischewitz - Creamy Wasabi, Original
Wegmans Brand - Prepared Horseradish
Hot Chocolate Mix... see Cocoa Mix
Hot Dog Buns... see Buns
Hot Dogs... see Sausage
Hot Sauce
Bone Suckin' - Habanero Sauce
Frank's RedHot -
Chile 'N Lime
Original
Xtra Hot
Frontera -
Chipotle
Habanero
Jalapeno
Red Pepper
Gifts Of Nature▲ - Sriracha Hot Sauce
La Victoria - Jalapeno, Salsa Brava
Mr. Spice Organic - Tangy Bang! Hot
Santa Barbara - Pepper Sauce (Original Blend California)
Texas Pete -
Garlic
Hotter Hot
Original

H The Wizard's - Hot Stuff

Trader Joe's - Jalapeno Hot

Trappey - Hot Sauce

Winn Dixie - Louisiana (Extra Hot, Hot)

Hummus

Athenos -

Hummus

Artichoke & Garlic

Black Olive

Greek Style

Original

Pesto

Roasted (Eggplant, Garlic, Red Pepper)

Spicy Three Pepper

NeoClassic Hummus

Original

Original w/Sesame Seeds & Parsley

Roasted Garlic w/Garlic & Parsley

Roasted Red Pepper w/Red Peppers & Parsley

Casbah Natural Foods - Hummus

Fantastic World Foods - Original Hummus

T. Marzetti -

Original

Roasted Garlic

Roasted Red Pepper

Tribe Mediterranean Foods - All Natural Hummus (All Varieties)

Wegmans - Smoked Jalapeno, Traditional

Wild Garden - Black Olive, Fire Roasted Red Pepper, Jalapeno, Red Hot Chili Pepper, Roasted Garlic, Sundried Tomato, Sweet 2 Pepper, Traditional

I

I

Ice Cream... (includes Frozen Desserts, Frozen Yogurt, Sherbet, Sorbet)

Albertsons - Twin Pops

Chapman's - Sorbet (Orange, Rainbow, Raspberry)

Cool Fruits - Fruit Juice Freezers (Grape & Cherry, Sour Apple)

Dreyer's -

Fruit Bars

Grape

Lemonade

Lime

Strawberry

Tangerine

Variety Pack (Lime, Strawberry & Wildberry)

Variety Pack No Sugar Added (Black Cherry, Mixed Berry, Strawberry, Strawberry Kiwi, Tangerine & Raspberry)

Edy's -

Fruit Bars

Grape

Lemonade

Lime

Strawberry

Tangerine

Variety Pack (Lime, Strawberry & Wildberry)

Variety Pack No Sugar Added (Black Cherry, Mixed Berry, Strawberry, Strawberry Kiwi, Tangerine & Raspberry)

Fla-Vor-Ice - Freezer Bars (Regular, Sugar Free)

Good Karma -

Chocolate Covered Bars (Chocolate Chocolate, Very Vanilla)

Organic Rice Divine (Banana Fudge, Carrot Cake, Chocolate Chip, Chocolate Peanut Butter Fudge, Coconut Mango, Key Lime Pie, Mint Chocolate Swirl, Mudd Pie, Very Cherry, Very Vanilla)

Hawaiian Punch - Freezer Bars
Hood -
Frozen Novelty Items
Hoodsie Pops 6 Flavor Assortment Twin Pops
Hy-Vee - Pops (Cherry, Grape, Orange, Root Beer)
Icee - Freezer Bars
It's Soy Delicious -
Almond Pecan●
Awesome Chocolate●
Black Leopard●
Carob Peppermint●
Chocolate (Almond●, Peanut Butter●)
Espresso●
Green Tea●
Mango Raspberry●
Pistachio Almond●
Raspberry●
Tiger Chai●
Vanilla●
Vanilla Fudge●
Jelly Belly - Freezer (Bars, Pops)
Kool Pops - Freezer Bars
Meijer Brand -
Juice Stix
Party Pops (No Sugar Added Assorted, Orange/Cherry/Grape,
RB/B/BR)
Red White & Blue Pops
Twin Pops
Minute Maid - Juice Bars
Natural Choice - All Full of Fruit Bars, All Sorbets

North Star -

Lotta Pops (Fruit, Juice, Regular, Sugar Free)

Pops (Assorted Twin, Banana Twin, Blue Raspberry Twin, Cherry Twin, Melon, Patriot Junior)

Otter Pops - Freezer Bars (Plus, Regular)

Philly Swirl -

Philly Swirl Sorbet/Italian Ice

Original Swirl Stix

Sugar Free Swirl Stix

Pop Ice - Freezer Bars

Publix -

Novelties

Banana Pops

Junior Ice Pops (Cherry, Grape, Orange)

Purely Decadent -

Bars (Purely Vanilla●, Vanilla Almond●)

Dairy Free Ice Cream

Belgian Chocolate●

Blueberry Cheesecake●

Cherry Nirvana●

Chocolate Obsession●

Coconut Craze●

Dulce De Leche●

Key Lime Pie●

Mint Chip●

Peanut Butter Zig Zag●

Pomegranate Chip●

Praline Pecan●

Purely Vanilla●

Rocky Road●

Snickerdoodle●
So Very Strawberry●
Turtle Trails●
Dairy Free Made w/Coconut Milk
Chocolate●
Chocolate Peanut Butter Swirl●
Coconut●
Cookie Dough●
Mint Chocolate Chip●
Mocha Almond Fudge●
Passionate Mango●
Vanilla Bean●

Rice Dream -
Non Dairy Frozen Desserts
Carob Almond
Cocoa Marble Fudge
Neapolitan
Orange Vanilla Swirl
Strawberry
Vanilla

Safeway Select -
Fruit Bars (Lemonade, Lime, Mandarin Orange, Strawberry)
Sorbet (Chocolate, Lemon, Mango, Peach, Pomegranate,
Raspberry, Strawberry, Tropical)

So Delicious Dairy Free -
Dairy Free Ice Cream Bars (Creamy Orange●, Creamy Raspberry●)
Dairy Free Kidz Pops (Assorted Fruit●, Fudge●)
Dairy Free Mini Fruit Bars (Orange Passion Fruit●, Raspberry●,
Strawberry●)
Dairy Free Sugar Free (Fudge Bar●, Vanilla Bar●)
Organic Bars (Creamy Fudge●, Creamy Vanilla●, Vanilla & Almonds●)

Organic Dairy Free
  Butter Pecan●
  Chocolate (Peanut Butter●, Velvet●)
  Creamy Vanilla●
  Dulce De Leche●
  Mint Marble Fudge●
  Mocha Fudge●
  Neapolitan●
  Strawberry●
Soy Dream -
  Non Dairy Frozen Desserts
    Butter Pecan
    Chocolate
    French Vanilla
    Green Tea
    Mocha Fudge
    Strawberry Swirl
    Vanilla (Fudge, Regular)
Sweet Nothings - Non Dairy (Fudge Bars●, Mango Raspberry●)
Tampico - All Freezer Bars
Trader Joe's - Sorbet (Double Rainbow)
Wegmans Brand - Sorbet (Green Apple, Lemon, Pink Grapefruit, Raspberry)
WholeSoy & Co. - All Frozen Yogurts
Winn Dixie -
  Assorted Juice Pops
  Assorted Junior Pops
  Fun Pops
  Red White & Blue Pops
  Sugar Free Pops
Wyler's - Italian Ice Freezer Bars

I

Ice Cream Cones... see Cones

Ice Cream Toppings... see also Syrup

J

Hershey's - Chocolate Syrup (Lite, Regular, w/Calcium)

Maple Grove Farms Of Vermont - Flavored Syrups (Apricot, Blueberry, Boysenberry, Raspberry, Strawberry)

Smucker's -

Special Recipe (Triple Berry)

Sundae Syrups (Strawberry)

Toppings (Apple Cinnamon, Marshmallow, Pecans In Syrup, Pineapple, Strawberry, Walnuts In Syrup)

Iced Tea/Iced Tea Mix... see Tea

Icing... see Baking Decorations & Frostings

Instant Coffee... see Coffee

Italian Dressing... see Salad Dressing

J

Jalapenos... *All **Fresh** Fruits & Vegetables Are **Gluten/Casein Free***

Chi-Chi's - Red

Great Value Brand (Wal-Mart) - Sliced Jalapenos En Rodajas, Whole Jalapenos

Old El Paso - Slices (Pickled)

Ortega - Hot (Sliced, Diced)

Safeway Brand - Sliced

Winn Dixie

Jalfrazi

Seeds Of Change - Jalfrezi Sauce

Sharwood's - Jalfrezi

Tamarind Tree - Vegetable Jalfrazi

Jam/Jelly

Baxters - Jelly (Cranberry, Mint, Red Currant)

Bionaturae - Fruit Spread (Apricot, Bilberry, Peach, Plum, Raspberry, Sicilian Oranges, Sour Cherry, Strawberry, Wild Berry, Wild Blackberry)

Cascadian Farm - Organic Fruit Spreads (Apricot, Blackberry, Blueberry, Concord Grape, Raspberry, Strawberry)

Eden Organic - Butter (Apple, Cherry)

Fischer & Wieser -

Jelly Texas (Mild Green Jalapeno)

Marmalade (Apricot Orange)

Preserves

Cinnamon Orange Tomato

Old Fashioned Peach

Southern Style Amaretto Peach Pecan

Southern Style Jalapeno Peach

Strawberry Rhubarb

Food Club Brand - Grape Jam, Grape Jelly, Organic Fruit Spread (Apricot, Raspberry, Strawberry, Wild Blueberry), Preserves (Apricot, Peach, Strawberry)

Full Circle - Fruit Spread (Raspberry, Strawberry)

Hannaford Brand - Jelly (Apple, Currant, Grape, Strawberry), Orange Marmalade, Preserves (Apricots, Blueberry, Grape, Red Raspberry)

Hy-Vee -

Jelly (Apple, Blackberry, Cherry, Grape, Plum, Red Raspberry, Strawberry)

Orange Marmalade

Preserves (Apricot, Cherry, Concord Grape, Peach, Red Raspberry, Strawberry)

Laura Lynn -

Grape Jam

Jelly (Apple, Grape)

Orange Marmalade

Preserves (Apricot, Peach, Red Raspberry, Strawberry)

J

Lowes Foods Brand - Jam (Grape), Jelly (Apple, Grape), Preserves (Strawberry)

Meijer Brand - Fruit Spread (Apricot, Blackberry Seedless, Red Raspberry, Strawberry), Jam (Grape), Jelly (Grape), Preserves (Apricot, Blackberry Seedless, Marmalade Orange, Peach, Red Raspberry, Red Raspberry w/Seeds, Strawberry)

Midwest Country Fare - Grape Jelly, Strawberry Preserves

O Organics - Preserves (Apricot, Blackberry, Blueberry, Raspberry, Strawberry)

Polaner - All (Jam, Jellies, Preserves)

Publix - All (Jam, Jellies, Preserves)

Safeway Brand - All (Jams, Jellies, Preserves)

Safeway Select - All (Jams, Jellies, Preserves)

Smucker's - All (Jams, Jellies, Marmalades, Preserves)

Spartan Brand - Jam (Grape), Jelly (Apple, Currant, Grape, Strawberry), Orange Marmalade, Preserves (Apricot, Blackberry, Cherry, Peach, Red Raspberry, Strawberry)

Stop & Shop Brand -

Jelly (Apple, Currant, Mint)

Preserves (Apricot, Grape, Peach, Pineapple, Red Raspberry, Seedless Blackberry, Strawberry)

Trader Joe's -

Organic Preserves Reduced Sugar (Blackberry, Blueberry, Raspberry, Strawberry)

Preserves (Apricots, Blackberries, Blueberries, Boysenberries, Raspberries)

Walden Farms - Spread (Apple Butter, Apricot, Blueberry, Grape, Orange Marmalade, Raspberry, Strawberry)

Wegmans Brand -

Fruit Spread

Apricot/Peach/Passion Fruit

Blueberry/Cherry/Raspberry

Organic (Red Raspberry, Strawberry)

J

> Raspberry/Strawberry/Blackberry
>
> Strawberry/Plum/Raspberry
>
> Jelly (Apple, Cherry, Concord Grape, Currant, Mint, Red Raspberry, Strawberry)
>
> Nature's Marketplace Organic Fruit Spread Jammin' (Red Raspberry, Strawberry)
>
> Preserves (Apricot, Cherry, Concord Grape, Peach, Red Raspberry, Seedless Blackberry, Strawberry)
>
> Sugar Free Fruit Spread
>
> > Apricot/Peach/Passion Fruit
> >
> > Raspberry/Wild Blueberry/Blackberry
> >
> > Strawberry/Plum/Raspberry

Welch's - All Jams, Jellies & Preserves

Jell-O... see Gelatin

Jerky/Beef Sticks

Applegate Farms - Joy Stick

Garrett County - Turkey Tom Tom Snack Sticks

Cary West

> Buffalo Strips
>
> Certified Angus Beef Steak Strips (All Varieties) *(Except Teriyaki)*
>
> Elk Strips
>
> Original Steak Strips (All Varieties) *(Except Teriyaki)*

Hormel - Dried Beef

Hy-Vee - Jerky (Original, Peppered)

Organic Prairie - Organic Beef Jerky 2 oz. (Prairie Classic, Smoky Chipotle, Spicy Hickory)

Shelton's - Beef Jerky, Turkey Jerky (Hot Turkey, Regular)

Juice... see Drinks/Juice

Juice Mix... see Drink Mix

K K

Kale... *All **Fresh** Fruits & Vegetables Are **Gluten/Casein Free***
  Pictsweet - Cut Leaf
Kasha
  Bob's Red Mill▲ - Organic
  Shiloh Farms - Organic
  Wolff's - Buckwheat Kasha
Ketchup
  Great Value Brand (Wal-Mart)
  Hannaford Brand
  Heinz -
    Hot & Spicy
    No Sodium Added
    Organic
    Reduced Sugar
    Regular
  Hy-Vee -
    Squeezable Thick & Rich Tomato
    Thick & Rich Tomato
  Meijer Brand - Regular, Squeeze, Tomato Organic
  Midwest Country Fare
  Muir Glen - Organic Tomato
  O Organics
  Organicville - Organic
  Publix
  Publix GreenWise Market - Organic
  Safeway Brand
  Trader Joe's - Organic
  Walden Farms
  Wegmans Brand - Organic
  Winn Dixie - Organic, Regular

K

L

   Woodstock Farms - Organic

Kielbasa... see Sausage

Kipper Snacks

   Crown Prince - Naturally Smoked (Natural, Regular)

   Ocean Prince -

     In Mustard

     Naturally Smoke

Kiwi... *All Fresh Fruits & Vegetables Are Gluten/Casein Free*

Kohlrabi... *All Fresh Fruits & Vegetables Are Gluten/Casein Free*

Korma

   Amy's - Indian Vegetable

L

Lamb... *All Fresh Meat Is Gluten/Casein Free (Non-Marinated, Unseasoned)*

Lasagna Noodles... see Pasta

Lemonade... see Drinks/Juice

Lemons... *All Fresh Fruits & Vegetables Are Gluten/Casein Free*

   Sunkist

Lentils... see also Beans

   Tasty Bite - Bengal, Jaipur Vegetables

Lettuce... *All Fresh Fruits & Vegetables Are Gluten/Casein Free*

Licorice... see Candy/Candy Bars

Limeade... see Drinks/Juice

Limes... *All Fresh Fruits & Vegetables Are Gluten/Casein Free*

   Sunkist

Liquid Aminos

   Bragg - Liquid Aminos

L Liverwurst

    Jones Dairy Farm -

M
        Chub Braunschweiger Liverwurst (Bacon & Onion●, Light●,
           Mild & Creamy●, Original●)

        Chunk Braunschweiger (Light●, Original●)

        Sliced Braunschweiger●

        Stick Braunschweiger●

Lobster... *All **Fresh** Shellfish Is **Gluten/Casein Free** (Non-Marinated, Unseasoned)*

Lunch Meat... see Deli Meat

M

Macaroni & Cheese

    Ian's - Wheat Free Gluten Free Mac & No Cheese

    Namaste Foods▲ - Say Cheez

    Road's End Organics -

        Dairy Free Mac & Chreese Alfredo

        Dairy Free Penne & Chreese

Macaroons... see Cookies

Mackerel... see also Fish... *All **Fresh** Fish Is **Gluten/Casein Free** (Non-Marinated, Unseasoned)*

    Chicken Of The Sea - Canned Jack Mackerel

    Crown Prince -

        Fillet of Mackerel In Soybean Oil

        Jack Mackerel

Makhani

    Tamarind Tree - Dal Makhani

Mandarin Oranges... *All **Fresh** Fruits & Vegetables Are **Gluten/Casein Free***

    Albertsons

Del Monte -
- Canned/Jarred Fruit (All Varieties)
- Fruit Snack Cups (Metal, Plastic)

Dole - All Fruits (Bowls, Canned, Dried, Frozen, Jars) *(Except Real Fruit Bites)*

Food Club Brand

Great Value Brand (Wal-Mart) - In Light Syrup

Hannaford Brand - In Light Syrup

Hy-Vee - Light Syrup, Orange Gel Cups, Regular Cups

Kroger Brand - Fruit (Canned, Cups)

Lowes Foods Brand - In Lite Syrup

Meijer Brand - Light Syrup

Publix - In Light Syrup

Spartan Brand - Fruit Cups

Trader Joe's - In Light Syrup

Wegmans Brand - Regular, Whole Segment In Light Syrup

Winn Dixie

Mango... *All Fresh Fruits & Vegetables Are Gluten/Casein Free*

Del Monte -
- Canned/Jarred Fruit (All Varieties)
- Fruit Snack Cups (Metal, Plastic)

Meijer Brand - Frozen (Chunks, Sliced)

Native Forest - Organic Mango Chunks

Stop & Shop Brand - Mango

Winn Dixie - Frozen Mango Chunks

Woodstock Farms - Organic Frozen Mango

Maple Syrup... see Syrup

Maraschino Cherries... see Cherries

Margarine... see Spread and/or Butter

M Marinades

Drew's All Natural -
    Garlic Italian
    Green Olive & Caper
    Honey Dijon
    Poppy Seed
    Raspberry
    Roasted Garlic & Peppercorn
    Rosemary Balsamic
    Smoked Tomato

Jack Daniel's EZ Marinades - Original No. 7 Recipe

Hy-Vee - Citrus Grill, Herb & Garlic, Lemon Pepper, Mesquite

Lawry's -
    Baja Chipotle
    Caribbean Jerk
    Havana Garlic & Lime
    Herb & Garlic
    Lemon Pepper
    Louisiana Red Pepper
    Mesquite
    Mexican Chile & Lime
    Tequila Lime

McCormick -
    Grill Mates
        Baja Citrus Marinade
        Chipotle Pepper Marinade
        Hickory BBQ Marinade
        Mesquite Marinade
        Mojito Lime
        Montreal Steak Marinade (25% Less Sodium, Original)
        Peppercorn & Garlic Marinade
        Southwest Marinade

M

Moore's Marinade - Original, Teriyaki

Mr. Spice Organic - Sauce & Marinade (Garlic Steak, Ginger Stir Fry, Honey BBQ, Honey Mustard, Hot Wing, Indian Curry, Sweet & Sour, Thai Peanut)

Newman's Own -
    Herb & Roasted Garlic
    Lemon Pepper
    Mesquite w/Lime

Safeway Brand - Caribbean Jerk, Lemon Garlic

San-J - Gluten Free (Sweet & Tangy●, Szechuan●, Teriyaki●, Thai Peanut●)

Weber Grill Creations - Chipotle Marinade

Wegmans Brand -
    Chicken BBQ
    Citrus Dill
    Fajita
    Greek
    Honey Mustard
    Italian
    Lemon & Garlic
    Mojo
    Rosemary Balsamic
    Santa Fe Medium
    Spiedie
    Steakhouse Peppercorn
    Tangy
    Zesty (Savory, Thai)

Winn & Lovett - Argentina, Cilantro Lime, Citrus, Garlic, Red Chili & Thyme

Winn Dixie - Mojo

Marmalade... see Jam/Jelly

Marshmallow Dip
    Jet Puffed - Marshmallow Crème
    Marshmallow Fluff - Original
    Walden Farms - Calorie Free Marshmallow Dip
Marshmallows
    Albertsons - Mini, Regular
    AllerEnergy
    Great Value Brand (Wal-Mart) - Regular
    Hannaford Brand - Miniature, Regular
    Hy-Vee - Colored Miniatures, Miniature, Regular
    Jet-Puffed -
        Chocomallows
        Coconut
        Funmallows
        Miniature
        Regular
        Strawberrymallows
        Swirlmallows Caramel & Vanilla
        Vanilla
    Marshmallow Fluff - Original
    Meijer Brand - Mini, Mini Flavored, Regular
    Publix
    Safeway Brand - Large, Mini
    Spartan Brand - Miniature, Regular
    Winn Dixie - Mini, Regular
Masala
    A Taste Of India - Masala Rice & Lentils
    Tamarind Tree - Channa Dal Masala
    Tasty Bite - Channa Masala
Mashed Potatoes
    Edward & Sons - Organic (Chreesy, Home Style, Roasted Garlic)

M

Meijer Brand - Instant Mashed Potatoes
Ore-Ida - Steam N' Mash (Cut Red, Cut Russet, Cut Sweet)
Safeway Brand - Instant Mashed Potatoes (Regular)
Spartan Brand - Instant

Mayonnaise

Albertsons
Bakers & Chefs - Extra Heavy
Best Foods - Canola, Light, Low Fat, Real
Cain's - All Natural, Sandwich Spread
Dietz & Watson - Sandwich Spread
Follow Your Heart - Vegenaise (Grapeseed Oil, High Omega, Organic, Original, Reduced Fat Flax Seed & Olive Oil)
Hannaford Brand - Lite, Regular, Squeeze
Hellmann's - Canola, Light, Low Fat, Real
Hy-Vee - Regular, Squeezable
Meijer Brand - Lite, Regular
Miracle Whip - Light, Regular
Nasoya - Nayonaise (Dijon Style, Fat Free, Original)
Publix
Safeway - Light, Regular
Simply Delicious - Organic Mayonnaise (Garlic, Lemon, Original)
Smart Balance - Omega Plus Light
Spartan Brand - Regular Squeeze
Spectrum -
  Canola (Light, Regular)
  Organic (Dijon, Omega 3 w/Flax Oil, Olive, Regular, Roasted, Wasabi)
Trader Joe's - Reduced Fat
Walden Farms - Mayo
Wegmans Brand - Classic, Light

Meals

    A Taste Of China - Sweet & Sour Rice, Szechuan Noodles

    A Taste Of India - Quick Meals (Masala Rice & Lentils)

    A Taste Of Thai - Quick Meal (Coconut Ginger Noodles, Pad Thai Noodles, Peanut Noodles, Red Curry Noodles, Vermicelli Rice Noodles, Wide Rice Noodles, Yellow Curry Noodles)

    Amy's - Kids Meals (Baked Ziti)

    Chi-Chi's - Fiesta Chicken Salsa Plate

    Del Monte - Harvest Selections Heat & Eat (Santa Fe Style Rice & Beans)

    Dinty Moore - Microwave Meals (Chicken w/ Rice)

    Gillian's Foods▲ - Chicken Cutlets

    Gluten Free Café - Asian Noodles●

    Glutino▲ -

        Frozen Meals

            Chicken Ranchero

            Pad Thai w/Chicken

            Pomodoro Chicken

    Hormel - Compleats (Santa Fe Style Chicken), Compleats Microwave 10 oz. Meals (Chicken & Rice, Santa Fe Style Chicken w/Beans & Rice)

    Ian's - Wheat Free Gluten Free (Mac & Meat Sauce, Mac & No Cheese)

    Kid's Kitchen - Beans & Wieners

    Mixes From The Heartland▲ -

        Meal Mix

            BBQ Beef N'Pasta●

            Beef Skillet●

            Cheeseburger Pie●

            Garden Meat Loaf●

            Green Chili●

            Green Chili Spaghetti●

            Mexican Chicken N' Rice●

    Mexican Style Casserole●

    Sausage Casserole●

    Southwest Potato Casserole●

    Taco Rice Skillet●

    Tex Mex (Meat Loaf●, Spaghetti●)

    Texas Bean Bake●

    Texas Goulash●

My Own Meals - Beef Stew, Chicken & Black Bean, Mediterranean Chicken Meal, My Kind Of Chicken, Old World Stew

Namaste Foods▲ - Pasta Meals (Pasta Pisavera, Say Cheez, Taco)

Old El Paso - Dinner Kit (Stand 'N Stuff Taco, Taco)

Orgran▲ -

    Pasta Ready Meal (Tomato & Basil, Vegetable Bolognese)

    Spaghetti In A Can

Ortega - Dinner Taco Kit

Smart Ones - Frozen Entrees Chicken (Lemon Herb Piccata, Santa Fe)

Tasty Bite -

    Aloo Palak

    Bombay Potatoes

    Mushroom Takatak

    Punjab Eggplant

    Spinach Dal & Basmati Rice

Thai Kitchen -

    Noodle Carts (Lemon & Chili, Pad Thai, Thai Peanut, Toasted Sesame)

    Stir Fry Rice Noodle Meal Kit (Lemongrass & Chili, Original Pad Thai, Thai Peanut)

    Take Out Box (Ginger & Sweet Chili, Original Pad Thai, Thai Basil & Chili)

Meatballs

    Aidells - Chipotle

Melon... *All Fresh Fruits & Vegetables Are **Gluten/Casein Free***

Milk Alternative

Amazake - Almond, Amazing Mango, Banana Appeal, Cool Coconut, Go (Go Green, Hazelnuts), Oh So Original, Rice Nog, Tiger Chai, Vanilla (Gorilla, Pecan Pie)

Better Than Milk -
Rice (Original, Vanilla)
Soy (Chocolate, Original, Vanilla)

Blue Diamond -
Almond Breeze (Chocolate, Original, Vanilla)
Almond Breeze Unsweetened (Chocolate, Original, Vanilla)

Dari Free - Non Dairy Milk Alternative (Chocolate, Original)

Eden Organic - EdenBlend, Edensoy (Unsweetened)

Good Karma - Organic Ricemilk (Chocolate, Original, Vanilla)

Imagine -
Organic Non Dairy Soy Beverage
Enriched (Chocolate, Original, Vanilla)
Original (Vanilla)

Lucerne - Soy Beverage (Low Fat Vanilla, Regular)

MimicCreme - Sugar Free Sweetened, Sweetened, Unsweetened

Nature's Promise -
Chocolate Soymilk
Organic Soymilk (Chocolate, Original, Vanilla)
Organic Valley Soy Milk (Chocolate, Original, Unsweetened, Vanilla)

Pacific Natural Foods -
Hemp Milk (Original, Vanilla)
Nut Beverages
Hazelnut (Chocolate, Original)
Organic Almond (Original, Vanilla)
Organic Almond Unsweetened (Original, Vanilla)

M

Rice Beverage
    Low Fat Rice Beverage (Plain, Vanilla)
Soy Beverage
    Organic Soy Unsweetened Original
    Select Soy (Plain, Vanilla)
    Ultra Soy (Plain, Vanilla)

Publix GreenWise Market -
Soy Milk
    Regular (Chocolate, Plain, Vanilla)
    Light (Chocolate, Plain, Vanilla)

Rice Dream -
Enriched (Chocolate, Organic Original, Vanilla)
Refrigerated Enriched Rice Drink (Original, Vanilla)
Shelf Stable Rice Drink
    Classic (Carob, Vanilla)
    Enriched (Original, Vanilla)
    Heartwise (Original, Vanilla)
    Horchata
    Original

Silk Soymilk -
Refrigerated Soymilk (Chocolate, Light (Chocolate, Plain, Vanilla), Plain, Silk Plus (Fiber, Omega 3 DHA), Vanilla, Very Vanilla)
Shelf Stable Soymilk (Chocolate, Plain, Unsweetened, Vanilla, Very Vanilla)

Soy Dream -
Refrigerated Non Dairy Soymilk
    Classic Original
    Enriched (Original, Vanilla)
Shelf Stable Non Dairy Soymilk
    Classic Vanilla
    Enriched (Chocolate, Original, Vanilla)

M **Sunrise** - Soya Beverage (Sweetened, Unsweetened)

Trader Joe's - Organic Soy Milk (Unsweetened)

Vitasoy - Soymilk (Chocolate Banana, Holly Nog, Peppermint, Chocolate, Strawberry Banana)

Wegman's Brand - Rice Milk (Original, Vanilla)

Westsoy -

Organic Soymilk (Original)

Organic Unsweetened Soymilk (Almond, Chocolate, Plain, Vanilla)

Soymilk Non Fat (Plain, Vanilla)

Soymilk Plus (Plain, Vanilla)

Wild Wood Organic - All Varieties

Zensoy -

Soy Milk (Cappucino, Chocolate, Plain, Vanilla)

Soy On The Go (Cappucino, Chocolate, Vanilla)

Millet

Arrowhead Mills - Hulled Millet, Millet Flour

Bob's Red Mill▲ - Flour, Grits/Meal, Hulled Millet

Mints... see also Candy/Candy Bars

Altoids - Large Tins (Peppermint, Wintergreen)

Safeway Brand - Dessert, Star Light

Vermints - Café Express, Chai, Cinnamint, Gingermint, Peppermint, Wintermint

Miso

Eden Organic - Organic Miso (Genmai, Shiro)

Edward & Sons - Miso Cup Savory Soup w/Seaweed

South River -

Azuki Bean

Dandelion Leek

Garlic Red Pepper

Golden Millet

Hearty Brown Rice

Sweet Tasting Brown Rice

Sweet White

Mixed Fruit... *All **Fresh** Fruits & Vegetables Are **Gluten/Casein Free***

Cascadian Farm - Organic Frozen Tropical Fruit Blend

Del Monte -

Canned/Jarred Fruit (All Varieties)

Fruit Snack Cups (Metal, Plastic)

Dole - All Fruits (Bowls, Canned, Dried, Frozen, Jars) *(Except Real Fruit Bites)*

Food Club Brand - Frozen Berry Medley, Triple Cherry Mixed Fruit (Fruit Cups)

Great Value Brand (Wal-Mart) -

Canned (Triple Cherry Fruit Mix In Natural Flavored Cherry Light Syrup, Tropical Fruit Salad in Light Syrup & Fruit Juices)

Frozen (Berry Medley)

Hannaford Brand - Light Syrup, No Sugar Added Chunky, Red Berry Fruit Blend, Triple Cherry Light Syrup, Tropical Fruit Blend

Home Harvest Brand

Hy-Vee - Fruit Cups (Mixed, Tropical), Mixed Fruit (Lite Chunk, Regular)

Laura Lynn - Canned

Lowes Foods Brand - Canned Fruit Cocktail (In Heavy Syrup, In Juice)

Meijer Brand - Frozen Tropical Fruit Blend, Mixed Fruit (Individually Quick Frozen, Regular)

Publix -

Canned (Chunky Mixed Fruit In Heavy Syrup, Fruit Cocktail In Heavy Syrup, Lite Chunky Mixed Fruit In Pear Juice)

Frozen (Mixed Fruit)

S&W - All Canned/Jarred Fruits

M

Spartan Brand - Frozen (Berry Medley, Mixed Fruit), In Heavy Syrup

Stop & Shop Brand - Fruit Mix In Heavy Syrup, Mixed Fruit, Very Cherry Fruit Mix In Light Syrup

Wegmans Brand - Fruit Cocktail (In Heavy Syrup, In Pear Juice, Regular)

Winn Dixie - Canned Chunky Mixed Fruit (Heavy Syrup, Light Syrup), Frozen (Berry Medley, Mixed Fruit), Fruit Cocktail (Heavy Syrup, Light Syrup)

Woodstock Farms - Tropical Fruit Mix

Mixed Vegetables... *All **Fresh** Fruits & Vegetables Are **Gluten/Casein Free**

Albertsons - Canned, Frozen **(Except Sweet Onion Rounds)**

Birds Eye - All Plain Frozen Vegetables

C & W - All Plain Frozen Vegetables

Cascadian Farm - Organic Frozen (California Style Blend, Gardener's Blend)

Del Monte - All Plain Canned Vegetables

Food Club Brand - Canned Mixed Vegetables, Frozen (California Style, Italian Style, Florentine Style, Mixed Vegetables)

Freshlike - Frozen Plain Vegetables **(Except Pasta Combos & Seasoned Blends)**

Full Circle - Organic Frozen 4 Vegetable Blend

Grand Selections - Frozen Vegetables (Caribbean Blend)

Great Value Brand (Wal-Mart) -
Frozen Vegetable Mix (California Style, Italian Style)

Green Giant - Frozen Mixed Vegetables

Hannaford Brand - Mixed Vegetables

Home Harvest Brand - Mixed Vegetables (Canned, Frozen)

Hy-Vee -
Canned Mixed Vegetables
Frozen
California Mix
Country Trio

M

Feast Blend

Mixed Vegetables

Oriental Vegetables

Stew Vegetables

Kroger Brand - All Plain Vegetables (Canned, Frozen)

Lowes Foods Brand - Frozen (California Blend, Fajita Blend, Italian Blend, Mixed Vegetables, Peking Stir Fry, Vegetables For Soup)

Meijer Brand -

Canned Mixed

Frozen

California Style

Fiesta

Florentine

Italian

Mexican

Mixed Vegetables (Organic, Regular)

Oriental

Parisian Style

Stew Mix

Stir Fry

Midwest Country Fare - Canned, Frozen (California Blend, Mixed Vegetables, Winter Mix)

O Organics - Frozen (California Style Vegetables, Mixed Vegetable Blend)

Pictsweet - All Plain Vegetables (Frozen)

Publix -

Canned Mixed

Frozen Blends

Alpine

California

Del Oro

Gumbo

M
Italian
Japanese
Mixed Vegetable
Peas & Carrots
Roma
Soup Mix w/Tomatoes
Succotash

S&W - All Plain Canned Vegetables

Safeway Brand - Frozen Blends (Asian Style, California Style, Santa Fe
Style, Stew Vegetables, Stir Fry, Tuscan Style Vegetables, Winter
Blend), Mixed Vegetables (Canned, Frozen)

Spartan Brand - Canned Mixed Vegetables, Frozen (Baby Pea Blend,
Baby Corn Blend, California Vegetables, Fiesta Vegetables, Italian
Vegetables, Mixed Vegetables, Oriental Vegetables, Pepper Stirfry,
Stew Mix Vegetables, Vegetables For Soup, Winter Blend)

Stop & Shop Brand -
Country Blend
Latino Blend
Mixed Vegetables (No Added Salt, Regular)
Stew Vegetables

Tasty Bite - Kerala Vegetables

Trader Joe's - All Plain Frozen Vegetables

Wegmans Brand -
Mix (Santa Fe, Southern, Spring)
Mixed Vegetables (Canned, Frozen)

Winn Dixie - Canned No Salt Added, Frozen Mixed Vegetables
(Organic, Regular)

Woodstock Farms - Organic Frozen Plain Mixed Vegetables

Molasses
Brer Rabbit - Molasses (Blackstrap, Full Flavor, Mild)
Grandma's - Original, Robust
Publix

M

Mousse

    Orgran▲ - Chocolate Mousse Mix

Muffins/Muffin Mix

    1-2-3 Gluten Free▲ - Meredith's Marvelous Muffin/Quickbread●

    Andrea's Fine Foods▲ - Banana, Chocolate Chunk, Pumpkin

    Aunt Gussie's▲ - English Muffins (Cinnamon Raisin, Original)

    Authentic Foods▲ - Blueberry Muffin Mix, Chocolate Chip Muffin Mix

    Breads From Anna▲ - Pancake & Muffin Mix (Apple, Cranberry, Maple)

    Cause You're Special▲ - Classic Muffin & Quickbread Mix, Lemon Poppy Seed Muffin Mix, Sweet Corn Muffin Mix

    Celiac Specialties▲ -

        English

        Mini Lemon Poppy

        Mini Pumpkin Chocolate

        Pumpkin

    El Peto▲ - Sugar Free Muffins (Banana, Blueberry, Carrot, Raisin/Rice Bran)

    Ener-G▲ - Brown Rice English Muffins w/Flax, English Muffins

    Flax4Life - Flax Muffins (Faithfull Carrot Raisin●, Tantalizing Cranberry & Orange●, Wild Blueberry●)

    Flour Nut - Muffin Mix (Austin's Maple Cinnamon, Maple Walnut)

    Foods By George▲ - Muffins (Cinnamon Currant English, English, No-Rye Rye English)

    Gluten Free Life▲ - The Ultimate Gluten Free Cake Muffin & Brownie Mix

    Gluten-Free Creations▲ - Chocolate Zucchini●, Cranberry Orange Pecan●, English Muffins●, Lemon Poppyseed●

    Gluten-Free Essentials▲ - Lemon Poppy Seed Bread & Muffin Mix●, Spice Cake & Muffin Mix●

    Gluten-Free Pantry▲ - Muffin & Scone Mix

    Glutino▲ - Premium English Muffins

    Good Juju Bakery▲ - Exceptional English Muffins

M

Hodgson Mill▲ - Apple Cinnamon Muffin Mix

Kinnikinnick▲ - Blueberry, Carrot, Chocolate Chip, Cranberry, Cornbread & Muffin Mix, Muffin Mix, Tapioca Rice English Muffin

Midge's Muffins - Banana, Cherry Apple, Chocolate Chip, Cranberry, Blueberry, Pumpkin

Namaste Foods▲ - Muffin Mix, Sugar Free

Only Oats - Muffin Mix (Cinnamon Spice●)

Orgran▲ - Muffin Mix (Chocolate, Lemon & Poppyseed)

Pitter Patties - Viva Vegan, Yammy Chicken

Really Great Food▲ - Apple Spice Muffin Mix, Cornbread Muffin Mix, English Muffin Mix, Maple Raisin Muffin Mix, Sweet Muffin Mix, Vanilla Muffin Mix

Simply Organic - Chai Spice Scone Mix●

Mushrooms... *All Fresh Fruits & Vegetables Are Gluten/Casein Free*

Albertsons - Pieces & Stems (No Salt, Regular)

Eden Organic - Maitake (Dried), Shiitake (Dried Sliced, Dried Whole)

Food Club Brand - Canned (Pieces & Stems, Whole)

Great Value Brand (Wal-Mart) - Canned Mushrooms Pieces & Stems

Green Giant - Canned/Jarred (Pieces & Stems, Sliced, Whole)

Hannaford Brand - Stems & Pieces (No Salt, Regular)

Hy-Vee - Sliced, Stems & Pieces

Lowes Foods Brand - Jar (Sliced, Whole)

Meijer Brand -
    Canned (Sliced, Whole)
    Canned Stems & Pieces (No Salt, Regular)

Midwest Country Fare - Mushrooms & Stems (No Salt Added, Regular)

Pennsylvania Dutchman - Sliced, Stems & Pieces, Whole

Publix - Sliced, Stems & Pieces

Safeway Brand - Canned (Button Sliced)

Wegmans Brand - Button, Pieces & Stems, Sliced

M

Winn Dixie - Button, Stems & Pieces

Woodstock Farms - Organic Frozen (Mixed, Shiitake)

Mustard

Annie's Naturals - Organic (Dijon, Honey, Horseradish, Yellow)

Best Foods - Deli Brown, Dijonnaise, Honey

Bone Suckin' - Sweet Hot

Di Lusso - Chipotle, Cranberry Honey, Deli Style, Dijon, Honey, Jalapeno

Dietz & Watson - Champagne Dill, Cranberry Honey, Jalapeno, Stone Ground, Sweet & Hot, Wasabi, Whole Grain Dijon

Eden Organic - Organic (Brown, Yellow)

Emeril's - Dijon (Kicked Up Horseradish, NY Deli Style, Smooth Honey, Yellow)

Fischer & Wieser - Smokey Mesquite, Sweet Heat, Sweet Sour & Smokey Sauce

French's - Classic Yellow, Honey, Honey Dijon, Horseradish, Spicy Brown

Frontera - Chipotle Honey Mustard Grilling Sauce

Great Value Brand (Wal-Mart) - Coarse Ground, Dijon, Honey, Southwest Spicy, Spicy Brown, Yellow

Grey Poupon - Country Dijon, Deli, Dijon, Harvest Coarse Ground, Hearty Spicy Brown, Savory Honey

Guldens - Natural Yellow, Spicy Brown, Zesty Honey

Hannaford Brand - Dijon, Honey, Spicy Brown, Yellow

Heinz - Dijon, Spicy Brown, Yellow

Hellmann's - Deli Brown, Dijonnaise, Honey

Hy-Vee - Dijon, Honey, Regular, Spicy Brown

Jack Daniel's - Hickory Smoke, Honey Dijon, Horseradish, Old No. 7, Spicy Southwest, Stone Ground Dijon

Lou's Famous - Hot Mustard w/Horseradish

Meijer Brand - Honey Squeeze, Hot & Spicy, Salad Squeeze, Spicy Brown Squeeze

M
N

Mr. Spice Organic - Honey Mustard Sauce & Marinade

O Organics - Dijon, Yellow

Publix - Classic Yellow, Deli Style, Dijon, Honey, Spicy Brown

Publix GreenWise Market - Creamy Yellow, Spicy Yellow, Tangy Dijon

Safeway Brand - Coarse Ground Dijon, Dijon, Honey Mustard, Spicy Brown, Stone Ground Horseradish, Sweet & Spicy

Spartan Brand - Dijon, Honey, Prepared, Spicy Brown, Sweet & Hot

Texas Pete - Honey Mustard

Trader Joe's - Dijon, Organic Yellow

Wegmans Brand - Classic Yellow, Dijon (Traditional, Whole Grain), Honey, Horseradish, Smooth & Tangy, Spicy Brown

Winn Dixie - Yellow

Woodstock Farms - Dijon, Stone Ground, Yellow

Mutter

Tamarind Tree - Dhingri Mutter

N

Nayonaise

Nasoya - Dijon Style, Fat Free, Original

Nectars

Bionaturae - Organic (Apple, Apricot, Bilberry, Carrot Apple, Peach, Pear, Plum, Sicilian Lemon, Sour Cherry, Strawberry, Wildberry)

Noodles... see also Pasta

A Taste Of Thai - Rice Noodles (Regular, Thin, Wide)

Annie Chun's - Rice Noodles (Maifun, Pad Thai)

Blue Chip Group - GF Rice Noodle Mix

Mixes From The Heatland▲ - Noodle Mix (Plain●, Spinach●)

Seitenbacher - Gourmet Noodles Gluten Free Golden Ribbon, Gluten Free Rigatoni

Sharwood's - Rice Noodles

N

Thai Kitchen -

Instant Noodle Bowls (Garlic & Vegetable, Lemongrass & Chili, Mushroom, Roasted Garlic, Spring Onion)

Noodle Carts (Pad Thai, Roasted Garlic, Thai Peanut, Toasted Sesame)

Rice Noodles (Stir Fry Rice Noodles, Thin Rice Noodles)

Stir Fry Rice Noodle Meal Kit (Lemongrass & Chili, Original Pad Thai, Thai Peanut)

Take Out Boxes (Ginger & Sweet Chili, Original Pad Thai, Thai Basil & Chili)

Thai Pavilion - Rice Noodles (Green Curry, Pad Thai, Spicy Pad Thai, Thai Peanut)

Nut Beverages

Blue Diamond - Almond Breeze (Chocolate, Original, Vanilla), Almond Breeze Unsweetened (Chocolate, Original, Vanilla)

Pacific Natural Foods - All Natural Hazelnut Original, Organic Almond (Chocolate, Original, Vanilla, Unsweetened)

MimicCreme - Sugar Free Sweetened, Sweetened, Unsweetened

Nut Butter... see Peanut Butter

Nutritional Supplements

MLO - Brown Rice Protein Powder

Odwalla -

All Natural Carrot Juice

All Natural Lemonade

All Natural Orange Juice

All Natural Smoothie (Mango Tango, Strawberry Banana)

B Monster (Blueberry B)

C Monster (Citrus C, Strawberry C)

Mo' Beta

Mojito Mambo

Pomegranate Strawberry

N

Serious Energy (Tropical Energy)

Serious Focus (Apple Raspberry)

Wholly Grain (Tropical Medley)

Ruth's - Organic Hemp Protein Powder (E3Live & Maca, Hemp Protein Power, Hemp w/Sprouted Flax & Maca)

Salba●

Nuts

Albertsons - Cashews (Halves & Pieces, Lightly Salted, Whole), Mixed Nuts (Deluxe, Lightly Salted, Regular), Peanuts (Dry Roasted, Dry Roasted Unsalted, Honey Roasted, Lightly Salted, Lightly Salted Party, Party)

Back To Nature - All Natural Nantucket Blend

Eden Organic - Tamari Dry Roasted Almonds

Emerald -

Glazed Pecans (Original, Pecan Pie)

Glazed Walnuts (Apple Cinnamon, Butter Toffee, Chocolate Brownie, Original)

Frito Lay -

Cashews

Deluxe Mixed Nuts

Honey Roasted (Cashews, Peanuts)

Hot Peanuts

Salted (Almonds, Peanuts)

Smoked Almonds

Great Value Brand (Wal-Mart) - Premium Pistachios

Hannaford Brand -

Almonds (Natural, Roasted & Salted, Smoked)

Cashews (Halves & Pieces, Lightly Salted, Unsalted, Whole)

Macadamia Dry Roasted

Mixed (Deluxe, Lightly Salted, Regular)

Peanuts (Dry Roasted, Honey Roasted, Party)

Pistachio Kernels

N

Hy-Vee -

Almonds (Dry Roasted, Honey Roasted, Natural, Raw, Roasted & Salted, Roasted Unsalted, Smoked)

Black Walnuts

Cashews (Halves & Pieces, Honey Roasted, Sea Salted, w/Almonds Whole, Whole Lightly Salted)

English Walnut Pieces

English Walnuts

Macadamia

Mixed Nuts (Deluxe Lightly Salted, Deluxe No Peanuts, Lightly Salted, Regular, w/Pistachios)

Natural Almonds (Regular, Sliced)

Peanuts (Dry Roasted, Dry Roasted Unsalted, Honey Roasted, Party)

Pecan (Pieces, Regular)

Raw Spanish Peanuts

Salted Peanuts (Blanched, Spanish)

Slivered Almonds

Katy Sweet - Nuts (Glazed Pecans, Holy Mole, Peppered Pecans, Sugar & Spice Pecans)

Mareblu Naturals -

Crunch (Almond, Almond Coconut, Cashew, Cashew Coconut, CranMango Cashew, Pecan Cinnamon, Pistachio)

Trail Mix Crunch (Blueberry Pomegranate, Cranberry Pomegranate, Cranblueberry Trail, Cranstrawberry Trail, Pecan Trail, Pistachio Trail)

Meijer Brand -

Almonds (Blanched Sliced, Blanched Slivered, Natural Sliced, Slivered, Whole)

Cashews (Halves w/Pieces, Halves w/Pieces Lightly Salted, Whole)

Mixed (Deluxe, Lightly Salted, Regular)

Nut Topping

Peanuts

N

    Blanched (Regular, Slightly Salted)

    Dry Roasted (Lightly Salted, Regular, Unsalted)

    Honey Roasted

    Spanish

  Pecan (Chips, Halves)

  Pine

  Walnuts (Black, Chips, Halves & Pieces)

Nut Harvest -

  Natural

    Honey Roasted Peanuts

    Lightly Roasted Almonds

    Nut & Fruit Mix

    Sea Salted Peanuts

    Sea Salted Whole Cashews

Planters - Cashews Halves & Pieces, Dry Roasted Peanuts, Extra Large Virginia Peanuts, Fancy Whole Cashews, Honey Roasted, Mixed Nuts, Pistachio Lovers Mix

Publix -

  Almonds (Natural Whole, Salted, Sliced, Smoked)

  Cashews (Halves & Pieces, Halves & Pieces Lightly Salted, Honey Roasted, Premium Salted Jumbo, Whole)

  Macadamia

  Mixed (Deluxe, Lightly Salted, Regular)

  Peanuts (Dry Roasted Lightly Salted, Dry Roasted Salted, Dry Roasted Unsalted, Honey Roasted, Oil Roasted, Premium Salted Jumbo, Salted Party)

  Pecan Halves

  Walnuts

Sabritas - Picante Peanuts, Salt & Lime Peanuts

Safeway Brand -

  Almonds (Roasted & Salted, Smoked Flavored, Whole Natural)

  Honey Roasted Party Peanuts

Mixed (Deluxe, Regular)

Nuts Cashews (Halves, Pieces, Whole)

Spartan Brand -

Cashews (Halves w/Pieces, Whole)

Mixed (Fancy w/Macadamias, Lightly Salted, Nature, Regular)

Peanuts (Blanched Roasted, Dry Roasted (Honey, Regular, Salted), Honey Roasted, Lightly Salted Dry Roasted, No Salt Dry Roasted, Spanish)

Sunkist - Gourmet Oven Roasted Almonds, Pistachios (Dry Roasted, Kernels)

Trader Joe's -

All Raw & Roasted Nuts

Almond Meal

Cinnamon Almonds

Marcona Almonds (All)

True North - Almond (Clusters, Almonds Pistachios Walnut Pecans), Peanut Clusters (Pecan Almond, Regular)

Wegmans Brand -

Cashews (Salted, Unsalted)

Dry Roasted (Macadamias, Seasoned Peanuts)

Honey Roasted (Peanuts, Whole Cashews)

Natural Whole Almonds

Party Peanuts (Roasted Lightly Salted, Salted)

Peanuts Dry Roasted (Lightly Salted, Seasoned, Unsalted)

Peanuts (Salted In The Shell, Unsalted In The Shell)

Pine Nuts (Italian Classics)

Roasted

Almonds (Salted)

Cashew Halves & Pieces Salted

Deluxe Mixed Nuts w/Macadamias Salted

Jumbo Cashew Mix w/ Almonds Pecans & Brazils

N

    Jumbo Cashews

    Mixed Nuts w/Peanuts (Lightly Salted)

    Party Mixed Nuts w/Peanuts (Salted, Unsalted)

    Party Peanuts Lightly (Salted, Lightly Salted)

    Spanish Peanuts Salted

    Whole Cashews (Salted, Unsalted)

Winn & Lovett - Coconut Almonds

Winn Dixie -

Cashews (Halves & Pieces Lightly Salted, Halves & Pieces Salted, Honey Roasted, Whole Salted)

Mixed Nuts (Deluxe, Regular)

Peanuts (Dry Roasted Lightly Salted, Dry Roasted Salted, Dry Roasted Unsalted, Green Boiled)

Roasted Pistachios

Woodstock Farms -

Almonds (Non Pareil, Roasted & No Salt, Roasted & Salt, Supreme, Tamari, Thick Sliced)

Brazil

Cashew (Large Whole (Regular, Roasted))

Cocoa Dusted Dark Chocolate Almonds

Deluxe Mixed Nuts Roasted

Extra Fancy Mixed Nuts

Hazelnut Filberts

Organic Nuts (Almonds (Dark Chocolate w/Evaporated Cane Juice, Regular), Brazil, Cashews (Large Whole (Regular, Roasted & Salt), Pieces), Pecan Halves, Pine, Pistachios (No Salt, Roasted & Salt), Soynuts (No Salt, Roasted), Walnuts Halves & Pieces)

Peanuts Honey Roasted

Pecan Halves

Pine

Soynuts Roasted (No Salt, Regular)

Walnuts Halves & Pieces

O

O

Oatmeal

Glutenfreeda▲ - Instant Oatmeal (Apple Cinnamon w/Flax, Banana Maple w/Flax, Maple Raisin w/Flax, Natural)

Oats

Bob's Red Mill▲ - Gluten Free Rolled Oats

Chateau Cream Hill Estates - Lara's Rolled Oats●

Gifts Of Nature▲ - Old Fashioned Rolled Oats●, Whole Oat Groats

Gluten-Free Oats▲ - Old Fashioned Rolled Oats●

Montana Monster Munchies - Whole Grain (Grab & Go●, Quick Oats●, Rolled Oats●)

Only Oats - Steel Cut Oat Pearls●

Oil

Albertsons - All Oil

Annies Naturals -

Olive Oil (Basil, Dipping, Roasted Pepper)

Olive Oil Extra Virgin (Roasted Garlic)

Bakers & Chefs - 100% Pure Clear Frying Oil

Bertolli - All Olive Oils

Bionaturae - Organic Extra Virgin Olive Oil

Bragg - Organic (Extra Virgin Olive Oil, Olive Oil)

Carapelli - Olive Oil

Crisco - 100% Pure Extra Virgin Olive, Frying Blend, Light Olive, Natural Blend, Pure (Canola, Corn, Olive, Peanut, Vegetable), Puritan Canola w/Omega 3DHA

Eden Organic -

Olive Oil Spanish Extra Virgin

Organic (Hot Pepper Sesame Oil, Safflower Oil, Sesame Oil Extra Virgin, Soybean Oil)

Toasted Sesame Oil

Food Club Brand - Canola, Corn, Vegetable

O

Full Circle - Organic (Canola, Extra Virgin Olive Oil)

Grand Selections - 100% Pure & Natural Olive Oil, Extra Light, Extra Virgin Olive Oil, Olive Oil (Basil, Chili, Garlic, Lemon)

Great Value Brand (Wal-Mart) - Canola Oil Blend, Olive Oil (Extra Virgin, Light Tasting), Pure Oil (Canola, Corn, Vegetable)

Hannaford Brand - Canola Oil, Corn Oil, Olive (Extra Virgin, Extra Virgin Imported, Light, Pure), Vegetable Oil

House of Tsang - Oil (Hot Chili Sesame, Mongolian Fire, Sesame, Wok)

Hy-Vee -

100% Pure Oil (Canola, Corn, Vegetable)

Natural Blend Oil

Kroger Brand - Canola, Corn, Olive, Sunflower, Vegetable

Laura Lynn - Blended, Canola, Corn, Peanut, Vegetable

Lee Kum Kee - Pure Sesame

Lowes Foods Brand - 100% Pure Olive, Canola, Corn, Extra Virgin Olive, Peanut

Manischewitz - Vegetable

Manitoba Harvest - Hemp Seed Oil (Organic, Regular)

Mazola - Canola, Cooking, Corn, Vegetable

Meijer Brand - Blended Canola/Vegetable, Canola, Corn, Oil Olive (100% Pure-Italian Classic, Extra Virgin (Italian Classic, Regular), Italian Select Premium Extra Virgin, Milder Tasting, Regular), Oil Olive Infused (Garlic & Basil Italian, Roasted Garlic Italian, Spicy Red Pepper Italian), Sunflower, Peanut, Vegetable

Member's Mark - 100% Pure Olive Oil

Midwest Country Fare - 100% Pure Vegetable Oil, Vegetable Oil

Newman's Own Organics - Extra Virgin Olive Oil

Nutiva - Organic (Extra Virgin Coconut Oil, Hemp Oil)

O Organics - Extra Virgin Olive Oil

Oskri Organics - Extra Virgin Olive Oil, Flaxseed Oil, Grapeseed Oil, Omega 3 Olive Oil, Sesame Seed Oil

Publix - Oil (Canola, Corn, Extra Virgin, Light Olive, Olive, Peanut, Pure Italian Olive, Vegetable)

O

Ruth's - Certified Organic Hemp Oil

Safeway Brand - Canola, Canola Vegetable Blend, Corn, Vegetable

Safeway Select - Olive Oil (Extra Light, Extra Virgin, Regular)

Simply Enjoy -
Apulian Regional Extra Virgin Olive Oil (Apulian, Sicilian, Tuscan, Umbrian)

Spartan Brand - Blended, Canola, Corn, Olive (Extra Virgin, Regular), Vegetable

Spectrum Organic Products -
Almond Refined

Apricot Kernel Refined

Avocado Refined

Canola (High Heat, Organic Refined, Regular)

Coconut Organic (Refined, Unrefined)

Corn Unrefined

Grapeseed Refined

Olive Oil (All Varieties)

Peanut Unrefined

Safflower (Organic High Heat Refined, Regular High Heat, Unrefined)

Sesame (Organic Unrefined, Organic Unrefined Toasted, Refined, Regular, Unrefined Toasted)

Soy Organic Refined

Sunflower Organic High Heat Refined

Walnut Refined

Star - Extra (Light, Virgin), Original

Stop & Shop Brand - Blended, Canola, Corn, Extra Light Olive, MiCasa (Corn, Vegetable), Pure Olive, Soybean, Vegetable

Tassos - Olive Oil (Extra Virgin, Fine, Organic Extra, Peza Crete Extra)

Trader Joe's - Cooking Oil (All Varieties)

O   **Wegmans Brand -**
  Basting w/Garlic & Herbs
  Canola
  Corn
  Extra Virgin (Black Truffle, Campania Style, Regular, Sicilian
    Lemon, Sicilian Style, Tuscany Style)
  Grapeseed
  Mild Olive
  Organic (Extra Virgin, Sunflower Oil)
  Peanut
  Pumpkin Seed
  Pure
  Submarine Sandwich
  Vegetable
Winn & Lovett - Extra Virgin Olive Oil
Winn Dixie - Canola, Corn, Olive, Peanut, Vegetable
Okra... *All **Fresh** Fruits & Vegetables Are **Gluten/Casein Free***
  Albertsons - Frozen (Cut, Whole)
  Lowes Foods Brand - Cut
  Meijer Brand - Frozen (Chopped, Whole)
  Pictsweet - All Plain Frozen Vegetables
  Publix - Frozen (Cut, Whole Baby)
  Safeway Brand - Frozen
  Spartan Brand - Cut, Whole
  Winn Dixie - Frozen (Cut, Diced, Whole)
  Woodstock Farms - Organic Frozen Cut Okra
Olive Oil... see Oil
Olives
  Albertsons
  Di Lusso - Green Ionian, Mediterranean Mixed

O

Food Club Brand - Pitted (Large, Medium)

Great Value Brand (Wal-Mart) -

Large Pitted Ripe

Medium Pitted Ripe

Minced Pimento Stuffed (Manzanilla, Queen)

Hannaford Brand - Pitted (Extra Large, Large, Medium, Small), Sliced (Ripe, Salad), Stuffed (Manzanilla, Queen)

Hy-Vee -

Chopped Ripe

Manzanilla Olives

Medium Ripe Black

Queen

Ripe Black (Jumbo, Large)

Sliced (Ripe Black, Salad)

Krinos - Imported Kalamata Olives

Meijer Brand - Manzanilla Stuffed (Placed, Thrown, Tree), Queen (Stuffed Placed, Whole Thrown), Ripe (Large, Medium, Pitted Jumbo, Pitted Small, Sliced), Salad, Salad Sliced

Midwest Country Fare - Large Ripe Black, Sliced Ripe Black

Peloponnese - Kalamata Olives

Publix - Colossal, Green, Large, Ripe, Small

Safeway Brand - Black Olives, Manzanilla

Santa Barbara Olive Co. - Garlic Stuffed

Spartan Brand - Ripe Pitted Olives (Jumbo, Large, Medium, Sliced, Small)

Tassos - Blonde Olives In Extra Virgin Olive Oil & Red Wine Vinegar, Evian Olives In Sea Salt Brine, Greek Black Olives In Extra Virgin Olive Oil & Red Wine Vinegar, Kalamata In Tassos Extra Virgin Olive Oil & Red Wine Vinegar, Stuffed Almond In Sea Salt Brine

Wegmans Brand -

Greek Mix

Kalamata (Pitted, Whole)

O

    Ripe (Pitted Colossal, Pitted Extra Large, Pitted Medium, Sliced)

    Spanish (Manzanilla, Queen, Salad)

    Stuffed w/ (Almonds, Garlic, Red Peppers)

Winn Dixie - Green (All Varieties), Ripe (All Varieties)

Onions... *All **Fresh** Fruits & Vegetables Are **Gluten/Casein Free***

  Albertsons - Frozen

  Birds Eye - All Plain Frozen Vegetables

  Lowes Foods Brand - Frozen Diced

  Meijer Brand - Frozen Chopped

  Publix - Frozen (Chopped, Diced)

  Trader Joe's - All Plain Frozen Vegetables

  Wegmans Brand - Whole Onions In Brine

  Winn Dixie - Frozen Pearl Onions

Orange Juice... see Drinks/Juice

Oranges... *All **Fresh** Fruits & Vegetables Are **Gluten/Casein Free***

  Sunkist

Oyster Sauce

  Panda Brand -

    Green Label Oyster Flavored Sauce

    Lo Mein Oyster Flavored Sauce

  Wok Mei - All Natural Oyster Flavored Sauce

Oysters... *All **Fresh** Seafood Is **Gluten/Casein Free (Non-Marinated, Unseasoned)***

  Bumble Bee - Smoked, Whole

  Chicken Of The Sea - Smoked (In Oil, In Water), Whole

  Crown Prince - Smoked In Cottonseed Oil, Whole Boiled

  Crown Prince Natural - Smoked In Pure Olive Oil, Whole Boiled In Water

  Great Value Brand (Wal-Mart) - Canned Smoked Oysters

  Ocean Prince -

    Fancy Whole Smoked In Cottonseed Oil

    Whole Boiled

pancakes/pancake mix & waffles/waffle mix

P

P

Pancakes/Pancake Mix & Waffles/Waffle Mix

1-2-3 Gluten Free▲ - Allie's Awesome Buckwheat Pancakes●

Arrowhead Mills - Gluten Free Pancake & Waffle Mix, Wild Rice Pancake & Waffle Mix

Authentic Foods▲ - Pancake & Baking Mix

Bob's Red Mill▲ - Gluten Free Pancake Mix

Breads From Anna▲ - Pancake & Muffin Mix (Apple, Cranberry, Maple)

Celiac Specialties▲ - Pancake Mix (Plain & Flaxseed)

Cherrybrook Kitchen - Gluten Free Pancake Mix *(Box Must Say Gluten-Free)*

El Peto▲ - Pancake Mix

Gluten-Free Creations▲ - Buckwheat Pancake Mix●, Mighty Mesquite Pancake Mix●

Gluten-Free Essentials▲ - Pancake & Waffle Mix●

Gluten Free Sensations - Pancake & Waffle Mix

Grandma Ferdon's▲ - Pancake/Waffle Mix

Hodgson Mill▲ - Gluten Free Pancake & Waffle Mix

Hol Grain - Pancake & Waffle Mix

Kinnikinnick▲ - Pancake & Waffle Mix

Laurel's Sweet Treats▲ - Bulk Pancake Mix, Pancake & Waffle Mix

Manischewitz - Pancake Mix (Potato, Sweetened Potato)

Maple Grove Farms Of Vermont - Gluten Free Pancake Mix

Mixes From The Heartland▲ - Pancake Mix (Apple Cinnamon●, Cornmeal●, Country●)

Namaste Foods▲ - Waffle & Pancake Mix

Nature's Path - Frozen Organic Waffles (Buckwheat Wildberry, Homestyle Gluten Free, Mesa Sunrise Omega 3)

Only Oats - Whole Oat Pancake Mix●

Orgran▲ - Apple & Cinnamon Pancake Mix, Buckwheat Pancake Mix, Plain Pancake Mix w/Sorghum

Pamela's Products ▲ - Baking & Pancake Mix●

P   **Really Great Food▲** - Classic Pancake Mix

Ruby Range - Southwest Pancakes Gluten Free Baking Mix●

Sylvan Border Farm - Pancake & Waffle Mix

Van's All Natural - Apple Cinnamon, Blueberry, Buckwheat, Flax, Homestyle, Mini

Papaya... *All Fresh Fruits & Vegetables Are Gluten/Casein Free*

   Native Forest - Organic Papaya Chunks

   Woodstock Farms - Organic Frozen Papaya Chunks

Pappadums

   Patak's - Pappadums (Black Peppercorn, Garlic, Plain)

   Sharwood's - Indian Puppodums (Crushed Garlic & Coriander, Plain)

Paprika... see Seasonings

Parmesan Cheese... see Cheese

Pasta

   Allegaroo▲ - Chili Mac, Spaghetti, Spyglass Noodles

   Ancient Harvest Quinoa - Elbows, Garden Pagodas, Linguine, Rotelle, Shells, Spaghetti, Veggie Curls

   Annie Chun's - Rice Noodles (Maifun, Pad Thai)

   Aproten - Fettuccine, Fusilli, Penne, Rigatini, Spaghetti, Tagliatelle

   Bi-Aglut - Fusilli, Maccheroncini, Penne, Spaghetti

   Bionaturae▲ - Organic Gluten Free (Elbow, Fusilli, Penne, Spaghetti)

   Conte's Pasta - Gnocchi, Potato Onion Pierogies

   Cornito - Elbow Macaroni, Mystic Flames Noodles, Rainbow Rotini, Rigatoni, Rotini, Sea Waves, Spaghetti

   DeBoles -

     Corn Pasta (Elbow Style, Spaghetti)

     Gluten Free Rice (Angel Hair & Golden Flax, Spirals & Golden Flax)

     Gluten Free Whole Grain (Penne, Spaghetti)

     Rice Pasta (Angel Hair, Fettuccini, Lasagna, Penne, Spaghetti, Spirals)

   Eden Organic - Bifun, Kuzu, Mung Bean

P

Ener-G▲ - White Rice (Lasagna, Macaroni, Small Shells, Spaghetti, Vermicelli)

Gillian's Foods▲ - Fetuccini, Fusilli, Penne, Spaghetti

Glutano▲ - Fusilli, Penne, Spaghetti

Glutino▲ - Brown Rice (Fusilli, Macaroni, Penne, Spaghetti)

Grandma Ferdon's▲ - Brown Rice (Chow Mein Noodles, Elbows, Fettuccini, Lasagna, Spaghetti)

Hodgson Mill▲ - Gluten Free Brown Rice (Angel Hair Pasta, Elbows, Linguine, Penne, Spaghetti)

Lundberg▲ - Organic Brown Rice Pasta (Elbow, Penne, Rotini, Spaghetti)

Mrs. Leeper's - Corn Pasta (Elbows, Rotelli, Spaghetti, Vegetable Radiatore), Rice Pasta (Alphabets, Elbows, Kids Shapes, Penne, Spaghetti, Vegetable Twists)

Namaste Foods▲ - Pasta Meals (Pasta Pisavera, Say Cheez, Taco)

Notta Pasta - Fettuccine, Linguine, Spaghetti

Orgran▲ -

Buckwheat Spirals

Buontempo Rice Pasta (Penne, Shells, Spirals)

Canned (Alternative Grain Spaghetti, Spaghetti In Tomato Sauce, Spirals In Tomato Sauce)

Corn & Spinach Rigati

Corn & Vegetable Pasta Shells

Corn Pasta Spirals

Essential Fibre (Penne, Spirals)

Garlic & Parsley Rice Pasta Shells

Italian Style Spaghetti

Pasta & Sauce (Tomato Basil)

Pasta Ready Meals (Tomato & Basil, Vegetable Bolognese)

Rice & Corn (Herb Pasta, Macaroni, Mini Lasagne Sheets, Penne, Risoni Garlic Herb, Spaghetti, Spirals, Tortelli, Vegetable Animal Shapes, Vegetable Corkscrews)

P

Rice & Millet Spirals

Rice Pasta Spirals

Super Grains Multigrain Pasta w/ (Amaranth, Quinoa)

Tomato & Basil Corn Pasta

Vegetable Rice (Penne, Spirals)

Pastariso▲ - Organic Brown Rice (Angel Hair, Elbows, Fettuccine, Lasagna, Linguine, Penne, Rotini, Spaghetti, Vermicelli), Spinach Spaghetti, Vegetable Rotini

Pastato▲ - Elbows, Shells, Spaghetti

Rizopia -

Brown Rice (Elbows, Fettuccine, Fusilli, Lasagne, Penne, Shells, Spaghetti, Spirals)

Organic Brown Rice (Elbows, Fantasia, Fettuccine, Fusilli, Penne, Spaghetti)

Organic Wild Rice (Elbows, Fusilli, Penne, Radiatore, Shells, Spaghetti)

Spinach Brown Rice Spaghetti

Vegetable Brown Rice Fusilli

White Rice Spaghetti

Sam Mills▲ - Corn Pasta (Conchigliette, Cornetti Rigati, Fusilli, Lasagna, Penne Rigate, Rigatoni, Tubetti Rigati)

Schar▲ - Anellini, Fusilli, Multigrain Penne Rigate, Penne, Spaghetti, Tagliatelle

Seitenbacher - Gourmet Noodles Gluten Free Golden Ribbon, Gluten Free Rigatoni

Tinkyada▲ -

Brown Rice (Elbows, Fettuccini, Fusilli, Grand Shells, Lasagne, Little Dreams, Penne, Shells, Spaghetti, Spirals)

Organic Brown Rice (Elbows, Lasagne, Penne, Spaghetti, Spirals)

Spinach Brown Rice Spaghetti

Vegetable Brown Rice Spirals

White Rice Spaghetti

Trader Joe's - Organic Brown Rice Pasta (All Varieties)
Westbrae - Corn Angel Hair Pasta
Pasta Sauce... see Sauces
Pastrami
   Dietz & Watson - Pastrami Brisket, Spiced Beef Pastrami
   Hormel - Deli Sliced Cooked
   Jennie-O Turkey Store - Refrigerated Dark Turkey Pastrami
   Perdue - Deli Dark Turkey Pastrami Hickory Smoked
   Wellshire Farms - Pastrami (Brisket, Round, Sliced Beef)
Pastry Mix
   Kinnikinnick▲ - Pastry & Pie Crust Mix
   Orgran▲ - All Purpose
Pate
   Kootenay Kitchen - Vege Pate (Curry, Herb, Jalapeno)
   Tartex - Pate (Herb Meadow, Mushroom, Original)
Pea Pods... see also Peas
   Meijer Brand - Frozen (Chinese)
Peaches... *All Fresh Fruits & Vegetables Are Gluten/Casein Free*
   Albertsons - All Canned Peaches, Frozen
   Cascadian Farm - Organic Frozen Sliced Peaches
   Del Monte -
      Canned/Jarred Fruit (All Varieties)
      Fruit Snack Cups (Metal, Plastic)
   Dole - All Fruits (Bowls, Canned, Dried, Frozen, Jars) *(Except Real Fruit Bites)*
   Food Club Brand - Fruit Cups Diced Peaches, Frozen Peaches, Halves In Heavy Syrup, Sliced In Heavy Syrup, Sliced Lite
   Hannaford Brand - Extra Light Syrup (Halves, Sliced), No Sugar Added Sliced, Sliced In Heavy Syrup
   Home Harvest Brand - Yellow Cling Peaches (In Light Syrup, Sliced)

P Hy-Vee -
   Diced
   Diced Fruit Cups
   Halves
   Lite (Diced, Halves, Slices)
   Peaches In Strawberry Gel
   Slices
Great Value Brand (Wal-Mart) -
   Cling Peach Halves In Light Syrup
   No Sugar Added Yellow Cling Peach Halves In Pear Juice From
      Concentrate & Water
Kroger Brand - Fruit (Canned, Cups)
Laura Lynn - Canned
Lowes Foods Brand - Slices (In Heavy Syrup, In Juice)
Meijer Brand -
   Cling Halves (In Heavy Syrup, In Juice Lite, In Pear Juice Lite)
   Cling Sliced (In Heavy Syrup, In Juice, In Pear Juice Lite)
   Frozen (Organic, Sliced)
   Pallet Mod
   Yellow Sliced In Heavy Syrup
Midwest Country Fare - Lite Peaches (Halves, Slices), Slices
Publix -
   Canned (Lite Yellow Cling Peaches in Pear Juice Halves & Slices,
      Yellow Cling Peaches In Heavy Syrup Halves & Slices)
   Frozen Sliced Peaches
S&W - All Plain Canned/Jarred Fruits
Safeway Brand - Canned Peaches (Halves, Halves Lite, Sliced, Sliced
   Lite), Frozen
Spartan Brand - Cling Halves (Heavy Syrup, Regular), Diced (Heavy
   Syrup, Light Syrup), Frozen, Lite Cling Halves, Sliced Cling Peaches
   In Pear, Yellow Cling Sliced
Thrifty Maid - Yellow Cling Halves & Slices

Wegmans Brand - Sliced Yellow Cling (In Heavy Syrup, Raspberry)

P

Winn Dixie - Frozen Sliced, Yellow Cling Halves & Slices (Heavy Syrup, Light Syrup)

Woodstock Farms - Organic Frozen Peach Slices

Peanut Butter... (includes Nut Butters)

Albertsons - Creamy, Crunchy, Reduced Fat (Creamy, Crunchy)

Arrowhead Mills -

Almond Butter (Creamy, Crunchy)

Cashew Butter (Creamy, Crunchy)

Honey Sweetened Peanut Butter (Creamy, Crunchy)

Organic Valencia Peanut Butter (Creamy, Crunchy)

Valencia Peanut Butter (Creamy, Crunchy)

Bee's Knees - All Varieties

Earth Balance - Creamy Natural Almond Butter, Natural Peanut Butter (Creamy, Crunchy)

Hannaford Brand - Creamy, Crunchy

Hy-Vee - Creamy, Crunchy, Reduced Fat

I.M. Healthy -

Soy Nut Butter

Chocolate

Honey (Chunky, Creamy)

Original (Chunky, Creamy)

Unsweetened (Chunky, Creamy)

Jif - Creamy, Extra Crunchy, Jif To Go, Peanut Butter & Honey, Reduced Fat Creamy, Reduced Fat Crunchy, Simply Jif

MaraNatha -

Natural Creamy (No Stir, With Salt)

Natural Crunchy (No Stir, With Salt)

Organic Creamy (No Salt, No Stir, With Salt)

Organic Crunchy (No Salt, No Stir, With Salt)

Organic No Stir Calcium

Meijer Brand - Creamy, Crunchy, Natural (Creamy, Crunchy)

P **Midwest Country Fare** - Creamy, Crunchy

Peanut Butter & Co. - All Varieties

Publix - All Natural (Creamy, Crunchy), Creamy, Crunchy, Reduced
Fat Spread (Creamy, Crunchy)

Safeway Brand - Creamy, Crunchy, Reduced Fat (Creamy, Crunchy)

Santa Cruz - Organic Dark Roasted (Creamy, Crunchy), Organic
Light Roasted (Creamy, Crunchy)

Skippy - Creamy, Extra Crunchy Super Chunk, Natural (Creamy,
Super Chunk), Reduced Fat (Creamy, Super Chunk), Roasted
Honey Nut (Creamy, Super Chunk)

Smart Balance - Omega (Chunky, Creamy)

Smucker's - Goober (Grape, Strawberry), Natural (Chunky, Creamy,
Honey, No Salt Added Creamy, Reduced Fat)

Spartan Brand - Crunchy, Smooth

Trader Joe's - All Nut Butters, Sunflower Seed

Walden Farms - Creamy Peanut Spread (Sugar Free)

Wegmans Brand -

Natural Peanut Butter (Creamy, Crunchy)

Organic Natural Peanut Butter w/Peanut Skins (Creamy,
Crunchy)

Organic No Stir (Creamy, Crunchy)

Peanut Butter (Creamy, Crunchy)

Woodstock Farms -

Non-Organic Nut Butters

Almond Butter (Crunchy Unsalted, Smooth Unsalted)

Cashew Butter Unsalted

Raw Almond

Tahini Unsalted

Organic Nut Butters

Almond Butter (Crunchy Unsalted, Smooth Unsalted)

Classic Peanut Butter (Crunchy Salted, Smooth Salted)

Easy Spread Peanut Butter (Crunchy (Salted, Unsalted), Smooth **P**
(Salted, Unsalted))

Peanut Butter (Crunchy (Salted, Unsalted), Smooth (Salted,
Unsalted))

Raw Almond

Tahini Unsalted

Peanut Sauce

A Taste Of Thai - Peanut Satay Sauce, Peanut Sauce Mix

Mr. Spice Organic - Thai Peanut Sauce & Marinade

San-J - Gluten Free Thai Peanut Marinade & Dipping Sauce●

Thai Kitchen - Peanut Satay

Peanuts... see Nuts

Pears... *All Fresh Fruits & Vegetables Are Gluten/Casein Free*

Albertsons - Canned

Del Monte -

Canned/Jarred Fruit (All Varieties)

Fruit Snack Cups (All Varieties)

Dole - All Fruits (Bowls, Canned, Dried, Frozen, Jars) *(Except Real Fruit
Bites)*

Food Club Brand - Fruit Cups (Diced Pears), Sliced

Full Circle - Organic (Halves In Juice, Sliced In Juice)

Great Value Brand (Wal-Mart) -

Bartlett Pear Halves In Heavy Syrup

Bartlett Sliced Pears In Heavy Syrup

No Sugar Added Bartlett (Chunky Mixed Fruits, Fruit Cocktail, Pear
Halves) In Pear Juice From Concentrate & Water

Hannaford Brand - Diced In Light Syrup, Extra Light Syrup (Halves,
Sliced), No Sugar Added (Halves, Sliced)

Home Harvest Brand - Whole Pears (In Light Syrup, Regular)

Hy-Vee - Bartlett Pears (Halves, Sliced), Diced Bartlett Pears Cups, Lite
Pears

P **Kroger Brand** - Fruit (Canned, Cups)

Laura Lynn - Canned Pears

Lowes Foods Brand - Halves (In Heavy Syrup, In Juice)

Meijer Brand - Halves (Heavy Syrup, In Juice, In Juice Lite, Lite), Slices (Heavy Syrup, In Juice Lite)

Midwest Country Fare - Bartlett Pear Halves In Light Syrup

Native Forest - Organic Sliced Asian Pears

Publix - Canned (Bartlett Pears In Heavy Syrup (Halves, Slices), Lite Bartlett Pear Halves In Pear Juice)

S&W - All Canned/Jarred Fruits

Safeway Brand - Canned Pears (Halves, Halves Lite, Sliced, Sliced Lite)

Spartan Brand - Halves (Heavy Syrup, Lite Syrup), Slices (Heavy Syrup, In Juice)

Stop & Shop Brand - Bartlett Pear Halves (Heavy Syrup, Light Syrup, Pear Juice, Splenda)

Thrifty Maid - Bartlett Halves & Slices

Wegmans Brand - Halves (Heavy Syrup, Regular), Sliced (Heavy Syrup, Regular)

Winn Dixie - Bartlett Halves & Slices (Heavy Syrup, Light Syrup)

Peas... *All Fresh Fruits & Vegetables Are Gluten/Casein Free*

Albertsons - Canned, Frozen

Birds Eye - All Plain Frozen Vegetables

C & W - All Plain Frozen Vegetables

Cascadian Farms - Organic Frozen (Garden Peas, Peas & Carrots, Peas & Pearl Onions, Purely Steam Petite Sweet Peas, Sugar Snap Peas, Sweet Peas)

Del Monte - All Plain Canned Vegetables

Food Club Brand - Canned Sweet, Frozen (Green Peas, Peas & Carrots, Sugar Snap)

Freshlike - Select (Petite Sweet Peas, Sweet Peas & Tiny Onions), Sweet Peas & Carrots, Tender Garden

Full Circle - Organic Frozen Peas, Organic Sweet Peas

Grand Selections - Frozen (Petite Green, Sugar Snap)

P

Great Value Brand (Wal-Mart) - Canned (Blackeye Peas, No Salt Added Sweet Peas, Sweet Peas), Frozen Sweet Peas, Microwaveable Plastic Cups Sweet Peas

Green Giant -

Canned Sweet Peas

Frozen

Simply Steam (Baby Sweet Peas, Sugar Snap Peas)

Sweet Peas

Halstead Acres - Blackeye Peas

Hannaford Brand - No Salt, Petite, Sweet

Health Market Organic - Sweet

Home Harvest Brand - Canned Sweet, Frozen

Hy-Vee - Black Eyed, Dry Green Split, Frozen Sweet, Steam In A Bag Frozen Peas, Sweet

Kroger Brand - All Plain Vegetables (Canned, Frozen)

Laura Lynn - Canned Blackeye Peas, Sweet Peas, Tiny June Peas

Lowes Foods Brand - Black Eyed, Frozen (Crowder, Field Peas, Green, Peas, Peas & Carrots, Tiny Green), Split Green Peas

Meijer Brand -

Canned (Blackeye, Peas & Sliced Carrots, Small, Sweet, Sweet No Salt, Sweet Organic)

Frozen Peas (Green, Green Petite, Organic Green, Peas & Sliced Carrots)

Midwest Country Fare - Frozen Green, Sweet

O Organics - Frozen Sweet Peas

Pictsweet - All Plain Vegetables (Frozen)

Publix -

Canned Sweet Peas (No Salt Added, Regular, Small)

Frozen (Green, Field Peas w/Snap, Original, Peas & Carrots, Petite)

Publix GreenWise Market - Organic Canned Sweet Peas

S&W - All Plain Canned Vegetables

P

Safeway Select - Frozen (Blackeyed, Green, Peas & Carrots, Petite),
Steam In Bag (Pod, Peas & Onions, Petite Green)

Spartan Brand - Canned (Green, Sweet), Dried (Blackeyed, Green
Split), Frozen (Blackeyed, Crowder, Peas, Peas & Carrots, Peas
w/Snaps, Petite, Sugar Snap, w/Snaps)

Trader Joe's - All Plain Frozen Vegetables

Wegmans Brand - Blackeye, Regular, Small Sweet, Sugar Snap
Frozen, Sweet (No Salt Added, Regular), Sweet Petite Frozen,
w/Pearl Onions Frozen

Winn Dixie -

Canned Green Peas (Large, Medium, No Salt Added, Small, Tiny)

Frozen (Crowder, Field w/Snaps, Green, Organic Green, Peas &
Carrots, Petite Green, Purple Hull)

Woodstock Farms - Organic Frozen (Green Peas, Peas & Carrots,
Petite Peas, Sugar Snap)

Wylwood - Blackeye Peas

Pepper Rings

Publix - Banana Pepper Rings Mild

Spartan Brand - Pepper Rings (Mild, Hot)

Vlasic - Hot Pepper Rings, Mild Pepper Rings

Pepper Sauce... see Chili Sauce and/or Hot Sauce

Pepperoni... see Sausage

Peppers... *All **Fresh** Fruits & Vegetables Are **Gluten/Casein Free***

Albertsons - Frozen Diced Green

B&G -

Giardiniera

Hot Cherry Peppers (Red & Green, Regular)

Hot Chopped Peppers (Regular, Roasted)

Hot Jalapenos (Cherry, Chopped)

Hot Pepper Rings

Pepperoncini

Roasted (w/Balsamic Vinegar, w/Oregano & Garlic)

Sweet (Cherry Peppers, Fried)

P

Birds Eye - All Plain Frozen Vegetables

Di Lusso - Roasted Red

Hannaford Brand - Whole Pepperoncini

Hy-Vee - Diced Green Chilies, Green Salad Pepperoncini, Hot Banana Peppers, Mild Banana Peppers, Salad Peppers, Sliced Hot Jalapenos, Whole Green Chilies

La Victoria - Diced Jalapenos, Nacho Jalapenos Sliced

Meijer Brand - Frozen Green Peppers Chopped

Peloponnese -
    Rainbow Peppers
    Roasted Florida Sweet Pepper Strips
    Whole Roasted Florida Sweet Peppers

Publix - Frozen Green Peppers (Diced)

Safeway Select - Fire Roasted, Frozen Pepper Strips

Spartan Brand - Jalapeno Peppers

Stop & Shop Brand - Chopped Green

Trader Joe's -
    All Plain Frozen Vegetables
    Artichoke Red Pepper Tapenade
    Fire Roasted Red (Regular, Sweet & Yellow)

Trappey - Jalapeno (Sliced, Whole)

Vlasic -
    Hot Chili Peppers
    Hot Pepper Rings
    Mild Pepper Rings
    Mild Pepperoncini Peppers
    Sweet Roasted Pepper Strips

Wegmans Brand - Clean & Cut Peppers & Onions (Diced, Sliced), Pepper & Onions Mix, Roasted Red Peppers Whole

Winn Dixie - Pepperoncini, Sliced Banana Peppers (Hot, Mild)

Woodstock Farms - Organic Frozen Tri Colored Peppers

P Picante Sauce
   Albertsons - Medium, Mild
   Chi-Chi's - Smooth & Spicy
   Hy-Vee - Hot, Medium, Mild
   Winn Dixie - Medium, Mild
Pickled Beets... see Beets
Pickles -
   Albertsons - All Varieties
   B&G -
      Bread & Butter
      Hamburger Dill
      Kosher Dill (Baby Gherkins, Gherkins, Original)
      Midget Gherkins
      NY Deli Dill
      Pickle In A Pouch
      Sour
      Sweet (Gherkins, Mixed, Mixed Pickles)
      Tiny Treats
      Unsalted (Bread & Butter, Kosher Dill)
      Zesty Dill
   Boar's Head - All Varieties
   Great Value Brand (Wal-Mart) -
      Bread & Butter
      Dill Spears
      Garlic Dill Slicers
      Hamburger Dill Chips
      Kosher Baby Dill
      Kosher Dill Spears
      Sweet (Gherkin, Pickle Relish)
      Whole Sweet

P

Hannaford Brand - Bread & Butter Chips, Bread & Butter Sandwich Slices, Kosher Baby Dills, Kosher Dill (Regular, Sandwich Slices, Spears), Kosher Petite, Polish Dill Spears, Sour Dill, Spear & Chips Sugar Free Bread & Butter, Sugar Free Sweet Gherkin, Sweet Gherkins (Midgets, Mixed Chips)

Hy-Vee -

Bread & Butter (Sandwich Slices, Sweet Chunk Pickles, Sweet Slices)

Dill (Kosher Sandwich Slices, Relish)

Fresh Pack Kosher Baby Dills

Hamburger Dill Slices

Kosher (Baby Dills, Cocktail Dills, Dill Pickles, Dill Spears)

Polish Dill (Pickles, Spears)

Refrigerated Kosher Dill (Halves, Sandwich Slices, Spears, Whole Pickles)

Special Recipe (Baby Dills, Bread & Butter Slices, Hot & Spicy Zingers, Hot & Sweet Zinger Chunks, Jalapeno Baby Dills, Sweet Garden Crunch)

Midwest Country Fare - Dill, Hamburger Dill Pickle Slices, Kosher Dill, Whole Sweet

Mrs. Renfro's - Green Tomato Pickles

Publix - All Varieties

Safeway Brand - All Varieties

Sharwood's - Lime

Spartan Brand -

Bread & Butter Pickle (Slices)

Hamburger Dill Slices

Kosher Dill (Baby, Slices, Spears, Whole)

Plain Baby Dills

Polish Dill (Regular, Spears)

Sweet (Gherkin Whole, Regular, Slices)

P   **Trader Joe's -** Organic Kosher Sandwich Pickles, Organic Sweet Bread & Butter Pickles

    Vlasic -

      Baby Kosher (Dills, Spears)

      Bread & Butter

      Hamburger Dill Chips

      Sweet & Crunchy Sweet

      Sweet Gherkins

      Sweet Midgets

      Zesty Dill

      Zesty Garlic

    Wegmans Brand -

      Hamburger Dill Slices

      Kosher Dill (Baby Dills, Slices, Spears, Spears Reduced Sodium, Whole)

      Polish Dill (Spears, Whole)

      Refrigerated Kosher Dills (Halves, Mini, Sandwich Slices, Spears, Whole)

    Winn Dixie - Dill (All Varieties), Sweet Pickles (All Varieties), Sweet Relish

    Woodstock Farms - Organic (Kosher Dill (Baby, Sliced, Whole), Sweet Bread & Butter)

Pie

    Amy's - Organic Mexican Tamale Pie, Shepherd's Pie (Light In Sodium, Regular)

    Mixes From The Heartland▲ - Pie Mix (Impossible Coconut●, Impossible Pumpkin●)

Pie Crust/Pie Crust Mix

    Authentic Foods▲ - Pie Crust Mix

    Breads From Anna▲ - Piecrust Mix

    El Peto▲ - Perfect Pie Crust Mix

    Gluten-Free Pantry▲ - Perfect Pie Crust

Hodgson Mill▲ - GF Pizza Crust Mix
Kinnikinnick▲ - Pastry & Pie Crust Mix
Mixes From The Heartland▲ - Pie Crust Mix●
Namaste Foods▲ - Biscuits Piecrust & More Mix

Pie Filling

Comstock - Apple, Blueberry, Cherry, Peach
Fischer & Wieser - Fredericksburg Golden Peach, Harvest Apple & Brandy
Great Value Brand (Wal-Mart) - Apple, Blueberry, Cherry, No Sugar Added (Apple, Cherry)
Hy-Vee - More Fruit Pie Filling/Topping (Apple, Cherry)
Jell-O -

Regular Cook & Serve
Banana Cream
Chocolate (Fudge, Regular)
Coconut Cream
Lemon
Vanilla
Regular Instant Pudding & Pie Filling
Banana Cream
Chocolate (Fudge, Regular)
Coconut Cream
Devil's Food
French Vanilla
Lemon
Pistachio
Pumpkin Spice
Vanilla
White Chocolate
Sugar Free Fat Free Cook & Serve
Chocolate
Vanilla

P

Lucky Leaf - Blueberry, Cherry, Chocolate Crème, Coconut Crème, Dark Sweet Cherry, Key Lime Pie Crème, Lemon, Lemon Crème, Lite (Apple, Cherry), Peach, Premium (Apple, Blackberry, Blueberry, Cherry, Red Raspberry), Strawberry

Midwest Country Fare - Apple, Cherry

My T Fine - Lemon, Vanilla

Musselman's - Apple, Cherries Jubilee, Cherry, Peach

Spartan Brand - Apple, Blueberry, Cherry (Lite, Regular)

Winn Dixie - Apple, Blueberry, Cherry

Pilaf

Trader Joe's - Thai Style Lime, Wild & Basmati Rice

Pimentos

Meijer Brand - Pieces, Sliced

Winn Dixie - Sliced

Pineapple... *All Fresh Fruits & Vegetables Are **Gluten/Casein Free***

Albertsons - All Varieties

Del Monte -

Canned/Jarred Fruit (All Varieties)

Fruit Snack Cups (Metal, Plastic)

Dole - All Fruits (Bowls, Canned, Dried, Frozen, Jars) *(Except Real Fruit Bites)*

Food Club Brand - Chunks, Crushed, Sliced, Tidbits

Great Value Brand (Wal-Mart) - Chunks, Pineapple In Unsweetened Pineapple Juice (Crushed, Slices), Tidbits

Hannaford Brand - Chunks, Crushed, No Sugar Added Sliced

Hy-Vee - Chunk, Crushed, In Lime Gel, Sliced, Tidbit Fruit Cup

Kroger Brand - Fruit (Canned, Cups)

Laura Lynn - Canned

Lowes Foods Brand - Chunks In Juice, Crushed In Juice, Sliced In Juice

Meijer Brand - Chunks (Heavy Syrup, In Juice), Crushed (Heavy Syrup, In Juice), Frozen Chunks, Sliced In (Heavy Syrup, Juice)

Midwest Country Fare - Chunks, Crushed, Slices, Tidbits

P

Native Forest - Organic (Chunks, Crushed, Slices)

Publix - Canned (All Varieties)

Safeway Brand - Chunks, Crushed, Sliced

Spartan Brand - Chunks, Crushed, Tidbits

Stop & Shop Brand - Frozen Pineapple

Wegmans Brand - Chunk, Crushed, Sliced (In Heavy Syrup, Regular), Tidbits

Winn Dixie - Chunks, Crushed, Sliced, Tidbits

Pistachio Nuts... see Nuts

Pizza

  Amy's - Rice Crust Pizza (Non Dairy Cheese, Spinach)

  Ian's - Wheat Free Gluten Free French Bread Pizza Soy Cheesy

Pizza Crust/Pizza Mix

  Arrowhead Mills - Gluten Free Pizza Crust Mix

  Authentic Foods▲ - Pizza Crust Mix

  Bob's Red Mill▲ - GF Pizza Crust Mix

  Celiac Specialties▲ - Pizza (6" Pizza Crust, 12" Pizza Crust)

  Chebe▲ - Pizza Mix

  El Peto▲ - Pre Baked (Basil, Millet, White)

  Ener-G▲ -
    Rice Pizza Shell (6", 10")
    Yeast Free Rice Pizza Shell (6", 10")

  Food-Tek Fast & Fresh - Dairy Free Minute Pizza Crust Mix

  Foods By George▲ - Pizza Crusts

   Bakery - Gluten Free Pizza Crust●

  Gillian's Foods▲ - Deep Dish Pizza Crust, Pizza Dough Mix

  Gluten Free & Fabulous▲ - Pizza Crust●

  Gluten-Free Creations▲ - Italian Seasoned Crust●, Simply Pizza Crust●, Whole Grain Crust●

  Gluten-Free Pantry▲ - French Bread & Pizza Mix

  Glutino▲ - Premium Pizza Crust

P Katz Gluten Free▲ - Pizza Crust
Kinnikinnick▲ - Pizza Crust (7", 10"), Pizza Crust Mix
Namaste Foods▲ - Pizza Crust Mix
Orgran▲ - Pizza & Pastry Multi Mix
Rose's Bakery▲ - All Varieties●
Rustic Crust▲ - Gluten Free Napoli Herb Pizza Crust●
Tastefully Gluten Free▲ - Pizza Crust Mix

Pizza Sauce... see also Sauces
Contadina
Eden Organic - Organic Pizza Pasta Sauce
Hannaford Brand
Hy-Vee
Meijer Brand
Muir Glen - Organic
Sauces 'N Love - Marinara Fresh
Spartan Brand - Regular
Trader Joe's - Fat Free
Winn Dixie

Plum Sauce
Sharwood's
Winn Dixie
Wok Mei - All Natural Plum Sauce

Plums... *All Fresh Fruits & Vegetables Are Gluten/Casein Free*
Hy-Vee - Purple Plums
Stop & Shop Brand - Whole Plums In Heavy Syrup
Winn Dixie - Canned Whole Plums

Polenta
Bob's Red Mill▲ - Gluten Free Corn Grits/Polenta
Food Merchants Brand - Ready Made Organic (Ancient Harvest Quinoa, Basil & Garlic, Chili Cilantro, Mushroom & Onion, Sun Dried Tomato, Traditional)
Trader Joe's - Organic Polenta

Pomegranate... *All **Fresh** Fruits & Vegetables Are **Gluten/Casein Free*** **P**
  Woodstock Farms - Organic Frozen Pomegranate Kernels
Pop... see Soda Pop/Carbonated Beverages
Popcorn
  Cracker Jack - Original Caramel Coated Popcorn & Peanuts
  Eden Organic - Organic Popping Kernels
  Farmer Steve's - Kernels, Organic Microwave
  Hannaford Brand - Kettle Corn, Natural, White Kernels, Yellow Kernels
  Herr's - Light
  Home Harvest Brand - Kernels (White, Yellow)
  Hy-Vee -
    Microwave
      Kettle
      Natural Flavor
    Regular (White, Yellow)
  Jolly Time -
    Microwave
      Healthy Pop (Kettle Corn)
      Kettle Mania
      Sassy Salsa
      Sea Salt & Cracked Pepper
    Kernel Corn (American's Best, Organic Yellow, White, Yellow)
  Kroger Brand - Plain Popcorn Kernels
  Meijer Brand -
    Microwave
      Kettle Sweet & Salty
      Natural Lite
    Regular (White, Yellow)
  Newman's Own - Regular (Raw Popcorn)
  Newman's Own Organics - Microwave Pop's Corn (No Butter No
  Salt 94% Fat Free)

P   **Pirate's Booty** -
Barbeque
Veggie
Safeway Brand - Yellow Kernels
Skeete & Ike's - Organic Sea Salt
Trader Joe's - Fat Free Caramel, Lite Popcorn
Wegmans Brand -
Microwave
Kettle Corn
Yellow Kernels
Winn-Dixie - Natural
Pork... *All Fresh Meat Is Gluten/Casein Free (Non-Marinated, Unseasoned)*
Always Tender -
Flavored Fresh Pork
Apple Bourbon
Citrus
Honey Mustard
Lemon Garlic
Mesquite
Mojo Criollo
Onion Garlic
Original
Peppercorn
Roast Flavor
Sun Dried Tomato
Dietz & Watson - Barbecue Roast Of Pork, Boneless Pork Chops w/Natural Juices, Italian Style Roast Pork, Pork Cello Butt, Roast Sirloin Of Pork
Ejay's So. Smokehouse - All Natural Salt Pork

P

Homestyle Meals - Pork Baby Back Ribs w/BBQ Sauce, Shredded Pork In BBQ Sauce, Whole Bulk St. Louis Ribs w/BBQ Sauce

Hormel -

Pork Rib Tips In Barbecue Sauce (Party Tray)

Pork Roast Au Jus (Fully Cooked Entrée)

Jones Dairy Farm -

All Natural

Hearty Pork Sausage Links●

Little Link Pork Sausage●

Light Pork Sausage & Rice Links●

Maple Sausage Patties●

Original Pork Roll Sausage●

Pork Sausage Patties●

All Natural Golden Brown Cooked & Browned Sausage Patties (Maple Fully●, Mild Fully●)

All Natural Golden Brown Light Fully Cooked & Browned Sausage & Rice Links●

Lloyd's - Pork Ribs w/Original BBQ Sauce, Shredded Pork In Original Barbecue Sauce

Organic Prairie -

Fresh Organic (Ground Pork 1 lb., Pork Loin, Pork Ribs, Pork Chops, Pork Loin Roast)

Frozen Organic Pork Chops 12 oz.

Publix - Deli Pre Pack Sliced Lunch Meats (Spanish Style Pork)

Saz's -

Barbecue Pork Meat Tub

Barbecued Baby Back Ribs

Wegmans Brand - Canned Pork & Beans In Tomato Sauce

Wellshire Farms - Whole Smoked Boneless Pork Loin

Potato Chips... see **Chips**

Potato Crisps... see **Crisps**

P Potatoes... *All **Fresh** Fruits & Vegetables Are **Gluten/Casein Free***

Albertsons - French Fries, Hash Browns (Country, Southern), Potato Rounds (Tator Tots), Potatoes O'Brien, Steak Fries

Alexia Foods -

Crispy Potatoes w/Seasoned Salt Waffle Fries

Julienne Fries Spicy Sweet Potato

Julienne Fries Sweet Potato

Julienne Fries w/Sea Salt Yukon Gold

Olive Oil & Sea Salt Oven Fries

Olive Oil Rosemary & Garlic Oven Fries

Olive Oil Sun Dried Tomatoes & Pesto Oven Reds

Organic (Oven Crinklesn Classic, Oven Crinkles Onion & Garlic, Oven Crinkles Salt & Pepper, Seasoned Salt Hashed Browns, Yukon Gold Julienne Fries w/Sea Salt)

Yukon Gold Potatoes w/Seasoned Salt Potato Nuggets

Cascadian Farm - Organic Frozen (Country Style Potatoes, Crinkle Cut French Fries, Hash Browns, Shoe String Fries, Spud Puppies, Straight Cut French Fries, Wedge Cut Oven Fries)

Funster - Natural Potato Letters (BBQ Lite, Original)

Great Value Brand (Wal-Mart) - Canned (Diced, Sliced, Whole New)

Hannaford Brand - Diced, Instant, Sliced, Whole

Hy-Vee - Canned (Sliced, Whole), Frozen (Country Style Hash Brown Potatoes, Crinkle Cut Fries, Criss Cut Potatoes, Curly Cut, Potatoes O'Brien, Regular, Steak Fries)

Ian's - Alphatots

Jimmy Dean -

Breakfast Skillets

Bacon

Ham

Sausage

Smoked Sausage

Manischewitz - Potato Mix (Homestyle Latke, Kugel, Mini Knish, Pancake, Sweetened Pancake)

P

Meijer Brand -

Canned White (Sliced, Whole)

Frozen French Fries (Crinkle Cut, Original, Quickie Crinkles, Shoestring, Steak Cut)

Frozen Hash Browns (Original, Shredded, Southern Style, Western Style)

Potatoes (Crinkle Cut, Tater Tots, Tater Treats)

Regular Hash Browns

Midwest Country Fare - Whole White Potatoes

Mixed From The Heartland ▲ - Texas Style Potatoes●

Ore-Ida -

Frozen

Cottage Fries

Country Style Steak Fries

Crispers

Extra Crispy Fast Food Fries

Fast Food Fries

Golden (Crinkles, Fries)

Hash Browns (Country Style, Original, Southern Style)

Pixie Crinkles

Potatoes O'Brien

Shoestrings

Steak Fries

Steam N' Mash (Cut Red, Cut Russet, Cut Sweet)

Tater Tots (ABC, Extra Crispy, Mini, Original Seasoned Shredded)

Publix -

Canned (Sliced & Whole, White)

Frozen (Crinkle Cut Fries, Extra Crispy Fries, Golden Fries (Fast Food Style, Regular), Original Cut Fries, Shoestring Fries, Southern Style Hash Browns, Steak Fries, Tater Bites)

P **S&W** - All Plain Canned Vegetables
Safeway Brand -
   Crinkle Cut
   French Fried
   Hashbrowns Southern Style
   Instant Potatoes
   Restaurant Style Crinkle Cut
   Shoestring
   Steak Cut
Spartan Brand -
   Frozen (Crinkle Cut Fries, Extra Crispy Fast Fries, French Fries, Hash Brown Patties, O'Brien Hash Browns, Shredded, Southern Style Hash Browns, Tater Puffs)
   Mashed Potatoes (Instant)
   White (Sliced, Whole Sliced)
Tasty Bite - Aloo Palak, Bombay, Mushroom Takatak
Trader Joe's - Frozen Crinkle Wedge Potatoes
Wegmans Brand -
   Frozen (Crinkle Cut, Steak Cut, Straight Cut, Tater Puffs)
   Frozen Hash Browns (Country Style, Hash Browns O'Brien, Regular)
   White Potatoes (Peeled, Sliced)
Winn Dixie -
   Instant (Mashed Regular)
   Frozen (Crinkle Cuts, French Fries, Matchstick Fries, Potato Crowns, Steak Fries, Tater Puffs)
Woodstock Farms - Organic Frozen (Crinkle Cut Oven Fries, Shredded Hash Browns, Tastee Taters)
Preserves... see Jam/Jelly
Pretzels
   Barkat - Pretzels (Sesame, Sticks, Regular)
   Ener-G▲ - Crisp Pretzels, Sesame Pretzel Rings, Wylde Pretzels (Poppy Seed, Regular, Sesame)

P

Dutch Country - Soft Pretzel Mix

Glutano▲ - Pretzels

Glutino▲ -

Family Bag (Sticks, Twists)

Sesame Ring, Snack Pack

Sticks

Twists

Unsalted Twists

Protein

Bob's Red Mill▲ -

Hemp Protein Powder

TSP (Textured Soy Protein)

TVP (Textured Vegetable Protein)

Living Harvest - Organic Hemp Protein Powder (Original, Vanilla Spice)

MLO - Brown Rice Protein Powder

Nutiva -

Hemp Protein Shake (Amazon Acai, Berry Pomegranate, Chocolate)

Protein Powder (Hemp, Hemp & Fiber)

Odwalla -

Super Protein Original

Super Protein Pumpkin Protein

Ruth's - Organic Hemp Protein Powder (E3Live & Maca, Hemp Protein Power, Hemp w/Sprouted Flax & Maca

Protein Shakes... see Shakes... see also Protein

Prunes

Great Value Brand (Wal-Mart) - Pitted Prunes

Hannaford Brand - Pitted

Meijer Brand - Pitted (Canister, Carton)

Spartan Brand - Prunes Pitted

Pudding

Hannaford Brand - Pudding Cook & Serve (Chocolate, Vanilla)

Hunt's - Pudding Snack Packs (Lemon, Lemon Meringue Pie)

Jell-O -

Regular Cook & Serve

Banana Cream

Chocolate (Fudge, Regular)

Coconut Cream

Lemon

Vanilla

Regular Instant Pudding & Pie Filling

Banana Cream

Chocolate (Fudge, Regular)

Coconut Cream

Devil's Food

French Vanilla

Lemon

Pistachio

Pumpkin Spice

Vanilla

White Chocolate

Sugar Free Fat Free Cook & Serve

Chocolate

Vanilla

Meijer Brand -

Cook & Serve (Butterscotch, Chocolate, Vanilla)

Mixes From The Heartland ▲ - Pudding Mix (Apple Cinnamon Rice●, Chocolate Delight●)

Mori-Nu - Mates Pudding Mix (Chocolate, Lemon Crème, Vanilla)

My T Fine - Lemon, Vanilla

P

Royal - All Instant Pudding (Regular, Sugar Free)
Spartan Brand - Cook & Serve (Chocolate, Vanilla)
ZenSoy - All Varieties

Q

Pumpkin... *All Fresh Fruits & Vegetables Are Gluten/Casein Free*
   Libby's -
     Canned
       100% Pure Pumpkin
       Easy Pumpkin Pie Mix
   Meijer Brand - Canned
   Safeway Brand - Canned
   Wegmans Brand - Solid Pack
Puppodums
   Patak's - Pappadums (Black Peppercorn, Garlic, Plain)
   Sharwood's - Indian Puppodums (Crushed Garlic & Coriander, Plain)

Q

Quinoa
   Ancient Harvest Quinoa -
     Inca Red Quinoa
     Quinoa Flakes
     Quinoa Flour
     Quinoa Pasta (Elbows, Garden Pagodas, Linguine, Rotelle, Shells, Spaghetti, Veggie Curls)
     Traditional Quinoa Grain
   Arrowhead Mills - Quinoa
   Gluten Free & Fabulous▲ - Bon Appetit! Quinoa w/Marinara●
   Seeds Of Change -
     Amantani Whole Grain Blend Quinoa & Wild Rice
     Cuzco Whole Grain Quinoa Blend

R R

Radishes... *All **Fresh** Fruits & Vegetables Are **Gluten/Casein Free***

Raisins

   Albertsons - Regular

   Food Club Brand

   Great Value Brand (Wal-Mart) - California Sun Dried Raisins (100% Natural)

   Hannaford Brand - Raisins

   Hy-Vee - California Sun Dried Raisins

   Meijer Brand - Canister, Seedless (Carton)

   Publix - Raisins

   Spartan Brand - Regular

   Sun-Maid - Raisins (Baking, Golden, Natural California, Regular), Zante Currants

   Wegmans Brand - Seedless

   Winn Dixie - Raisins (Organic, Regular)

   Woodstock Farms - Organic (Dark Chocolate Raisins w/Evaporated Cane Juice, Raisins (Jumbo Thompson, Select Thompson)), Raisins (Jumbo Flame)

Raspberries... *All **Fresh** Fruits & Vegetables Are **Gluten/Casein Free***

   Cascadian Farm - Organic Frozen Raspberries

   Food Club Brand - Frozen Red Raspberries

   Full Circle - Organic Raspberries

   Hannaford Brand - In Syrup, Regular

   Hy-Vee - Frozen Red Raspberries

   Meijer Brand - Frozen (Organic, Regular), Red Individually Quick Frozen

   Publix - Frozen Raspberries

   Safeway Brand - Frozen Red Raspberries

   Spartan Brand - Frozen Red Raspberries

   Stop & Shop Brand - Raspberries, Raspberries In Syrup

   Wegmans Brand - Raspberries (Regular, w/Sugar)

R

___

Winn Dixie - Frozen Red Raspberries

Woodstock Farms - Organic Frozen Red Raspberries

Raspberry Vinaigrette... see Salad Dressing

Refried Beans... see Beans

Relish

　Albertsons - Sweet

　B&G - Dill, Emerald, Hamburger, Hot Dog, India, Piccalilli, Sweet, Unsalted

　Cascadian Farms

　Hannaford Brand - Dill, Hot Dog, Sweet, Sweet Squeeze

　Heinz - Hot Dog, India, Sweet

　Mrs. Renfro's - Corn, Hot Chow Chow, Hot Tomato, Mild Chow Chow, Mild Tomato

　Spartan Brand - Dill, Sweet

　Vlasic - Sweet

　Wegmans Brand - Dill, Hamburger, Sweet

　Woodstock Farms - Organic (Spicy Chipotle Sweet, Sweet Relish)

Ribs... *All Fresh Meat Is Gluten/Casein Free (Non-Marinated, Unseasoned)*

　Homestyle Meals - Pork Baby Back w/BBQ Sauce, Whole Bulk St. Louis Ribs w/BBQ Sauce

　Saz's - Barbecued Baby Back Ribs

Rice

　A Taste Of India - Masala Rice & Lentils

　A Taste Of Thai - Rice (Coconut Ginger, Garlic Basil, Jasmine, Yellow Curry)

　Albertsons - Boil In A Bag, Brown, White (Instant, Regular)

　Annie Chun's - Sprouted Brown Rice, Sticky White Rice

　Arrowhead Mills - Brown Basmati, Long Grain Brown, Short Brown, White Basmati

　Dinty Moore - Microwave Meal (Rice w/Chicken)

R

Eden Organic -
> Organic Canned
>> Curried Rice & Lentils
>> Mexican Rice & Black Beans
>> Moroccan Rice & Garbanzo Beans
>> Rice & Cajun Small Red Beans
>> Rice & Caribbean Black Beans
>> Rice & Garbanzo Beans
>> Rice & Kidney Beans
>> Rice & Lentils
>> Rice & Pinto Beans
>> Spanish Rice & Pinto Beans

Fantastic World Foods - Arborio, Basmati, Jasmine

Food Club Brand - Instant Rice

Full Circle - Organic (Basmati Brown, Basmati White, Long Grain Brown, Long Grain White)

Gluten-Free Essentials▲ - Exotic Curry●, Italian Herb & Lemon●, Southwest Chipotle & Lime●

Go Go Rice - Organic Steamed Rice Bowls (Brown, White), Organic White Rice

Golden Star - Jasmine Rice

Hannaford Brand - Enriched Long Grain, Frozen Steam In Bag White Rice, Instant

Home Harvest Brand - 50% Broken Long Grain, Instant, Long Grain

Hormel -
> Compleats Microwaveable Meals
>> Chicken & Rice
>> Sante Fe Style Chicken w/Beans & Rice

Hy-Vee -
> Boil In Bag Rice
> Enriched Extra Long Grain (Instant, Regular)
> Extra Long Grain

Instant Brown
Natural Long Grain Brown
Spanish

Konriko -
Original Brown Rice (Bag)
Wild Pecan Rice (Box, Burlap Bag)

Kraft Minute Rice - Brown, White

Laura Lynn - Boil N' Bag, Instant, Long Grain White

Lotus Foods - Forbidden Black

Lowes Foods Brand - Boil N Bag, Instant (Brown, White), Long Grain

Lundberg▲ - All Varieties Of Plain Rice

Meijer Brand - Brown, Instant (Boil In Bag, Brown), Long Grain, Medium Grain

Midwest Country Fare - Pre Cooked Instant Rice

Minute Rice - Brown, White

Nishiki - Sushi Rice

O Organics - Long Grain (Brown, Thai Jasmine)

Ortega - Spanish

Publix -
Long Grain (Brown, Enriched)
Medium Grain White
Pre Cooked Instant (Boil in Bag, Brown, White)
Yellow Rice Mix

Royal - Basmati Rice

S&W - Natural Brown, White

Safeway Brand - Brown, Instant, Long Grain, Rice Pouch Gently Milled Bran Rice, White

Seeds Of Change -
Amantani Whole Grain Blend Quinoa & Wild Rice
Cuzco Whole Grain Quinoa Blend
Havana Cuban Style Whole Grain Rice & Beans

R   Microwaveable (Dharamsala Aromatic Indian Rice Blend,
        Rishikesh Whole Grain Brown Basmati Rice, Tapovan White
        Basmati Rice)

Velleron French Style Herb Whole Grain Blend

Shiloh Farms - Brown Basmati Rice, Brown Rice, California Wild Rice

Spartan Brand -

4% Broken Long Grain

Instant (Boil In Bag, Brown Box, Regular Box)

Stop & Shop Brand -

Instant Brown

Organic Long Grain (Brown & White)

Success - Boil In Bag (Jasmine Rice, Whole Grain Brown Rice, White Rice)

Tasty Bite - Basmati Rice & Spinach Dal

Thai Kitchen -

Jasmine Rice Mixes

Jasmine Rice

Roasted Garlic & Chili

Thirsty Maid - Boil In A Bag

Trader Joe's - All Plain Grain Rice

Uncle Ben's -

Boil In Bag

Fast & Natural Instant Brown Rice

Instant Rice

Original Converted Brand Rice

Ready Rice (Original Long Grain Rice 8.8 oz & 14.8 oz)

Wegmans Brand -

Arborio Italian Style

Basmati

Boil In Bag

Enriched (Long, Long Grain White, Medium)

Instant (Brown, Regular)

R

Jasmine
Long Grain (Brown, Regular)
Medium Grain White

Rice Beverages

  Amazake -
    Almond
    Amazing Mango
    Banana Appeal
    Cool Coconut
    Go (Go Green, Hazelnuts)
    Oh So Original
    Rice Nog
    Tiger Chai
    Vanilla (Gorilla, Pecan Pie)
  Better Than Milk - Rice (Original, Vanilla)
  Eden Organic - EdenBlend
  Good Karma Organic Ricemilk (Chocolate, Original, Vanilla)
  Pacific Natural Foods - Low Fat Rice Beverage (Plain, Vanilla)
  Rice Dream -
    Enriched
      Organic Original
      Chocolate
      Vanilla
    Refrigerated Enriched Rice Drink (Original, Vanilla)
    Shelf Stable Rice Drink
      Classic (Carob, Vanilla)
      Enriched (Organic Original, Original, Vanilla)
      Heartwise (Original, Vanilla)
      Horchata
      Original
  Wegman's Brand - Rice Milk (Original, Vanilla)

R Rice Cakes
    Hannaford Brand - Fat Free Apple Cinnamon
    Hy-Vee - Lightly Salted
    Kroger Brand - Plain, Salted
    Lundberg▲ -
      Eco Farmed
        Apple Cinnamon
        Brown Rice (Lightly Salted, Salt Free)
        Honey Nut
        Sesame Tamari
        Toasted Sesame
      Organic
        Brown Rice (Lightly Salted, Salt Free)
        Koku Seaweed
        Mochi Sweet
        Rice w/Popcorn
        Sesame Tamari
        Sweet Green Tea w/Lemon
        Tamari w/Seaweed
        Wild Rice
    Spartan Brand - Salt Free
    Stop & Shop Brand - Rice Cakes (Plain Salted, Plain Unsalted,)
    Trader Joe's - Lightly Salted Rice Cakes
Rice Crackers... see Crackers
Rice Cream
    Erewhon - Brown Rice Cream
Rice Noodles... see Noodles... see also Pasta
Rice Syrup... see Syrup
Rice Vinegar... see Vinegar
Risotto
    Lundberg▲ - Organic (Florentine, Tuscan)

Roast Beef... see Beef
Rolls... see Bread
Rum... *All **Distilled** Alcohol Is **Gluten/Casein Free** [2]
Rusks
   Glutino▲ - Gluten Free Rusks
Rutabaga... *All **Fresh** Fruits & Vegetables Are **Gluten/Casein Free**

S

Salad... *All **Fresh** Fruits & Vegetables Are **Gluten/Casein Free**
   Mixes From The Heartland▲ - Pasta Salad (Corn N'Pasta●, Dilled●)
   Safeway Select - Mediterranean Salad
Salad Dressing
   A Taste Of Thai - Peanut Salad Dressing Mix
   Annie's Naturals -
     Natural Dressings
       Balsamic Vinaigrette
       Lemon & Chive
       Lite Vinaigrette (Honey Mustard, Raspberry)
       Roasted Red Pepper Vinaigrette
       Tuscany Italian
     Organic
       Balsamic Vinaigrette
       French
       Green Garlic
       Maple Ginger
       Oil & Vinegar
       Papaya Poppyseed
       Pomegranate Vinaigrette

S

Red Wine & Olive Oil

Roasted Garlic Vinaigrette

Sesame Ginger w/Chamomile

Bakers & Chefs - Italian

Bragg - Organic (Ginger & Sesame, Healthy Vinaigrette)

Briannas -

Champagne Caper Vinaigrette

Dijon Honey Mustard

New American

Rich Poppy Seed

Santa Fe

Vinaigrette (Blush Wine, Real French)

Zesty French

Cardini's -

Honey Mustard

Italian

Vinaigrette (Balsamic, Light Balsamic, Pear, Raspberry
Pomegranate)

Consorzio - Fat Free (Mango, Raspberry & Balsamic, Strawberry &
Balsamic)

Drew's All Natural -

Classic Italian

Green Olive & Caper

Honey Dijon

Poppy Seed

Raspberry

Roasted Garlic & Peppercorn

Rosemary Balsamic

Smoked Tomato

Emeril's - Caesar, Vinaigrette (Balsamic, House Herb, Italian,
Raspberry Balsamic)

salad dressing

Fischer & Wieser - Original Roasted Raspberry Chipotle Vinaigrette **S**

Follow Your Heart -

Honey Mustard

Lemon Herb

Sesame (Dijon, Miso)

Thousand Island

Girard's -

Champagne (Light, Regular)

Fat Free (Balsamic Vinaigrette, Raspberry)

Honey Dijon Peppercorn

Olde Venice Italian

Original French

Raspberry

Spinach Salad Dressing

Vinaigrette (Balsamic Basil, Wasabi Ginger, White Balsamic)

Glutino ▲ - French Herb Balsamic, Naturally Italian, Peppercorn Garlic

Hannaford Brand - Balsamic Vinaigrette, California French Style, Deluxe French, Fat Free Sweet Vinegar & Olive Oil, Honey Dijon, Light Italian, Old World Greek, Raspberry Vinaigrette, Robust Italian, Thousand Island, Vidalia Onion, Zesty Italian

Health Market Organic - Balsamic, Honey Mustard, Raspberry Vinaigrette

Henri's -

Classic Original French

Homestyle Sweet & Tangy

Honey Mustard Fat Free

Hy-Vee -

Dressing (French, Italian, Lite Salad, Raspberry Vinaigrette, Salad, Thousand Island, Zesty Italian)

Light Dressing (Thousand Island)

Light Salad Dressing (French, Italian, Thousand Island)

Squeezable Salad Dressing (Light, Right)

S Ken's Steak House -
  Chef's Reserve
    Creamy Balsamic
    French w/Applewood Smoke Bacon
    Golden Vidalia Onion
    Honey Dijon
    Russian
  Fat Free Dressings (Raspberry Pecan, Sun Dried Tomato)
  Healthy Options
    Balsamic Vinaigrette
    Honey (Dijon, French)
    Olive Oil & Vinegar
    Raspberry Walnut
    Sweet Vidalia Onion Vinaigrette
  Lite Dressings
    Balsamic & Basil
    Country French w/Vermont Honey
    Honey Mustard
    Italian
    Raspberry Walnut
    Sweet Vidalia Onion
    Vinaigrette (Balsamic, Olive Oil)
  Regular
    Balsamic & Basil
    Country French w/Vermont Honey
    Honey Mustard
    Italian & Marinade
    Red Wine Vinegar & Olive Oil
    Russian
    Thousand Island

salad dressing

S

    Sweet Vidalia Onion

    Zesty Italian

Kraft -

Balsamic Vinaigrette

Catalina

Creamy Italian

Dressing Made w/Extra Virgin Olive Oil (Classic Balsamic Vinaigrette, Italian Vinaigrette)

Free (Catalina, French, Thousand Island, Zesty Italian)

Honey Dijon

Light (Balsamic Vinaigrette, Catalina, Creamy French Style, Italian House, Raspberry Vinaigrette, Sicilian Roasted Garlic Balsamic Vinaigrette, Thousand Island)

Seven Seas Viva Italian

Sweet Honey Catalina

Tangy Tomato Bacon

Thousand Island

Vidalia Onion Vinaigrette

Zesty Italian

Lily's Gourmet Dressings -

Balsamic Vinaigrette

Poppyseed

Raspberry Walnut Vinaigrette

Litehouse -

Balsamic Vinaigrette

Organic Raspberry Lime Vinaigrette

Pomegranate Blueberry Vinaigrette

Poppyseed

Red Wine Olive Oil Vinaigrette

Spinach Salad

Thousand Island

Zesty Italian Vinaigrette

S **Maple Grove Farms Of Vermont** -
All Natural
Blueberry Pomegranate
Champagne Vinaigrette
Ginger Pear
Maple Fig
Strawberry Balsamic
Fat Free
Cranberry Balsamic
Greek
Honey Dijon
Lime Basil
Vinaigrette (Balsamic, Raspberry)
Organic (Dijon, Italian Herb, Vinaigrette (Balsamic, Raspberry))
Regular & Lite
Balsamic Maple
Sweet N' Sour
Sugar Free (Italian Balsamic, Vinaigrette (Balsamic, Raspberry))
Marzetti -
Refrigerated Dressings
Honey Balsamic
Honey Dijon (Light, Regular)
Honey French (Light, Regular)
Poppyseed
Slaw (Light, Regular)
Spinach Salad
Sweet Italian
Thousand Island
Venice Italian
Vinaigrette (Balsamic, Light Balsamic, Light Raspberry Cabernet,
Strawberry Chardonnay)

Shelf Stable
- California French
- Country French
- Honey Balsamic
- Honey Dijon (Fat Free, Mustard)
- Italian (House)
- Poppyseed
- Potato Salad
- Slaw (Light, Low Fat, Original, Southern Recipe)
- Sweet & Sour (Fat Free, Regular)
- Thousand Island
- Venice Italian
- Vinaigrette (Balsamic, Light Balsamic, Organic Balsamic, Peppercorn, Strawberry)

Midwest Country Fare - French, Italian, Thousand Island

Miracle Whip - Lite, Regular

Nasoya -
Vegi Dressings
- Creamy Dill
- Creamy Italian
- Garden Herb
- Sesame Garlic
- Thousand Island

Newman's Own -
Light
- Balsamic Vinaigrette
- Cranberry Walnut
- Italian
- Lime Vinaigrette
- Raspberry & Walnut
- Red Wine Vinegar & Olive Oil
- Roasted Garlic Balsamic

S

Organic Light Balsamic Vinaigrette

Regular

    Balsamic Vinaigrette

    Olive Oil & Vinegar

    Orange Ginger

    Two Thousand Island

Salad Mist (Balsamic, Italian)

O Organics - Light Balsamic, Red Wine Vinegar, Thousand Island, Tuscan Italian

Olde Cape Cod -

    All Natural (Cabernet Sauvignon Tomato Basil, Chardonnay Ginger Sesame, Lite Raspberry Vinaigrette)

    Fat Free Balsamic Vinaigrette

    Sundried Tomato Olive Oil & Basil

    Vineyard Lite Honey French

Organicville -

    Organic

        French

        Herbs De Provence

        Miso Ginger

        Non Dairy Ranch

        Olive Oil & Balsamic

        Orange Cranberry

        Pomegranate

        Sesame (Goddess, Tamari)

        Sundried Tomato & Garlic

        Tarragon Dijon

Pfeiffer -

    California French

    Cole Slaw

    French

    Honey Dijon

salad dressing

S

Italian (Fat Free, Light, Regular)
Poppyseed
Russian
Sweet 'N Sour
Thousand Island (Light, Regular)
Tuscan Italian
Vinaigrette (Balsamic, Red Wine, Roasted Garlic)
Zesty Garlic Italian

Publix -
California French
Italian (Fat Free, Regular)
Lite Raspberry Walnut
Tangy Balsamic
Thousand Island
Zesty Italian

Safeway Brand -
1000 Island (Fat Free, Regular)
California
Zesty Italian (Light, Regular)

Safeway Select -
Balsamic & Olive Oil Vinaigrette
Raspberry Vinaigrette
Salad Dressing

San-J -
Gluten Free Asian Dressing
Tamari Ginger●
Tamari Sesame●

Seeds Of Change - Balsamic Vinaigrette, French Tomato, Italian Herb, Roasted Red Pepper

Spartan Brand - French, Italian (Light, Regular, Zesty), Thousand Island

S **Spectrum** - Organic Dressing Omega 3 (Asian Ginger, Golden Balsamic Vinaigrette, Lemon Sesame, Pomegranate Chipotle)

Teresa's Select Recipes -
Blackberry Poppyseed
Fat Free Honey Dijon
Raspberry White Balsamic
Strawberry Chardonnay
Vinaigrette (Balsamic, Roasted Garlic, Sun Dried Tomato)

Trader Joe's -
Dressings
Balsamic Vinaigrette (Fat Free, Regular)
Organic Red Wine and Olive Oil Vinaigrette
Raspberry
Refrigerated Dressings
Red Wine & Olive Oil Vinaigrette

Walden Farms -
Single Serve Packets (Creamy Bacon, Honey Dijon, Italian, Ranch, Thousand Island)
Sugar Free No Carb
Asian
Bacon Ranch
Balsamic Vinaigrette
Blue Cheese
Coleslaw
Creamy (Bacon, Italian)
French
Honey Dijon
Italian
Italian w/Sun Dried Tomato
Ranch

salad dressing

S

    Raspberry Vinaigrette
    Russian
    Sweet Onion
    Thousand Island
    Zesty Italian

Wegmans Brand -

    Balsamic w/Garlic Chunks
    Fat Free (Red Wine Vinegar, Roasted Red Pepper)
    Light Italian
    Organic (Balsamic Vinaigrette, Honey Mustard, Italian, Raspberry Vinaigrette, Sun Dried Tomato Vinaigrette)
    Sun Dried Tomato Vinaigrette
    Tarragon Vinaigrette
    Thousand Island (Light, Regular)
    Traditional Italian
    Three Spice Garden French

Wild Thymes - Salad Refresher (Black Currant, Mango, Meyer Lemon, Morello Cherry, Passion Fruit, Pomegranate, Raspberry, Tangerine), Vinaigrette (Fig Walnut, Mandarin Orange Basil, Mediterranean Balsamic, Parmesan Walnut Caesar, Raspberry Pear Balsamic, Roasted Apple Shallot, Tahitian Lime Ginger, Tuscan Tomato Basil)

Winn Dixie -

    Balsamic Vinaigrette
    California French
    Creamy French
    Fat Free (Italian, Thousand Island)
    Honey Dijon
    Italian (Lite, Regular)
    Robust Italian
    Thousand Island
    Zesty Italian

S Wish-Bone -
  Balsamic Oil & Herbs
  Balsamic Vinaigrette
  Deluxe French (Regular)
  Italian (Fat Free, Regular, Robusto)
  Raspberry Hazelnut Vinaigrette
  Western (Low Fat, Sweet & Smooth)

Salami... see Sausage

Salmon... see also Fish... *All Fresh Fish Is Gluten/Casein Free (Non-Marinated, Unseasoned)*
  Chicken Of The Sea -
    Canned (Pink Salmon Chunk Style In Water, Pink Salmon Traditional Style)
    Pouch (Skinless & Boneless Pink Salmon, Smoked Pacific Salmon)
  Crown Prince - Pink (Fancy Alaskan)
  Crown Prince Natural - Alaskan Pink, Alder Wood Smoked Alaskan Coho, Skinless & Boneless Pacific Pink
  Full Circle - All Natural Alaskan Sockeye Salmon Fillets
  Great Value Brand (Wal-Mart) - Canned Alaskan Pink Salmon
  Hannaford Brand - Canned Pink Salmon
  Hy-Vee - Frozen
  Publix - Coho Salmon Fillets, Sockeye Salmon Fillets

Salsa
  Albertsons - Chunky (Medium, Mild)
  Amy's - Organic (Black Bean & Corn, Fire Roasted Vegetable, Medium, Mild, Spicy Chipotle)
  Bone Suckin' - Salsa
  Bravos - Hot, Medium, Mild
  Chi-Chi's - Fiesta, Garden, Original
  Dei Fratelli - Black Bean 'N Corn Medium, Casera (Medium Hot, Mild), Chipotle Medium, Original (Medium, Mild)

Drew's - Organic (Black Bean Cilantro & Corn Medium, Chipotle Lime Medium, Double Fire Roasted Medium, Hot, Medium, Mild) **S**

Eat Smart - Garden Style Sweet

Emeril's - Gaaahlic Lovers Medium, Kicked Up Chunky Hot, Original Recipe Medium, Southwest Style Medium

Fischer & Wieser - Artichoke & Olive, Black Bean & Corn, Chipotle & Corn, Das Peach Haus Peach, Havana Mojito, Hot Habanero, Salsa A La Charra, Salsa Verde Ranchera, Sicilian Tomato Pesto, Timpone's Organic Salsa Muy Rica

Frontera - Gourmet Mexican Salsa (Chipotle, Corn & Poblano, Double Roasted, Guajillo, Habanero, Jalapeno Cilantro, Mango Key Lime, Medium Chunky Tomato, Mild Chunky Tomato, Red Pepper & Garlic, Roasted Tomato, Tomatillo)

Grand Selections - Black Bean & Corn (Medium, Mild)

Green Mountain Gringo - All Varieties

Herdez - Salsa Casera Mild

Herr's - Chunky (Medium, Mild)

Hy-Vee - Thick & Chunky (Hot, Medium, Mild)

La Victoria - Cilantro (Medium, Mild), Hot, Jalapena Extra Hot (Green, Red), Salsa Ranchera, Salsa Ranchera Hot, Salsa Victoria Hot, Suprema (Medium, Mild), Thick 'N Chunky (Hot, Medium, Mild), Verde (Medium, Mild)

Meijer Brand -

Original (Hot, Medium, Mild)

Restaurant Style (Hot, Medium, Mild)

Santa Fe Style (Medium, Mild)

Thick & Chunky (Hot, Medium, Mild)

Miguel's - Black Bean & Corn, Chipotle, Medium, Mild, Roasted Garlic

Mrs. Renfro's - Black Bean, Chipotle Corn, Garlic, Green, Habanero, Hot, Mango Habanero, Medium, Mexican (Hot, Mild), Mild, Peach, Pineapple, Pomegranate, Raspberry Chipotle, Roasted, Tequila

Muir Glen - Organic (Medium, Medium Black Bean & Corn, Medium Garlic Cilantro, Mild)

S **Nature's Promise** - Organic (Chipotle, Medium, Mild)

Newman's Own - Black Bean & Corn, Farmer's Garden, Hot, Mango, Medium, Mild, Organic (Cilantro, Medium), Peach, Pineapple, Roasted Garlic, Tequila Lime

Old Dutch - Restaurante Salsa (Medium, Mild)

Old El Paso - Salsa Thick N' Chunky (Hot, Medium, Mild)

Organicville - Medium, Mild, Pineapple

Ortega - Garden Medium, Original (Medium, Mild), Roasted Garlic, Salsa Verde, Thick & Chunky (Medium, Mild)

Pace -
    Chunky Salsa (Medium, Mild)
    Pico De Gallo
    Salsa Verde

Publix -
    All Natural (Hot, Medium, Mild)
    Thick & Chunky (Hot, Medium, Mild)

Publix GreenWise Market - Organic (Medium, Mild)

Safeway Select - 3 Bean Medium, Garlic Lovers, Peach Pineapple Medium, Roasted Tomato Medium, Southwest (Hot, Medium, Mild), Verde Medium

Salpica -
    Cilantro Green Olive
    Fall Harvest
    Garlic Chipotle
    Habanero Lime
    Mango Peach
    Roasted Corn & Bean
    Rustic Tomato
    Spring Break
    Summer Of Love
    Tomato Jalapeno

Taco Bell - Thick 'N Chunky (Medium, Mild)

Tostitos - All Natural (Hot Chunky, Medium Chunky, Mild Chunky)   **S**

Trader Joe's -

    3 Pepper

    Corn & Chili Tomatoless

    Double Roasted

    Fire Roasted Tomato

    Pineapple

    Spicy Smoked Peach

    Verde

UTZ - Mt. Misery Mike's Salsa Dip, Sweet Salsa Dip

Wegmans Brand - Hot, Medium, Mild, Organic (Hot, Mango, Medium, Mild), Roasted (Chipotle, Salsa Verde, Sweet Pepper, Tomato), Santa Fe Style

Winn Dixie -

    Black Bean & Corn (Medium)

    Chunky (Medium, Mild)

    Fire Roasted Pepper (Medium)

    Roasted Chipotle

    Roasted Green

    Roasted Sweet Pepper

    Roasted Tomato

Salt

Albertsons - Iodized, Regular

Great Value Brand (Wal-Mart) - Iodized, Plain

Hannaford Brand - Iodized, Regular

Kroger Brand

Lawry's - Seasoned

Manischewitz

Meijer Brand - Iodized, Plain

Morton - Coarse Kosher Salt, Iodized Table Salt, Lite Salt Mixture, Plain Table Salt, Salt Substitute, Sea Salt (Coarse, Fine)

S   Nu Salt - Salt Substitute

Publix

Safeway Brand - Iodized, Plain

Spartan Brand - Garlic, Iodized, Plain

Stop & Shop Brand - Iodized, Plain

Wegmans Brand - Iodized, Plain

Winn Dixie - Iodized, Plain

Sandwich Meat... see Deli Meat

Sardines... *All Fresh Fish Is Gluten/Casein Free (Non-Marinated, Unseasoned)*

Bumble Bee - Canned In Water

Chicken Of The Sea - In Mustard Sauce, In Oil Lightly Smoked, In Water, Regular

Crown Prince -

Crosspacked Brisling In Olive Oil

One Layer Brisling In (Mustard, Oil No Salt Added, Soybean Oil, Tomato)

Two Layer Brisling In (Olive Oil, Soybean Oil)

Crown Prince Natural - Skinless & Boneless In (Pure Olive Oil, Water)

Ocean Prince -

In (Louisiana Hot Sauce, Mustard, Spring Water, Tomato Sauce)

Lightly Smoked (In Oil, With Green Chilies)

Premium Skinless & Boneless In Oil

Sauces... (includes Marinara, Pasta, Tomato, etc.)

A Taste Of Thai - Curry Paste (Green, Red, Yellow), Fish Sauce, Garlic Chili Pepper Sauce, Pad Thai, Peanut Satay Sauce, Peanut Sauce Mix, Sweet Red Chili Sauce

Amy's -

Family Marinara

Light In Sodium Marinara

Roasted Garlic

Tomato Basil (Low Sodium, Regular)

S

Baxters - Mint Sauce

Bertolli -

Marinara w/Burgundy Wine

Tomato & Basil

Vidalia Onion w/Roasted Garlic

Bove's Of Vermont - All Natural (Marinara, Mushroom & Wine, Roasted Garlic)

Classico - Bruschetta Sauce (Basil & Tomato, Extra Garlic), Red Sauce (Tomato & Basil, Traditional Sweet Basil)

Colameco's - Pomodoro Sauce

Contadina -

Pizza Sauce (Original, Pizza Squeeze)

Tomato Paste (Italian Paste & Roasted Garlic, Regular)

Tomato Sauce (Extra Thick & Zesty, Garlic & Onion Tomato, Regular, w/Italian Herbs)

Sweet & Sour Sauce

Daddy Sam's - Bar B Que Sawce (Medium Ginger Jalapeno, Original), Salmon Glaze

Dave's Gourmet - Organic Red Heirloom, Spicy Heirloom Marinara

Del Monte - Garlic & Herb Chunky, Garlic & Onion, Green Peppers & Mushroom, Mushroom, No Salt Added Tomato, Regular Tomato, Tomato & Basil, Traditional

Di Lusso - Sweet Onion Sauce

Eden Organic - Apple Cherry Sauce, Spaghetti Sauce (No Salt Added, Regular)

Emeril's -

Pasta Sauce

Home Style Marinara

Kicked Up Tomato

Roasted (Gaahlic, Red Pepper)

Sicilian Gravy

Tomato & Basil

S **Fischer & Wieser** -

Charred Pineapple Bourbon

Chipotle Sauce (Original Roasted Raspberry, Plum Chipotle BBQ, Pomegranate & Mango, Roasted Blackberry, Roasted Blueberry)

Mango Ginger Habanero

Mom's Garlic & Basil Spaghetti

Mom's Organic (Roasted Pepper, Traditional)

Papaya Lime Serrano

Steak & Grilling

Sweet & Savory Onion Glaze

Texas 1015 Onion Glaze

Traditional Steak & Grilling

Frank's RedHot -

Chile 'N Lime

Original

Xtra Hot

Frontera -

Cocktail & Ceviche Sauce (Cilantro Lime, Tomato Chipotle)

Cooking Sauce (Red Chile & Roasted Garlic, Roasted Garlic & Chipotle, Roasted Tomato & Cilantro)

Enchilada Sauce (Chipotle Garlic, Classic Red Chile)

Grilling Sauce (Chipotle Honey Mustard, Red Pepper Sesame)

Hot Sauce (Chipotle, Habanero, Jalapeno, Red Pepper)

Taco Sauce (Chipotle Garlic, Roasted Tomato)

Hannaford Brand - Mushroom & Olive, Mushroom & Onion, Onion & Garlic, Roasted Garlic, Sweet Pepper & Onion, Tomato & Basil, Tomato & Onion & Garlic, Tomato Paste, Tomato Sauce, Traditional

Health Market - Organic Tomato Basil, Mushroom Onion

House Of Blues - Bayou Heat Hot Sauce

Hunt's -

Organic Pasta Sauce (Regular, w/Roasted Garlic)

S

Spaghetti Sauce (Garlic & Herb, Traditional)

Tomato Sauce (Basil Garlic & Oregano, Regular, Roasted Garlic)

Hy-Vee - Spaghetti Sauce (Garden, Mushroom, Traditional, w/Meat)
Tomato Onion Garlic Pasta Sauce

Las Palmas - Red Chile, Red Enchilada

Lee Kum Kee -

Panda Brand Green Label Oyster Flavored

Shrimp

Meijer Brand -

Extra Chunky Spaghetti Sauce (Garden Combo, Mushroom &
Green Pepper)

Pasta Sauce Select (Marinara, Mushroom & Olive, Onion & Garlic,
Original)

Tomato Sauce (Regular, Organic)

Midwest Country Fare -

Spaghetti Sauce

All Natural Garlic & Onion

Garden Vegetable

Garlic & Herb

Meat Flavor

Mushroom

Roasted Garlic & Onion

Tomato Sauce

Traditional

Moore's Marinade - Honey BBQ Wing, Original, Teriyaki

Mr. Spice Organic - Sauce & Marinade (Garlic Steak, Ginger Stir Fry,
Honey BBQ, Honey Mustard, Hot Wing, Indian Curry, Sweet & Sour,
Thai Peanut)

Muir Glen - Organic (Beef Bolognese, Cabernet Marinara, Chunky
Tomato & Herb, Fire Roasted Tomato, Garden Vegetable, Garlic
Roasted Garlic, Italian Herb, Italian Sausage w/Peppers, Portobello
Mushroom), Tomato Sauce (Chunky, No Salt Added, Regular)

S **Nature's Promise** - Organic Pasta Sauce (Plain)
Newman's Own -
Bombolina
Cabernet Marinara
Fire Roasted Tomato & Garlic
Fra Diavolo
Italian Sausage & Peppers
Marinara (Regular, w/Mushroom)
Organic (Marinara, Tomato Basil, Traditional Herb)
Pesto & Tomato
Roasted Garlic
Sockarooni
Sweet Onion & Roasted Garlic
Patak's - Sauces (Madras, Rogan Josh)
Patsy's Pasta Sauce - Marinara, Tomato Basil
Prego -
Chunky Garden (Combo, Mushroom & Green Pepper, Mushroom
Supreme w/Baby Portobello, Tomato Onion & Garlic)
Flavored w/Meat
Fresh Mushroom
Italian Sausage & Garlic
Marinara
Mushroom & Garlic
Roasted Garlic & Herb
Tomato Basil Garlic
Traditional
Publix -
Garden Style
Mushrooms
Tomato Sauce
Tomato & Garlic & Onion

S

Ragu -
> Chunky (Garden Combination, Mushroom & Green Pepper, Super Chunky Mushroom, Tomato & Garlic & Onion)
> Light Tomato & Basil
> Organic Garden Veggie
> Robusto (7 Herb Tomato, Roasted Garlic, Sautéed Onion & Garlic)

Rao's - Homemade (Arrabbiata, Cuore Di Pomodoro, Marinara, Puttanesca, Roasted Eggplant, Southern Italian Pepper & Mushroom, Vodka)

Safeway Brand - Sloppy Joe

Safeway Select -
> Chili Sauce
> Gourmet Dipping Sauces (Honey Mustard, Sweet & Sour)
> Pasta Sauce
>> Arrabiatta
>> Chunky Vegetable
>> Mushroom/Onion
>> Roasted Garlic
>> Spicy Red Bell Pepper
>> Sun Dried Tomatoes & Olives
> Taco Sauce Mild

San-J - Gluten Free (Asian BBQ●, Sweet & Tangy●, Szechuan●, Thai Peanut●, Teriyaki●)

Sauces 'N Love - Arrabbiata, Barely Bolognese, Fresh Marinara & Pizza Sauces, Mint Pesto, Parsley Chimichurri, Pesto, Pink Pesto, Pomodoro & Basilico, Puttanesca, Sugo Rosa, Tuscan Vodka

Scarpetta - Arrabbiata, Barely Bolognese, Bruschetta Toppings (Tomato & Artichoke, Tomato & Capers), Fresh Marinara & Pizza Sauces, Puttanesca, Spreads (Artichoke & Olive, Asparagus, Olive & Almond, Red Pepper & Eggplant, Spicy Red Pepper), Tomato & Arugula, Tuscan Vodka

S **Seeds Of Change** -
Indian Simmer Sauce (Jalfrezi, Madras)
Pasta Sauce
  Arrabiatta Di Roma
  Marinara Di Venezia
  Tomato Basil Genovese
  Tuscan Tomato & Garlic
Sharwood's - Balti, Bhuna, Jalfrezi, Kaffir Lime & Coriander, Madras, Plum Sauce, Rogan Josh, Sweet Chilli & Lemongrass
Simply Boulder - Culinary Sauce (Coconut Peanut●, Honey Dijon●, Lemon Pesto●, Pineapple Ginger●, Truly Teriyaki●)
Spartan Brand - Chili, Pizza Sauce, Sloppy Joe, Spaghetti Sauce (Traditional, w/Meat, w/Mushroom), Tomato Sauce
Stonewall Kitchen Sauce - Roasted Garlic Basil, Traditional Marinara
Taste Of Inspirations - Roasted Red Pepper & Tomato Bruschetta, Sun Dried Tomato Bruschetta
Texas Pete - Garlic Hot Sauce, Hotter Hot Sauce, Original Hot Sauce, Pepper, Seafood
Thai Kitchen -
Fish Sauce
Original Pad Thai
Peanut Satay
Simmer Sauce Curry (Green, Panang, Red, Yellow)
Spicy Thai Chili
Sweet Red Chili
Trader Joe's -
Organic
  Marinara Sauce (Fat Free No Salt Added, Low Fat, Regular)
  Red Wine & Olive Oil Vinaigrette
  Spaghetti Sauce
  Tomato Basil Marinara

S

Regular
  Bruschetta
  Chili Pepper
  Pizza Fat Free
  Roasted Garlic Spaghetti
  Rustico
  Tomato Basil (Marinara, Pasta Sauce)
  Traditional Marinara
  Tuscano Marinara Low Fat
  Whole Peeled Tomatoes w/Basil (All)

Walden Farms - Bruschetta, Marinara, Scampi

Wegmans Brand -
  Bruschetta Topping (Roasted Red Pepper, Traditional Tomato)
  Diavolo Sauce
  Italian Classics (Arrabbiata, Marinara, Seasoned Tomato)
  Lemon & Caper Sauce
  Prepared Horseradish
  Remoulade
  Roasted Garlic Pasta Sauce
  Tomato (& Basil, Regular, w/Italian Sausage)

Wild Thymes -
  Dipping Sauce (Indian Vindaloo, Moroccan Spicy Pepper, Thai Chili Roasted Garlic)
  Tropical Mango Lime Marinade

Winn & Lovett - Balsamic & Olive Oil, Grilling Sauce (Apple Spice, Molasses Horseradish, Roasted Onion & Balsamic), Mandarin Poppy Seed, Sun Dried Tomato & Basil, Thick & Hearty All Purpose, Vidalia Onion

Winn Dixie - Classic (Fra Diavolo, Home Style, Marinara, Peppers & Onions), Classic Style (Double Garlic, Fat Free), Pizza Sauce, Tomato Sauce

Woodstock Farms - Tomato Sauce (Chunky, No Salt, Original)

S Sauerkraut
  B&G
  Boar's Head
  Cortland Valley Organic
  Eden Organic - Organic
  Flanagan
  Great Value Brand (Wal-Mart) - Canned
  Hannaford Brand
  Hy-Vee - Shredded Kraut
  Krrrrisp Kraut
  Meijer Brand
  Safeway Brand
  Silver Floss
  Spartan Brand
  Wegmans Brand
  Willie's
  Winn Dixie
Sausage
  Abraham - Diced Prosciutto
  Aidells -
    Artichoke & Garlic
    Bier
    Cajun Style Andouille
    Chicken & Apple Breakfast Links
    Habanero & Green Chile
    Mango
    Smoked Chorizo
  Applegate Farms -
    Genoa Salami (Hot, Natural, Organic)
    Joy Stick
    Natural Uncured Hot Dogs (Beef, Big Apple, Chicken, Turkey)

S

Organic (Andouille, Chicken & Apple, Fire Roasted Red Pepper, Smoked Pork Andouille, Smoked Pork Bratwurst, Smoked Pork Kielbasa, Sweet Italian)

Organic Uncured Hot Dogs (Beef, Chicken, Stadium Style, The Great Organic, Turkey)

Pancetta

Pepperoni

Sopressata (Hot, Regular)

The Greatest Little Organic Smokey Pork Cocktail Franks

Turkey Salami

Butterball - Turkey Sausage (Fresh Bratwurst, Fresh Breakfast, Fresh Hot Italian, Fresh Sweet Italian, Polska Kielbasa Dinner, Smoked Dinner, Smoked, Smoked Hot)

Canino's - Bratwurst●, Breakfast Sausage●, German Brand Sausage●, Hot Chorizo●, Hot Italian Sausage●, Mild Italian Sausage●, Polish Sausage●, Spicy Cajun Style Sausage●, Sweet Italian Sausage●

Dietz & Watson -

Beef Franks (New York Deli) *(Except Fat Free & Gourmet Lite)*

Black Forest Knockwurst

Bologna (German Brand)

Bratwurst

Honey Roll

Lunch Roll

Pepper & Onion Sausage

Wieners

Empire Kosher - Deli Slices (Turkey Bologna, Turkey Salami), Turkey Franks

Farmer John -

Breakfast Sausage Links & Patties (Firehouse Hot Roll, Firehouse Hot Skinless Links, Old Fashioned Maple Skinless, Original Roll, Original Skinless, Premium Original Chorizo, Premium PC Links Lower Fat, Premium Sausage Patties Lower Fat, Premium SC Links, Premium Spicy Hot Chorizo, Premium Traditional Chorizo, Quick Serve Fully Cooked)

S

California Natural Chicken Sausage (Apple Chicken Smoked, Cajun Style Smoked, Chicken Brat Smoked, Lemon Cracked Pepper Chicken Smoked, Mango & Habanero Smoked)

Cotto Salami

Dinner Sausage (Hot Louisiana Smoked, Jalapeno Pepper Premium Rope, Jalapeno Pepper Premium Smoked, Premium Beef Rope, Premium Polish, Premium Pork Rope, Red Hots Extra Hot Premium Smoked)

Franks & Wieners (Dodger Dogs, Premium Beef Franks, Premium Jumbo Beef Franks, Premium Jumbo Meat Wieners, Premium Meat Wieners, Premium Quarter Pounder Beef Franks)

Garrett County Farms -

Andouille Sausage

Chorizo Sausage

Franks (4XL Big Beef, Chicken, Old Fashioned Beef, Original Deli, Premium Beef, Turkey)

Kielbasa (Polska, Turkey)

Sliced Beef (Bologna, Salami)

Sliced Uncured Pepperoni

Hebrew National - Franks (Beef, Cocktail, Jumbo Beef)

Hertel's - All Original Fresh Sausages *(Except British Bangers)*

Hillshire Farms -

Lit'l Beef Franks

Lit'l Polskas

Lit'l Smokies (Beef, Chipotle Hot, Regular)

Lit'l Wieners

Polska Kielbasa (Beef, Pork Turkey & Beef, Turkey)

Smoked Bratwurst

Smoked Sausage (Beef, Hot Chipotle, Italian, Lite, Original, Pork Turkey & Beef)

Turkey Smoked Sausage

Homeland - Hard Salami

Honeysuckle White -

S

Hardwood Smoked Turkey Franks

Hickory Smoked Cooked Turkey Salami

Turkey Sausage (Bratwurst, Breakfast Sausage (Links, Patties), Italian Sausage (Hot, Sweet), Poblano Pepper Links)

Turkey Sausage Rolls (Breakfast, Mild Italian)

Hormel -

Deli Sliced Cooked Pastrami

Little Sizzlers (Links, Patties)

Natural Choice (Hard Salami)

Pepperoni (Pillow Pack, Sliced)

Smokies

Hy-Vee - Beef, Cooked Salami, Little Smokies (Beef, Regular), Polish (Link, Rope), Smoked Bratwurst

Ian's - Wheat Free Gluten Free Recipe Popcorn Turkey Corn Dogs

Jennie-O Turkey Store -

Fresh

Breakfast Sausage (Mild Links, Mild Patties)

Dinner Sausage (Lean Turkey Bratwurst, Sweet Italian)

Frozen

Italian Style Meatballs

Turkey Franks

Jimmy Dean -

All Natural Pork Roll Sausage (Hot, Regular)

Fully Cooked Links (Original, Turkey)

Fully Cooked Patties (Hot, Original, Sandwich Size, Turkey)

Heat N Serve Sausage Links (Hot, Maple, Regular)

Heat N Serve Sausage Patties

Original (Links, Patties)

Premium Pork Roll Sausage (Bold Country, Extra Mild Country, Hot, Italian, Light, Maple, Mild Country, Regular, Sage)

S   Johnsonville -
   Bratwurst (Butcher Shop Style Cooked, Hot 'N Spicy, Original,
      Smoked, Stadium Style)
   Butcher Shop Style Wieners
   Chorizo
   Hearty Beef Bologna
   Irish O'Garlic
   Italian (Hot, Mild, Sweet)
   Italian Ground Sausage (Hot, Mild, Sweet)
   New Orleans Brand Smoked
   Original (Breakfast (Links, Patties), Ring Bologna)
   Polish
   Vermont Maple Syrup (Links, Patties)
Jones Dairy Farm -
   All Natural
      Hearty Pork Sausage Links●
      Light Pork Sausage and Rice Links●
      Little Link Pork Sausage●
      Maple Sausage Patties●
      Original Pork Roll Sausage●
      Pork Sausage Patties●
   All Natural Golden Brown Cooked & Browned Sausage Patties
      (Maple Fully●, Mild Fully●)
   All Natural Golden Brown Fully Cooked & Browned Turkey●
   All Natural Golden Brown Light Fully Cooked & Browned Sausage
      & Rice Links●
   All Natural Golden Fully Cooked & Browned Sausage Links (Made
      From Beef●, Maple●, Mild●, Spicy●)
Lou's Famous - Chicken Sausage (Apple, Peppers & Onion, Roasted
   Red Pepper & Garlic, Spicy Italian, Sundried Tomato)
Maluma - All Bison Sausage

S

Midwest Country Fare - Hot Dogs, Sliced Cooked Salami

Nature's Promise -
Mild Italian Chicken
Spiced Apple Chicken
Sun Dried Tomato & Basil Chicken

Organic Prairie -
Frozen Organic (Bratwurst 12 oz., Breakfast Sausage 12 oz., Brown N Serve Breakfast Links 8 oz., Italian Sausage 12 oz.)

Oscar Mayer -
Beef Franks (Bun Length, Jumbo, Light, Regular)
Little (Smokies, Wieners)
Mini Beef Hot Dogs
Salami (Cotto, Deli Thin Beef, Hard)
Smokies (Beef, Sausage)
Summer Sausage (Beef, Regular)
Turkey Franks (Bun Length, Regular)
Variety Pak (Bologna/Ham/Salami)
Wieners (98 % Fat Free, Bun Length, Jumbo, Light, Regular, Turkey Franks)
XXL Hot Dogs (Deli Style Beef, Hot & Spicy, Premium Beef, Smoked)

Primo Naturale -
Chorizo (Sliced Dried, Stick Dried)
Chub Salami (Genoa, Original, w/Black Pepper, w/Herbs)
Pepperoni (Pillow Pack, Sliced Dried, Stick, Whole Large Diameter)
Sliced Salami (Hard, Original, Premium Genoa, w/Black Pepper, w/Herbs)
Sopressata (Regular, Sliced)
Whole Chorizo
Whole Salami (Black Pepper, Genoa, Hard, Herb & Wine, Original)

Primo Taglio - Salami (Peppered Coated w/Gelatin & Black Pepper)

S **Publix** -
   Bratwurst
   Chorizo
   Franks (Beef, Meat)
   Fresh Turkey Italian (Hot, Mild)
   Hot Dogs (Beef, Meat)
   Italian (Hot, Mild)
Publix GreenWise Market - Pork Sage Sausage
Safeway Select -
   Beef Franks
   Bratwurst
   Italian (Hot, Mild, Pork)
   Polish
   Regular Hot Dogs
Shelton's -
   Bologna Uncured Turkey
   Franks (Smoked Chicken, Smoked Turkey, Uncured Chicken, Uncured Turkey)
   Turkey Sausage (Breakfast, Italian, Patties)
   Turkey Sticks (Pepperoni, Regular)
SPAM - Classic, Less Sodium, Lite, Oven Roasted Turkey, Smoke Flavored
Spartan Brand - Breakfast (Maple, Original), Hot, Mild
Sweetbay - Blueberry & Cinnamon, Chorizo, Country, Hot Italian, Mild Italian, Pepper & Onion
Thrifty Maid - Vienna Sausage (Chicken, Original)
Wegmans Brand -
   Beef Hot Dogs (Skinless)
   Red Hot Dogs Skinless (Lite)
   Uncured Beef Hot Dogs (Skinless)

S

Wellshire Farms -
Beef Franks Hot Dogs (4XL Big, The Old Fashioned, The Premium)
Cocktail Franks
Frozen
Chicken Apple Sausage (Links, Patties)
Country Sage Sausage (Links, Patties)
Original Breakfast Sausage (Links, Patties)
Sunrise Maple Sausage (Links, Patties)
Turkey (Burgers, Maple Sausage (Links, Patties))
Morning Maple Turkey Breakfast Link Sausage
Original Matt's Select Pepperoni Steaks
Polska Kielbasa
Pork Andouille Sausage
Pork Sausage (Chorizo, Linguica)
Sliced (Beef Pepperoni, Beef Salami)
Smoked Bratwurst
The Original Deli Franks
Turkey
Andouille Sausage
Dinner Link Sausage Mild Italian Style
Franks
Kielbasa
Tom Toms (Hot & Spicy, Original)
Wellshire Organic - Organic (Andouille Sausage (Pork, Turkey), Franks (Beef, Chicken, Turkey), Kielbasa (Polska, Turkey))
Winn Dixie -
Beans & Wieners
Beef
Ground Mild Italian

S

Hot

Hot Dogs (Beef, Beef/Pork/Turkey, Chicken, Turkey)

Kielbasa

Original Bratwurst

Smoked Hot

Smoked Original

Turkey

w/Green Onion

Scallops... *All **Fresh** Seafood Is **Gluten/Casein Free** (Non-Marinated, Unseasoned)*

Hy-Vee - Frozen

Publix - Sea Scallops

Whole Catch - Sea Scallops

Seafood Sauce

Frontera - Cocktail & Ceviche Sauce (Cilantro Lime, Tomato Chipotle)

Hannaford Brand - Cocktail Sauce

Heinz - Cocktail Sauce (Original)

Hy-Vee - Cocktail Sauce For Seafood

Lee Kum Kee - Shrimp Sauce

Lou's Famous - Cocktail Sauce

McCormick -

Extra Hot

Gold Dipt (Regular)

Original

Seafood Sauce (Cajun Style, Lemon Herb, Mediterranean, Santa Fe Style)

Old Bay

Safeway Brand - Cocktail

Spartan Brand

Texas Pete - Seafood Cocktail

Walden Farms

Seasoning Packets... see Seasonings

Seasonings

Accent - Flavor Enhancer (All Varieties)

Albertsons - Bay Leaves, Black Pepper, Cinnamon, Garlic Powder, Garlic Salt, Ginger, Minced Onion, Nutmeg, Onion Powder, Paprika, Parsley Flakes

Arora Creations -

Organic Seasoning Packets (Bhindi Masala, Chicken Tikka, Goan Shrimp Curry, Gobi, Punjabi Chhole, Rajmah, Tandoori Chicken)

Regular Seasoning Packets (Bhindi Masala, Chicken Tikka, Goan Shrimp Curry, Gobi, Punjabi Chhole, Rajmah, Tandoori Chicken, Tikka Masala)

Bone Suckin' - Seasoning & Rub

Bragg - Sea Kelp Delight, Sprinkle Seasoning

Cali Fine Foods▲ - Gourmet Seasoning Packets (Dill Delight●, Garlic Gusto●, Herb Medley●, Spicy Fiesta●, Sweet & Spicy BBQ●)

Chi-Chi's - Fiesta Restaurante Seasoning Mix

Durkee - All Food Coloring, All Liquid Extracts, All Liquid Flavorings, Allspice, Alum, Anise Seed, Arrowroot, Basil, Bay Leaves, Caraway Seed, Cardamom, Cayenne Pepper, Celery Salt, Celery Seed, Chicken Seasoning, Chili Powder, Chives, Cilantro, Cinnamon, Cloves, Coriander, Cream Of Tartar, Crushed Red Pepper, Cumin, Curry Powder, Dill Seed/Weed, Fennel, Garlic Minced, Garlic Pepper, Garlic Powder, Garlic Salt, Ginger, Italian Seasoning, Jamaican Jerk Seasoning, Lemon & Herb, Lemon Pepper, Lime Pepper, Mace, Marjoram, Meat Tenderizer, Mint Leaves, MSG, Mustard, Nutmeg, Onion Minced, Onion Powder, Onion Salt, Oregano, Paprika, Parsley, Pepper Black/White (All), Pickling Spice, Poppy Seed, Rosemary, Sage, Salt Free Garden Seasoning, Salt Free Garlic & Herb, Salt Free Lemon Pepper, Salt Free Original All Purpose Seasoning, Salt Free Vegetable Seasoning, Sesame Seed, Six Pepper Blend, Steak Seasoning, Tarragon, Thyme, Turmeric

Emeril's -

Essence (Bayou Blast, Italian, Original, Southwest)

Rubs (Chicken, Fish, Rib, Steak, Turkey)

S **Food Club Brand** - Black Pepper, Cinnamon, Iodized Salt, Pure Vanilla
Extract, Salt

Gayelord Hauser - Spike Magic (5 Herb, Garlic, Hot N Spicy, Original,
Salt Free, Veggi)

Hannaford Brand -

Basil Leaves, Bay Leaves, Celery Salt, Chili Powder, Crushed Red
Pepper, Garlic Powder, Garlic Salt, Ground Black Pepper, Ground
Cinnamon, Ground Ginger, Ground Mustard, Ground Nutmeg,
Minced Onion, Oregano Leaves, Paprika

Rubs (Bayou Cajun, Cabo Chipotle, Chicago Steakhouse,
Fisherman's Wharf, Monterey Citrus Pepper, Mushroom Truffle,
Northwoods Garlic Pepper, Sweet Southern BBQ)

Hy-Vee - Basil Leaf, Bay Leaves, Black Pepper, Chicken Grill
Seasoning, Chili Powder, Chopped Onion, Dill Weed, Garlic
Powder, Garlic Salt, Grinders (Black Peppercorn, Peppercorn
Melange, Sea Salt), Ground Cinnamon, Ground Cloves, Ground
Mustard, Iodized Salt, Italian Seasoning, Lemon Pepper, Meat
Tenderizer, Oregano Leaf, Paprika, Parsley Flakes, Plain Salt, Red
Crushed Pepper, Rosemary, Salt & Pepper Shaker, Seasoned Salt,
Steak Grilling Seasoning, Thyme

Konriko - Chipotle All Purpose Seasoning, Creole Seasoning

Laura Lynn - Black Pepper

Lawry's -

Black Pepper Seasoned Salt, Garlic Pepper, Garlic Powder
w/Parsley, Garlic Salt, Lemon Pepper, Salt Free 17, Seasoned
Pepper, Seasoned Salt

Seasoning Mixes (Chicken Fajitas, Fajitas, Guacamole, Sloppy Joes,
Tenderizing Beef Marinade Mix)

Litehouse - Freeze Dried (Basil, Chives, Cilantro, Dill, Garlic, Parsley)

Lowes Foods Brand - Black Pepper, Cinnamon Ground, Paprika, Salt
& Pepper Shaker Set

Mayacamas - Chicken BBQ, Curry Blend, Herb Mix, Savory Salt

McCormick -

Grill Mates Dry Rub (Chicken, Pork, Seafood, Steak, Sweet
Smoky)

seasonings

S

Grill Mates Grinders (Montreal Chicken Seasoning, Montreal Steak Seasoning)

Grill Mates Seasoning Blends (25% Less Sodium Montreal Chicken, 25 % Less Sodium Montreal Steak, Barbecue, Mesquite)

Roasting Rub (Cracked Peppercorn Herb, French Herb, Savory Herb)

Seasoning Packets (Fajitas, Salsa, Tex Mex Chili)

Spices (Alum, Anise Seed, Apple Pie Spice, Basil Leaves, Bay Leaves, Caraway Seed, Celery Flakes, Celery Seed, Chili Powder, Chives, Cilantro Leaves, Cinnamon Sticks, Cinnamon Sugar, Cream of Tartar, Cumin Seed, Curry Powder, Dill Seed, Dill Weed, Fennel Seed, Ground Allspice, Ground Cinnamon, Ground Cloves, Ground Cumin, Ground Ginger, Ground Mace, Ground Marjoram, Ground Mustard, Ground Nutmeg, Ground Oregano, Ground Sage, Ground Thyme, Ground Turmeric, Hot Mexican Style, Italian Seasoning, Marjoram Leaves, Mixed Pickling Spice, Mustard Seed, Oregano, Oregano Leaves, Paprika, Parsley Flakes, Poppy Seed, Poultry Seasoning, Pumpkin Pie Spice, Rosemary Leaves, Rubbed Sage, Sage Leaves, Sesame Seed, Tarragon Leaves, Whole Allspice, Whole Cloves, Whole Mexican)

Meijer Brand - Black Pepper, Chili Powder, Cinnamon, Garlic Powder, Garlic Salt, Minced Onion, Onion Salt, Oregano Leaves, Paprika, Parsley Flakes, Seasoned Salt

Midwest Country Fare - Chili Powder, Chopped Onion, Cinnamon, Garlic Powder, Garlic Salt, Ground Black Pepper, Onion Powder, Parsley Flakes, Pure Ground Black Pepper, Season Salt

Morton -

Canning & Pickling Salt

Garlic Salt

Hot Salt

Lite Salt Mixture

Nature's Seasons Seasoning Blend

Popcorn Salt

Salt & Pepper Shakers

S

Sausage & Meat Loaf Seasoning

Seasoned Salt

Smoke Flavored Sugar Cure

Sugar Cure

Tender Quick

Mrs. Dash - Caribbean Citrus, Extra Spicy, Fiesta Lime, Garlic & Herb, Grilling Blends, Lemon Pepper, Onion & Herb, Original Blend, Southwest Chipotle, Table Blend, Tomato Basil Garlic

Nantucket Off-Shore - Rub (Bayou, Dragon, Garden, Holiday Turkey, Mt. Olympus, Nantucket, Prairie, Pueblo, Raj, Rasta, Renaissance, St. Remy), Shellfish Boil

Nielsen-Massey - Madagascar Bourbon Pure Vanilla Powder●

O Organics - Basil Leaves, Bay Leaves, Cayenne Peppers, Ground Cinnamon, Ground Cloves, Ground Cumin, Ground Nutmeg, Paprika

Old Bay - 30% Less Sodium, Blackened Seasoning, Garlic & Herb, Lemon & Herb, Original, Rub, Seafood Steamer

Ortega - Chipotle Mix, Taco Seasoning Mix

Publix - Adobo Seasoning w/Pepper, Adobo Seasoning w/o Pepper, Ajoen Polvo Garlic Powder, Basil, Bay Leaves, Black Pepper, Chili Powder, Cinnamon, Comino Molido Ground Cumin, Condimento Completo Seasoning, Garlic Powder, Garlic Powder w/Parsley, Garlic Salt, Ground Cumin, Ground Ginger, Ground Mustard, Ground Nutmeg, Ground Red Pepper, Italian Seasonings, Minced Onion, Onion Powder, Oregano, Paprika, Parsley Flakes, Salt, Seasoned Salt, Whole Black Pepper

Safeway Brand - Fajita Seasoning Mix

Sharwood's - Curry Powder (Hot, Medium, Mild)

Spartan Brand - Black Pepper, Chili Powder, Cinnamon, Garlic Powder, Garlic Salt, Ground Nutmeg, Imitation Vanilla, Iodized Salt, Iodized Salt Crystals, Minced Onion, Oregano Leaves, Paprika, Parsley Flakes, Salt, Vanilla Extract

Spice Islands - All Food Coloring, All Liquid Extracts, All Liquid Flavorings, Allspice, Alum, Anise Seed, Arrowroot, Basil, Bay Leaves, Caraway Seed, Cardamom, Cayenne Pepper, Celery Salt, Celery

seasonings

S

Seed, Chicken Seasoning, Chili Powder, Chives, Cilantro, Cinnamon, Cloves, Coriander, Cream Of Tartar, Crushed Red Pepper, Cumin, Curry Powder, Dill Seed/Weed, Fennel, Garlic Minced, Garlic Pepper, Garlic Powder, Garlic Salt, Ginger, Italian Seasoning, Jamaican Jerk Seasoning, Lemon & Herb, Lemon Pepper, Lime Pepper, Mace, Marjoram, Meat Tenderizer, Mint Leaves, MSG, Mustard, Nutmeg, Onion Minced, Onion Powder, Onion Salt, Oregano, Paprika, Parsley, Pepper Black/White (All), Pickling Spice, Poppy Seed, Rosemary, Sage, Salt Free Garden Seasoning, Salt Free Garlic & Herb, Salt Free Lemon Pepper, Salt Free Original All Purpose Seasoning, Salt Free Vegetable Seasoning, Sesame Seed, Six Pepper Blend, Steak Seasoning, Tarragon, Thyme, Turmeric

Spice Islands Specialty - Beau Monde, Chili Powder, Crystallized Ginger, Garlic Pepper Seasoning, Fine Herbs, Italian Herb Seasoning, Old Hickory Smoked Salt

Thai Kitchen - Beef & Broccoli Seasoning Mixes

Tones - All Food Coloring, All Liquid Extracts, All Liquid Flavorings, Allspice, Alum, Anise Seed, Arrowroot, Basil, Bay Leaves, Caraway Seed, Cardamom, Cayenne Pepper, Celery Salt, Celery Seed, Chicken Seasoning, Chili Powder, Chives, Cilantro, Cinnamon, Cloves, Coriander, Cream Of Tartar, Crushed Red Pepper, Cumin, Curry Powder, Dill Seed/Weed, Fennel, Garlic Minced, Garlic Pepper, Garlic Powder, Garlic Salt, Ginger, Italian Seasoning, Jamaican Jerk Seasoning, Lemon & Herb, Lemon Pepper, Lime Pepper, Mace, Marjoram, Meat Tenderizer, Mint Leaves, MSG, Mustard, Nutmeg, Onion Minced, Onion Powder, Onion Salt, Oregano, Paprika, Parsley, Pepper Black/White (All), Pickling Spice, Poppy Seed, Rosemary, Sage, Salt Free Garden Seasoning, Salt Free Garlic & Herb, Salt Free Lemon Pepper, Salt Free Original All Purpose Seasoning, Salt Free Vegetable Seasoning, Sesame Seed, Six Pepper Blend, Steak Seasoning, Tarragon, Thyme, Turmeric

Tropical Sun Spices - Caribbean Garlic Lemon Herb, Caribbean Guava Delite, Caribbean Seasoning Salt, Caribbean Tangerine Pepper, Citrus Delite Spice, Creole Spice, Cuban Rum Spice, Fisherman's Seasoning, Jamaican Black Pepper, Key Lime Jerk

S

Seasoning, Mesquite Grilling Spice, Pizza Pasta Spice, Salsa Seasoning Spice, Sexy Spice, Spanish Sazon Completa, Southwest Santa Fe Spice, Strawberry Spice Rub, Sweet Orange Habanero Spice

Watkins - Organic Beef Seasoning

Weber Grill Creations -

Club Pack Seasoning (Gourmet Burger, Smokey Mesquite)

Grinders (Chicago Steak, Gourmet Burger, Kick 'N Chicken, N'Orleans Cajun, Smokey Mesquite, Veggie Grill, Zesty Lemon Seasoning)

Rub (Burgundy Beef, Classic BBQ)

Seasoning (Chicago Steak, Gourmet Burger, Kick 'N Chicken, Mango Lime, N'Orleans Cajun, Roasted Garlic & Herb, Seasoning Salt, Smokey Mesquite, Veggie Grill)

Wegmans Brand - Bay Leaves, Black Pepper, Cinnamon, Cloves, Cracked Pepper Blend, Fleur De Sel (Sea Salt), Minced Onions, Nutmeg, Oregano, Paprika, Parsley Flakes, Sage (Ground & Rubbed)

Seaweed -

Eden Organic - Agar Agar Bars, Agar Agar Flakes

Nagai's - Sushi Nori Roasted Seaweed

Yaki - Sushi Nori Roasted Seaweed

Yamamotoyama - Sushi Party Toasted Seaweed, Toasted Seaweed Nori

Seeds

Arrowhead Mills - Flax, Golden Flax, Mechanically Hulled Sesame, Sunflower, Unhulled Sesame

Durkee - Anise, Caraway, Celery, Dill, Poppy, Sesame

Eden Organic - Pumpkin (Dry Roasted & Salted, Spicy Dry Roasted w/Tamari)

Frito Lay - Flamin' Hot Flavored Sunflower Seeds, Sunflower Seed Kernels, Sunflower Seeds

Goraw - Seeds (Sprouted Pumpkin●, Sprouted Sunflower●), Seed Mix (Simple●, Spicy●)

Hy-Vee - Dry Roasted Sunflower Kernels

shortening

S

Meijer Brand - Sunflower (Plain, Salted In Shell)

Publix - Sunflower Seeds

Shiloh Farms - Black Sesame Seeds

Spice Island - Anise, Caraway, Celery, Dill, Poppy, Sesame

Tones - Anise, Caraway, Celery, Dill, Poppy, Sesame

Woodstock Farms -

Non Organic Seeds (Pumpkin (Regular, Roasted Salted)), Sunflower Hulled (Regular, Roasted No Salt, Roasted Salted)

Organic Seeds (Flax, Pumpkin, Sesame, Sunflower (Hulled, Hulled Roasted No Salt, Roasted & Salted, Tamari), Tamari Pumpkin, White Quinoa)

Sesame Oil... see Oil

Sesame Seeds... see Seeds

Shakes... see also Smoothies

Amazake -

Almond

Amazing Mango

Banana Appeal

Chocolate (Almond, Chimp)

Cool Coconut

Go (Go Green, Hazelnuts)

Oh So Original

Rice Nog

Tiger Chai

Vanilla (Gorilla, Pecan Pie)

Nasoya - Silken Creations Non Dairy Starter For Smoothies & Desserts

Shortening

Albertsons

Crisco - Regular

Earth Balance - Vegetable Shortening

Great Value Brand (Wal-Mart) - Vegetable Shortening

S

Meijer Brand

Publix - Vegetable Shortening

Spartan Brand - All Vegetable, Butter Flavored Vegetable Shortening

Spectrum - Palm Oil Shortening

Wegmans Brand - Vegetable

Winn Dixie

Shrimp... *All Fresh Seafood Is Gluten/Casein Free (Non-Marinated, Unseasoned)*

Captain's Choice - Cooked Tail On Shrimp

Chicken Of The Sea - All Shrimp Products

Crown Prince - Shrimp (Broken, Tiny)

Great Value Brand (Wal-Mart) - Canned Tiny Shrimp

Hy-Vee - Frozen Cooked, Platter

Publix - Cooked (All Sizes), Fresh (All Sizes)

Publix GreenWise Market - All Sizes (Cooked, Fresh)

Starfish - Just Grilled Shrimp●

Wegmans - Shrimp From Belize Uncooked

Shrimp Sauce... see Cocktail Sauce

Sloppy Joe/Sloppy Joe Sauce

Hannaford Brand

Heinz

Hormel - Not So Sloppy Joe

Hy-Vee

Meijer Brand - Sloppy Joe Sauce

Safeway

Spartan Brand

Winn Dixie - Sloppy Joe Sauce

Smoke

Colgin - Natural Liquid Smoke (Apple, Hickory, Mesquite, Pepper)

Wright's - Liquid Smoke (Hickory, Mesquite)

Smoked Sausage... see Sausage

Smoked Turkey... see Turkey

Smoothies... see also Shakes

    Ella's Kitchen - Smoothie Fruits (The Green One, The Purple One, The Red One, The Yellow One)

    Hansen's Smoothie Nectar - Energy Island Blast, Guava Strawberry, Mango Pineapple, Peach Berry, Pineapple Coconut, Strawberry Banana

    Silk Live! Smoothies - All Varieties

    V8 Splash - Strawberry Banana, Tropical Colada

    Whole Soy & Co. - All Varieties

    Zola - Antioxident, Energy, Immunity

Snacks

    Annie's - Organic Bunny Fruit Snacks (Berry Patch, Tropical Treat)

    Baken-Ets - Cracklins Hot 'N Spicy, Pork Skins (BBQ, Fried, Hot 'N Spicy)

    Betty Lou's - Krispy Bites, Nut Butter Balls Chocolate Walnut

    Carole's - Soycrunch (Coconut, Cinnamon Raisin, Original, Sesame, Toffee)

    Cheetos - Chile Limon

    Corn Nuts - Barbeque, Chile Picante, Original

    Cracker Jack - Original Caramel Coated Popcorn & Peanuts

    Deep River Snacks - Asian Sweet & Spice, Mesquite BBQ, Original Salted, Reduced Fat Original Salted, Salt & Cracked Pepper, Sweet Maui Onion Baked Fries, Sweet Maui Onion, Zesty Jalapeno

    Eat Smart - Veggie Crisps (Regular, Sun Dried Tomato & Pesto)

    Eden Organic - All Mixed Up (Regular, Too), Wild Berry Mix

    Glenny's - Brown Rice Marshmallow Treat (Chocolate●, Peanut Caramel●, Raspberry Jubilee●, Vanilla●)

    Glutano▲ - Snacks

    Goraw - Flax Snax (Pizza●, Simple●, Spicy●, Sunflower●), Ginger Snaps●, Granola (Apple Cinnamon●, Live●, Live Chocolate●, Simple●), Seed Mix (Simple●, Spicy●), Seeds (Sprouted Pumpkin●, Sprouted Sunflower●), Super Chips (Pumpkin●, Spirulina●)

S Herr's -
Pork Rinds (BBQ Flavored, Original)
Potato Sticks

Hy-Vee -
Corn Chips (Regular, Scoop)
Fruit Snacks (Build A Bear, Curious George, Dinosaurs, Mayor & Miguel, Peanuts, Sharks, Variety Pack)
Nut Trail Mix (Raisin)
Tropical Fruit Mix

Krinkle Sticks - Sea Salt

Mareblu Naturals -
Crunch (Almond, Almond Coconut, Cashew, Cashew Coconut, CranMango Cashew, Pecan Cinnamon, Pistachio)
Trail Mix Crunch (Blueberry Pomegranate, Cranberry Pomegranate, Cranblueberry Trail, Cranstrawberry Trail, Pecan Trail, Pistachio Trail)

Meijer Brand -
Fruit Rolls
Justice League Galactic Berry
Rescue Heroes
Strawberry (Garfield, Regular)
Wildberry Rush
Fruit Snacks
African Safari
Curious George
Dinosaurs
Jungle Adventure
Justice League (Big Box, Regular)
Mixed Fruit
Peanuts
Rescue Heroes Big Box

    Sharks
    Underwater World
    Variety Pack (Big Boy, Regular)
    Veggie Tales
  Snacks
    Potato Sticks

Mrs. May's Naturals - Crunch (Almond●, Black Sesame●, Cashew●, Coconut Almond●, Cran Blueberry●, Cran Tropical●, Pom Raspberry●, Pumpkin●, Strawberry Pineapple●, Sunflower●, Ultimate●, Walnut●, White Sesame●)

Munchos - Regular Potato Crisps

Nonuttin' Foods▲ - Fruit Snacks, Sulfite Free Dried Apples

Nu-World Foods -
  Mini Ridges (Rosemary Basil●, Sun Dried Tomato●)
  Snackers (BBQ Sweet Sassy●, Chili Lime●, French Onion●)

Original Tings - Crunchy Corn Sticks

Oskri Organics - Almond Honey Crunch, Cashew Honey Crunch w/Cranberries, Pecan Honey Crunch w/Cinnamon

Pirate's Booty - Barbeque, Carmel, Veggie

Publix - Fruit Snacks (Curious George, Dinosaurs, Sharks, Snoopy, Veggie Tales)

Spartan Brand - Fruit Snacks (Build A Bear, Curious George, Dinosaurs, Maya Miquel, Veggie Tales)

Trader Joe's - Sea Salt & Pepper Rice Crisp

True North - Almond Clusters, Almonds Pistachios Walnut Pecans, Peanut Clusters (Pecan Almond, Regular)

Winn Dixie - Fruit Snacks (Dinosaurs, Sharks, Veggie Tales), Pork Rinds (BBQ, Hot, Regular), Potato Sticks

Wise - Onion Flavored Rings

Woodstock Farms - Organic Snack Mixes (California Supreme, Campfire, Cape Cod Cranberry, Cascade, Cranberry (Cove, Walnut Cashew), Goji Berry Power, Gourmet Trail, In The Raw, On The Trail, Organic, Tamari Delight, Tropical Delight, Tropical Fruit)

S Snaps

Edward & Sons - Brown Rice Snaps (Black Sesame, Onion Garlic, Plain (Unsalted), Salsa, Sesame (Tamari, Unsalted), Tamari Seaweed, Toasted Onion, Vegetable)

Soda Pop/Carbonated Beverages

7up - All Varieties

A & W - Root Beer

Aquafina -

FlavorSplash (Citrus Blend, Raspberry, Wild Berry)

Boylan's - Soda (Bottleworks, Seltzers)

Canada Dry -

Club Soda (All Varieties)

Ginger Ale (Diet, Regular)

Tonic Water (All Varieties)

Coca-Cola -

Cherry Coke (Diet, Regular, Zero)

Classic Coke (Caffeine Free, Regular, w/Lime, Zero)

Diet Coke (Caffeine Free, Plus, Regular, w/Lime, w/Splenda)

Vanilla Coke (Regular, Zero)

Crush - All Varieties

Dasani - Essence, Regular

Dr. Pepper -

Caffeine Free (Diet, Regular)

Cherry Vanilla (Diet, Regular)

Diet

Regular

Enviga - Sparkling Green Tea (Berry, Green, Pomegranate)

Fanta - Grape, Orange (Regular, Zero)

Fresca

Hannaford Brand - Cola, Cream Soda, Ginger Ale, Grape, Lemon Lime, Orange, Orange Pineapple, Peach, Root Beer, Strawberry

Hansen's - All Sodas

soda pop/carbonated beverages

S

Hires - Root Beer
Hy-Vee -
    Black Cherry (Diet, Regular)
    Cherry Cola
    Club Soda
    Cola (Diet, Regular)
    Cream Soda
    Diet Tonic
    Dr. Hy Vee
    Fruit Punch (Coolers, Regular)
    Gingerale
    Grape
    Hee Haw (Diet, Regular)
    Lemon Lime
    Orange (Diet, Regular)
    Root Beer (Diet, Regular)
    Sour
    Strawberry
    Tonic Water
    Water Cooler (Black Cherry, Key Lime, Kiwi Strawberry, Mixed
      Berry, Peach, Peach Melba, Raspberry, Strawberry, White Grape)
I.B.C. - Root Beer
Mountain Dew -
    Caffeine Free
    Caffeine Free Diet
    Code Red (Diet, Regular)
    Diet
    Live Wire
    Regular
Mug - Cream Soda (Diet, Regular), Root Beer (Diet, Regular)

S   **Orangina** - Sparkling Citrus Beverage

Pepsi -
  Caffeine Free (Diet, Regular)
  Lime (Diet, Regular)
  One
  Pepsi (Diet, Regular)

Publix -
  Black Cherry Soda
  Cherry Cola
  Club Soda
  Cola (Caffeine Free, Regular)
  Cream Soda
  Diet (Cola, Ginger Ale, Tonic Water)
  Dr. Publix
  Fruit Punch
  Ginger Ale
  Grape Soda
  Lemon Lime Seltzer
  Lemon Lime Soda (Diet, Regular)
  Raspberry Seltzer
  Root Beer (Diet, Regular)
  Seltzer
  Tonic Water

Safeway Select - Clear Sparkling Water (Cranberry Raspberry, Grapefruit Tangerine, Key Lime, Raspberry Black Cherry, Strawberry Kiwi, Strawberry Watermelon, Tangerine Lime, Wild Cherry) Sodas (All Varieties)

Schweppes - All Varieties

Sierra Mist - Cranberry Splash (Diet, Regular), Free, Regular, Ruby Splash (Diet, Regular)

Slice - Grape, Orange (Diet, Regular), Peach, Red

soda pop/carbonated beverages

S

Sprite - Diet, Regular, Zero
Sunkist - Cherry Limeade, Grape, Orange, Strawberry
Tab - All Varieties
Trader Joe's - Sparkling Juice Beverages (Apple Cider, Blueberry, Cranberry, Pomegranate)
Tubz - Diet Root Beer
Vernors - Diet, Regular
Virgil's - Root Beer
Wegmans Brand -
    Frizzante European Soda
        Blood Orange
        Blueberry Lemon
        Sicilian Lemon
        Sour Cherry Lemon
    Soda
        Black Cherry
        Cherry (Regular, Wedge Diet)
        Club Soda
        Cola (Caffeine Free, Caffeine Free Diet, Diet, Lime, Regular)
        Diet (Lime)
        Dr. W (Regular)
        Fountain Root Beer (Diet, Regular)
        Ginger Ale (Diet, Regular)
        Green Apple Sparkling Soda (Diet, Regular)
        Mango
        Mountain Citrus
        Mt. W
        Orange (Diet, Regular)
        Tonic (Diet, Regular)
        W UP (Diet, Regular)
        Wedge Diet (Cherry Grapefruit)

S

Sparkling Beverage
- Black Cherry
- Cranberry Raspberry (Diet, Regular)
- Key Lime (Diet, Regular)
- Kiwi Strawberry (Diet, Regular)
- Lemonade
- Mixed Berry (Diet, Regular)
- Peach (Diet, Diet Wedge, Grapefruit (Diet, Regular), Regular)

Sparkling Beverage w/Sweeteners (Black Cherry, Key Lime, Tangerine Lime, White Grape)

Welch's - All Varieties

Winn Dixie -
- Black Cherry Soda
- Club Soda
- Cola (Caffeine Free, Cherry, Diet Vanilla, Regular, Vanilla)
- Cream Soda
- Diet (Chek, Kountry Mist Soda, Lemon Lime, Orange Soda, Root Beer, Strawberry Soda, Vanilla Cola)
- Ginger Ale
- Grape Soda
- Green Apple Soda
- Kountry Mist Soda
- Lemonade
- Lemon Lime Soda
- Orange Pineapple Soda
- Orange Soda
- Peach Soda
- Premium Draft Style Root Beer
- Punch
- Red (Alerts Soda, Cream Soda)

Root Beer

Seltzer Water

Sparkling Water (Country Strawberry, Green Apple, Key Lime, Mandarin Orange, Mellow Peach, White Grape, Wild Cherry, Zesty Raspberry)

Strawberry Soda

Sorghum

Shiloh Farms - Sorghum Grain

Soup

A Taste Of Thai - Coconut Ginger Soup Mix

Amy's -

Black Bean Vegetable

Chunky Vegetable

Fire Roasted Southwestern Vegetable

Lentil (Curried, Light Sodium, Regular)

Lentil Vegetable (Light Sodium, Regular)

Split Pea (Light In Sodium, Regular)

Thai Coconut

Tuscan Bean & Rice

Baxters -

Favorites

Chicken Broth

Cock A Leekie

Lentil & Bacon

Pea & Ham

Scotch Vegetable

Healthy Choice

Chicken & Vegetable

Chunky (Chicken & Vegetable Casserole, Country Vegetable, Smoked Bacon & Three Bean)

Puy Lentil & Tomato

S   Spicy Tomato & Rice w/Sweetcorn

Tomato & Brown Lentil

Luxury Consomme (Beef, Chicken)

Soup Bowl (Smoked Bacon & Mixed Bean Soup)

Vegetarian (Carrot & Butterbean, Mediterranean Tomato, Tomato
& Butterbean)

Dinty Moore - Beef Stew

Dr. McDougall's - Black Bean, Black Bean & Lime, Chunky Tomato,
Lentil, Pad Thai Noodle, Roasted Red Pepper, Spring Onion,
Tamale w/Baked Chips, Tortilla w/Baked Chips, Vegetable

Edward & Sons - Miso Cup (Golden, Japanese Restaurant Style,
Organic Traditional w/Tofu, Reduced Sodium, Savory Seaweed)

El Peto▲ - Onion, Tomato, Tomato Vegetable, Vegetable

Full Flavor Foods▲ - Soup Mix (Beef●, Chicken●)

Fungus Among Us - Organic Soup Mix (Moroccan Porcini & Green
Lentil, Spicy Shiitake & Vegetable)

Glutino▲ - Soup Base (Onion)

Health Valley -

Fat Free (5 Bean Vegetable, 14 Garden Vegetable, Black Bean &
Vegetable, Corn & Vegetable, Lentil & Carrots, Split Pea & Carrots,
Tomato Vegetable)

Organic (Lentil, Potato & Leek, Split Pea)

Organic No Salt Added (Black Bean, Lentil, Potato Leek, Split Pea,
Tomato, Vegetable)

Imagine -

Organic Canned

Chicken & Wild Rice

Country Split Pea

Lentil Apple

Southwestern Tortilla

Organic Creamy

Acorn Squash & Mango

Broccoli

S

  Butternut Squash
  Garden Broccoli
  Garden Tomato Light In Sodium
  Harvest Corn Light In Sodium
  Portobello Mushroom
  Potato Leek
  Red Bliss Potato Light In Sodium
  Sweet Pea
  Sweet Potato (Light In Sodium, Regular)
  Tomato (Basil, Regular)

Kettle Cuisine - Angus Beef Steak Chili w/Beans●, Chicken Soup w/Rice Noodles●, Organic Carrot & Coriander Soup●, Roasted Vegetable Soup●, Three Bean Chili●, Tomato Soup w/Garden Vegetables●

Lipton - Recipe Secrets Onion Soup & Dip Mix

Manischewitz - Borscht, Condensed Clear Chicken, Split Pea w/Seasoning Cello Mix

Meijer Brand - Condensed Chicken w/Rice, Homestyle Chicken w/Rice

Mixes From The Heartland ▲ -
  Cajun Bean●
  Cajun Pastalava●
  Chicken Veggie●
  Cowboy●
  Green Chili Hamburger●
  Green Chili Stew●
  Hamburger Pasta●
  Harvest Chicken N' Rice●
  Italian Bean●
  Minestrone●
  Navy Bean●
  Pasta Veggie●

S

    Southwestern Chicken Stew●

    Tex Mex Pasta●

    Texas Sausage N' Bean●

    Tortilla Pasta●

Orgran▲ - Cup Of Soup (Garden Vegetable, Sweet Corn, Tomato)

Pacific Natural Foods -

    Cashew Carrot Ginger

    Curried Red Lentil

    Organic Creamy Butternut Squash

    Organic Light Sodium Creamy Butternut Squash

    Organic Savory Chicken & Wild Rice

    Organic Spicy (Black Bean w/Chicken Sausage, Chicken Fajita)

Progresso -

    Microwaveable Bowl

        Chicken & Wild Rice Soup

    Traditional

        Chicken & Wild Rice

        Chicken Rice w/Vegetables

        Green Split Pea w/Ham *(Vegetable Classics Style NOT Gluten/Casein Free)*

        Southwestern Style Chicken

    Vegetable Classics

        Garden Vegetable

        Hearty Black Bean w/Bacon

        Lentil

Safeway Brand - Condensed (Chicken w/Rice), Onion Soup Mix

Safeway Select - Chicken w/Rice

Shari - Organic (Italian White Bean, Split Pea, Tomato w/Roasted Garlic)

Shelton's - Black Bean & Chicken, Chicken Corn Chowder, Chicken Rice, Chicken Tortilla

Spartan Brand - Canned Beef Stew

S

Thai Kitchen -
  Instant Noodle Bowls (Garlic & Vegetable, Lemongrass & Chili, Mushroom, Roasted Garlic, Spring Onion)
  Soup Cans (Coconut Ginger, Hot & Sour)

Trader Joe's -
  Organic Soup
    Black Bean
    Split Pea
  Regular Soup
    Garden Patch Veggie
    Instant Rice Noodle Soup (Mushroom, Spring Onion)
    Latin Black Bean

Wegmans Brand - Chili Soup (Vegetarian), Gazpacho, Moroccan Lentil w/Chick Pea

Sour Cream

  Follow Your Heart - Vegan Gourmet Sour Cream

Soy Beverage/Soy Milk

  Better Than Milk Soy (Chocolate, Original, Vanilla)

  Eden Organic - EdenBlend, Edensoy (Unsweetened)

  Imagine -
    Organic Non Dairy Soy Beverage
    Enriched (Chocolate, Original, Vanilla)
    Original Vanilla

  Lucerne - Soy Beverage (Low Fat Vanilla, Regular)

  Nature's Promise -
    Chocolate Soymilk
    Organic Soymilk (Chocolate, Original, Vanilla)

  Organic Valley - Chocolate, Original, Unsweetened, Vanilla

  Pacific Natural Foods -
    Organic Soy Unsweetened Original
    Select Soy (Plain, Vanilla)
    Ultra Soy (Plain, Vanilla)

S

Publix GreenWise Market -

> Soy Milk
>> Regular (Chocolate, Plain, Vanilla)
>> Light (Chocolate, Plain, Vanilla)

Silk Soymilk -

> Refrigerated Soymilk (Chocolate, Light (Chocolate, Plain, Vanilla), Plain, Silk Plus (Fiber, Omega 3 DHA), Vanilla, Very Vanilla
>
> Shelf Stable Soymilk (Chocolate, Plain, Unsweetened, Vanilla, Very Vanilla)

Soy Dream -

> Refrigerated Non Dairy Soymilk (Classic Original, Enriched (Original, Vanilla))
>
> Shelf Stable Non Dairy Soymilk (Classic Vanilla, Enriched (Chocolate, Original, Vanilla))

Sunrise - Soya Beverage (Sweetened, Unsweetened)

Trader Joe's - Organic Soy Milk (Unsweetened)

Vitasoy - Soymilk (Chocolate Banana, Holly Nog, Peppermint Chocolate, Strawberry Banana)

Wegmans Brand - Organic (Chocolate, Original, Vanilla)

Westsoy -

> Organic Soymilk (Original)
>
> Organic Unsweetened Soymilk (Almond, Chocolate, Plain, Vanilla)
>
> Soymilk Non Fat (Plain, Vanilla)
>
> Soymilk Plus (Plain, Vanilla)

Wild Wood Organic - All Varieties

Zensoy -

> Soy Milk (Cappucino, Chocolate, Plain, Vanilla)
>
> Soy On The Go (Cappucino, Chocolate, Vanilla)

Soy Burgers... see Burgers

Soy Crisps... see Crisps

Soy Flour... see Flour

S

Soy Sauce
  Eden Organic - Organic Tamari Soy Sauce *(Brewed In USA)*
  Hannaford Brand
  Hy-Vee
  LaChoy - Lite, Regular
  San-J - Organic Tamari Wheat Free Soy Sauce (Reduced Sodium●, Regular●)
  Spartan Brand - Original

Soy Yogurt... see Yogurt

Soybeans... see Beans and/or Edamame... *All Fresh Fruits & Vegetables Are Gluten/Casein Free*

Soymilk... see Soy Beverage/Soy Milk

Spaghetti... see Pasta

Spaghetti Sauce... see Sauces

Spices... see Seasonings

Spinach... *All Fresh Fruits & Vegetables Are Gluten/Casein Free*
  Birds Eye - All Plain Frozen Vegetables
  C & W - All Plain Frozen Vegetables
  Cascadian Farms - Chopped, Organic Frozen Cut Spinach
  Del Monte - All Plain Canned Vegetables
  Food Club Brand - Canned Cut Leaf
  Freshlike - All Frozen Plain Vegetables *(Except Pasta Combos & Seasoned Blends)*
  Great Value Brand (Wal-Mart) - Canned Whole Leaf Spinach
  Green Giant - Frozen Spinach No Sauce
  Hannaford Brand - Whole Leaf
  Hy-Vee - Canned, Frozen (Chopped, Leaf)
  Laura Lynn - Canned
  Lowes Foods Brand - Frozen (Chopped, Leaf)
  Meijer Brand - Canned (Cut Leaf, No Salt, Regular), Frozen Spinach (Chopped, Leaf)
  O Organics - Chopped, Frozen

S **Pictsweet** - All Plain Frozen Vegetables

Publix -

Canned Spinach

Frozen (Chopped, Cut Leaf, Leaf)

Publix GreenWise Market - Organic (Baby Spinach Blend, Baby Spinach Salad, Spinach)

S&W - All Plain Canned Vegetables

Safeway Brand - Canned Leaf, Frozen Chopped

Spartan Brand - Canned, Frozen (Chopped, Cut, Leaf)

Stop & Shop Brand - Chopped, Cut, Leaf, No Salt Added, Regular

Tasty Bite - Spinach Dal

Trader Joe's - All Plain Frozen Vegetables

Wegmans Brand - Chopped Spinach (Frozen), Cut Leaf (Frozen), Whole Leaf

Winn Dixie -

Canned (No Salt Added, Regular)

Frozen (Chopped, Cut Leaf)

Woodstock Farms - Organic Frozen Cut Spinach

Sports Drinks

Gatorade -

Extremo (Fierce Strawberry, Mango Electrico, Tropical Intenso)

Fierce Thirst Quencher (Grape, Melon, Wild Berry)

Frost (Glacier Freeze, Riptide Rush)

G Thirst Quencher (Fruit Punch, Lemon Lime, Orange, Riptide Rush)

Instant Mix (Fruit Punch, Lemon Lime, Orange)

Propel Fitness Water (Berry, Black Cherry, Grape, Kiwi Strawberry, Lemon, Mandarin Orange, Mango, Melon, Mixed Berry, Orange, Peach, Tropical Citrus)

Rain Thirst Quencher (Berry, Lime, Tangerine)

Powerade - Grape, Ion 4, Mountain Blast

S

Wegmans Brand -

MVP Sport Drink (Blue Freeze, Fruit Punch, Grape, Green Apple, Lemon Lime, Orange, Raspberry Lemonade)

Velocity Fitness Water (Berry, Black Cherry, Grape, Kiwi Strawberry, Lemon)

Spread

Benecol - Light, Regular

Bionaturae - Fruit Spread (All Varieties)

Dietz & Watson - Sandwich Spread

Earth Balance -

Natural Buttery Spread

Olive Oil

Original

Soy Free

Soy Garden

Natural Shortening

Organic Buttery Spread (Original Whipped)

Vegan Buttery Sticks

Eden Organic - Butter (Apple, Cherry)

Ian's - Soy Butter 4 ME

Manischewitz - Apple Butter Spread

Maple Grove Farms Of Vermont - Blended Maple, Honey Maple, Pure Maple

Odell's - Clarified Butter, Popcorn Butter, Seafood Butter

Peloponnese - Kalamata Olive Spread

Purity Farms - Organic Ghee (Clarified Butter)

Shedd's - Willow Run Soy Bean Margarine Sticks

Spectrum - Essential Omega 3, Naturals

Underwood Spreads - Deviled Ham

Walden Farms - Spreads (Apple Butter, Apricot, Blueberry, Grape, Orange Marmalade, Raspberry, Strawberry)

S Sprinkles... see Baking Decorations & Frostings

Squash... *All Fresh Fruits & Vegetables Are Gluten/Casein Free*

    Albertsons - Frozen

    C & W - All Plain Frozen Vegetables

    Cascadian Farms - Organic Frozen (Winter Squash)

    Meijer Brand - Frozen Squash (Cooked)

    Pictsweet - All Plain Frozen Vegetables

    Publix - Frozen (Cooked Squash, Yellow Sliced)

    Spartan Brand - Frozen Yellow

    Stop & Shop Brand

    Trader Joe's - All Plain Frozen Vegetables

    Winn Dixie - Frozen Yellow

Starch

    AgVantage Naturals▲ - Tapioca

    Argo - Corn

    Authentic Foods▲ - Corn, Potato

    Bob's Red Mill▲ - Arrowroot, Corn, Potato

    El Peto▲ - Arrowroot, Corn, Potato, Tapioca

    Ener-G▲ - Potato

    Expandex▲ - Modified Tapioca Starch●

    Hodgson Mill▲ - Pure Corn

    Hy-Vee - Corn

    Kinnikinnick▲ - Corn, Potato, Tapioca

    Manischewitz - Potato

    Meijer Brand - Corn

    Safeway Brand - Corn

    Spartan Brand - Corn

    Winn Dixie - Corn

Steak... *All Fresh Cut Meat Is Gluten/Casein Free (Non-Marinated, Unseasoned)*

S

Steak Sauce
  A-1
  Fischer & Wieser - Jethro's Heapin' Helping, Steak & Grilling Sauce
  Hannaford Brand
  Jack Daniel's - Original, Smokey
  Lea & Perrins - Traditional
  Meijer Brand
  Mr. Spice Organic - Garlic Steak
  Publix
  Safeway Select - Bold, Original
  Spartan Brand - Original
  Wegmans Brand - Regular
  Winn & Lovett
Stew
  Dinty Moore - Beef, Microwave Meals Beef Stew
Stir Fry Sauce
  Mr. Spice Organic   Ginger Stir Fry Sauce & Marinade
  Wegmans Brand - Sweet & Sour
Stir Fry Vegetables... see also Mixed Vegetables
  Albertsons - Stir Fry Vegetable Blend
  Amy's - Asian Noodle, Thai
  Cascadian Farm - Organic Frozen (Chinese Style, Thai Style)
  Wegmans Brand - Asian, Cleaned And Cut Stir Fry Vegetables, Far
    East, Hong Kong
Stock
  Emeril's - Beef, Vegetable
  Full Flavor Foods▲ - Soup Stock Mix (Beef●, Chicken●)
  Imagine - Organic (Beef, Beef Flavored Low Sodium, Chicken,
    Chicken Low Sodium, Vegetable)
  Kitchen Basics - Beef, Chicken, Clam, Ham, Pork, Seafood, Turkey,
    Unsalted (Beef, Chicken), Vegetable

S **Massel** - Advantage Stock Powder (Beef Style, Chicken Style), Gourmet Plus Light Stock (Chicken Style, Vegetable), Perfect Stock Powder (Beef Style, Chicken Style, Vegetable Style), Stock Powder (Beef, Chicken, Vegetable)

Swanson - Beef (Carton), Chicken (Carton)

Wegmans Brand - Culinary Stock (Beef Flavored, Chicken, Thai, Vegetable)

Winn Dixie - Resealable Boxes (Beef, Chicken, Vegetable)

Strawberries... *All **Fresh** Fruits & Vegetables Are **Gluten/Casein Free***

Albertsons - Frozen (Sliced w/Sugar, Whole)

Cascadian Farm - Organic Frozen Strawberries

Food Club Brand - Frozen

Full Circle - Organic Whole Strawberries

Great Value Brand (Wal-Mart) - Frozen (Sliced, Sliced w/Sugar, Whole)

Hannaford Brand - Sliced (w/NutraSweet, w/Sugar, Whole)

Hy-Vee - Frozen (Sliced, w/Sugar, Whole)

Kroger Brand - Plain Frozen Fruit

Meijer Brand - Frozen (Organic, Sliced), Whole Individually Quick Frozen

Publix - Frozen (Sliced, Sweetened, Whole)

Safeway Brand - Frozen (Sliced w/Sugar, Sliced w/Sweetener, Whole)

Spartan Brand - Sliced, Whole

Stop & Shop Brand - Sliced Strawberries (In Sugar, Regular), Whole

Trader Joe's - Frozen

Wegmans Brand - Frozen Sliced w/Sugar

Winn Dixie - Frozen (Sugar Whole, Whole)

Woodstock Farms - Organic Frozen Whole Strawberries

Stuffing

Andrea's Fine Foods▲ - Stuffing Croutons

Deerfields Bakery▲ - Stuffing Cubes

El Peto▲ - Stuffing

Gluten-Free Pantry▲ - GF Stuffing

Succotash... *All **Fresh** Fruits & Vegetables Are **Gluten/Casein Free**

S

    Publix - Frozen Vegetable Blend

    Spartan Brand - Frozen

    Winn Dixie - Frozen Yellow

Sugar

    Albertsons - Granulated, Light Brown, Powdered

    Diamond Falls - Brown, Granulated, Powdered

    Domino - Confectioners, Cubes, Dark Brown, Granulated, Light Brown, Pure Cane

    Food Club Brand - Granulated, Light Brown, Powdered

    Full Circle - Organic Cane Sugar

    Great Value Brand (Wal-Mart) - Confectioners Powdered, Extra Fine Granulated, Light Brown, Pure Cane

    Hannaford Brand - Dark Brown, Granulated, Light Brown, Powdered

    Home Harvest Brand - Confectioners Powdered, Dark Brown, Granulated, Light Brown

    Hy-Vee - Confectioners Powdered, Dark Brown, Light Brown, Pure Cane

    Kroger Brand - Dark Brown, Granulated, Light Brown, Powdered

    Laura Lynn - Brown, Confectioners, White

    Lowes Foods Brand - Granulated, Light Brown, Powdered

    Meijer Brand - Confectioners, Dark Brown, Granulated, Light Brown

    Midwest Country Fare - Granulated, Light Brown, Powdered

    O Organics

    Publix - Dark Brown, Granulated, Light Brown, Powdered

    Safeway Brand - Brown (Dark, Light), Granulated, Powdered

    Spartan Brand - Confectioners Powdered, Granulated, Light Brown

    Stop & Shop Brand - Granulated

    Tops - Light Brown

    Trader Joe's - All Varieties

S **Wegmans Brand** - Cocktail Sugar (Cosmopolitan, Lemon, Mandarin), Dark Brown, Granulated White, Light Brown

Winn Dixie - Granulated, Light Brown, Powdered

Woodstock Farms - Organic Sugar (Brown, Powdered, Pure Cane, Turbinado)

Sugar Substitute/Sweetener

Albertsons - Aspartame, Saccharin

Equal

Great Value Brand (Wal-Mart) - Calorie Free Sweetener

Hy-Vee - Aspartame Sweetener

NutraSweet - Original

Spartan Brand

Splenda - Brown Sugar Blend, Café Sticks, Flavors For Coffee (French Vanilla, Hazelnut, Mocha), No Calorie Sweetener (Granulated), Sugar Blend

Sweet and Low

Sweet Fiber - All Natural Sweetener●

Wegmans Brand - Sugar Substitute w/Saccharin

Wholesome Sweeteners - All Varieties *(Except Organic Light Corn Syrup)*

Winn Dixie - Sweetener w/Aspartame

Sunflower Seeds... see Seeds

Sweet & Sour Sauce

Contadina

LaChoy - Regular, Sweet & Sour Duck Sauce

Mr. Spice Organic - Sweet & Sour Sauce & Marinade

San-J - Gluten Free Sweet & Tangy●

Wegmans

Sweet Potatoes... *All **Fresh** Fruits & Vegetables Are **Gluten/Casein Free***

Hannaford Brand - Sweet Potatoes

Meijer Brand - Cut (Light Syrup)

Sweetener... see Sugar Substitute/Sweetener

Swiss Chard... *All **Fresh** Fruits & Vegetables Are **Gluten/Casein Free*** **S**

Swordfish... see also Fish... *All **Fresh** Fish Is **Gluten/Casein Free** (Non-Marinated, Unseasoned)*

   Full Circle - All Natural Swordfish Steaks

   Wegmans - Swordfish

   Whole Catch - Fillet

Syrup

   Albertsons - Chocolate, Strawberry Pancake (Buttery, Light, Original)

   Beehive - Corn Syrup

   Cabot - Vermont Pure Maple Syrup

   Crown - Corn Syrup

   Golden Griddle - Original Syrup

   Grand Selections - 100% Pure Maple

   Hannaford Brand - Pancake (2% Maple, Lite)

   Hershey's - Chocolate (Lite, Regular)

   Hy-Vee - Butter Flavor, Chocolate, Lite, Pancake & Waffle, Strawberry

   Karo - Corn Syrup w/Brown Sugar, Dark Corn, Lite Corn, Pancake Syrup

   Lily White - Corn Syrup

   Log Cabin - Butter Flavored, Lite, Original, Sugar Free

   Lundberg▲ - Sweet Dreams Brown Rice Syrup (Eco Farmed, Organic)

   Maple Grove Farms Of Vermont -

     Flavored Syrups (Apricot, Blueberry, Boysenberry, Raspberry, Strawberry)

     Pure & Organic Maple Syrup

     Sugar Free Syrup (Maple Flavor, Vermont)

   Meijer Brand - Butter, Chocolate, Lite, Lite Butter, Lite Corn, Regular)

   Midwest Country Fare - Pancake & Waffle (Butter, Original)

   Mrs. Renfro's - Cane, Country

   Nescafe - Ice Java Coffee Syrup (Cappuccino Fat Free, Chocolate Mocha, French Vanilla Café Fat Free)

S **O Organics** - 100% Pure Maple
Old Tyme - Original, No Sugar Added
Organic Nectars - Chocagave, Vanillagave
Publix -
   Butter Maple (Lite, Regular)
   Chocolate (Regular, Sugar Free)
   Pancake (Lite, Regular)
Safeway Brand - Butter Light, Chocolate, Light, Old Fashioned
Smucker's -
   Fruit Syrup (Blackberry, Blueberry, Boysenberry, Red Raspberry,
      Strawberry)
   Sugar Free Breakfast Syrup
Spartan Brand - 2% Real Maple, Artificial Butter, Corn Syrup, Reduced
   Calorie (Butter, Lite)
Trader Joe's - Maple Syrup
Uncle Luke's - 100% Pure Maple Syrup
Vermont Maid - Butter Lite, Original
Walden Farms -
   Fruit Syrups (Blueberry, Strawberry)
   Single Serve Packets (Chocolate, Pancake)
   Syrup (Chocolate, Pancake)
Wegmans Brand -
   Butter Flavor (Light)
   Chocolate Flavored
   Pancake (Light, Regular)
   Pure Maple (Organic Dark Amber, Regular)
   Sugar Free
Winn & Lovett - 100% Pure Maple (Dark, Medium), Blackberry,
   Blueberry, Maple Praline Sugar Free, Raspberry
Winn Dixie - Butter Flavor, Chocolate, Lite, Regular, Strawberry

T   T

Taco Sauce

   Chi-Chi's - Taco Sauce

   Frontera - Taco Sauce (Chipotle Garlic, Roasted Tomato)

   Hy-Vee - Medium, Mild

   La Victoria - Green (Medium, Mild), Red (Medium, Mild)

   Old El Paso - Hot, Medium, Mild

   Ortega - Original (Hot, Medium, Mild)

   Safeway Brand

   Spartan Brand - Fat Free (Medium, Mild)

   Taco Bell - Restaurant Sauce (Hot, Medium, Mild)

Taco Seasoning... see also Seasonings

   Chi-Chi's - Fiesta Restaurante Seasoning Mix

   Old El Paso - Taco Seasoning Mix (40% Less Sodium, Hot & Spicy, Mild, Original)

   Ortega - Chipotle Mix, Jalapeno & Onion Mix, Taco Seasoning Mix

Taco Shells

   Hy-Vee - Taco Dinner, Taco Shells, White Corn Tortilla

   Old El Paso - Stand 'N Stuff Yellow Corn Taco Shells, Taco Shells (Super Stuffer, White Corn, Yellow Corn), Tostada Shells

   Ortega - Hard Shells (Yellow, White), Tostada Shells, Whole Grain

   Safeway Brand - Taco Shells (Jumbo, White Corn)

   Taco Bell - Taco Shells (12 ct, 18 ct)

   Winn Dixie - White Corn

Tahini

   Arrowhead Mills - Organic Sesame Tahini

   MaraNatha - Natural w/Salt (Raw, Roasted)

   Woodstock Farms - Organic Sesame Tahini (Unsalted)

Tamales

   Amy's - Black Bean Verde, Roasted Vegetable

T Tangerines... *All **Fresh** Fruits & Vegetables Are **Gluten/Casein Free***

Tapioca
   Let's Do...**Organic** - Organic (Granules, Pearls, Starch)

Taquitos
   Delimex - Chicken Taquitos (12 ct., 25 ct., 36 ct., Costco 66 ct.)
   El Monterey - Taquitos Corn Tortillas (Chicken, Shredded Steak)

Tartar Sauce
   Best Foods
   Heinz
   Hellmann's
   McCormick - Fat Free, Original
   Old Bay
   Spartan Brand
   Wegmans Brand

Tarts
   Crave Bakery▲ - Lemon, Pumpkin

Tater Tots... see Potatoes

Tea
   Bigelow Tea -
      American Classical Tea (Charleston Breakfast, Governor Gray,
         Plantation Peach Tree, Regular, Rockville Raspberry)
      Chinese Oolong
      Darjeeling
      Decaffeinated
         Constant Comment
         Earl Grey
         English Teatime
         French Vanilla
         Green Tea (Regular, w/Lemon)
         Lemon Lift
         Spiced Chai
      Earl Grey

English Breakfast
English Teatime
Flavored Tea
   Cinnamon Stick
   Eggnogg'n Tea
   French Vanilla
   Plantation Mint
   Raspberry Royale
   Spiced Chai
   Vanilla Caramel
   Vanilla Chai
Green Tea
   Constant Comment Green
   Earl Grey Green
   Green Tea w/(Chai, Chinese Oolong, Jasmine, Lemon (Decaf, Regular), Mango, Mint, Peach, Pomegranate)
   Regular
Herb Plus
   Cranberry & Ginseng
   Lemon Ginger
   Pomegranate Blueberry
   Wild Berry Acai
Herbal Tea
   Apple Cider
   Berri Good
   Blueberry
   Chamomile Lemon
   Chamomile Mint
   Cozy Chamomile
   Fruit & Almond
   Ginger Snappish

T

I Love Lemon w/Vitamin C
Mint Medley
Orange & Spice
Peppermint
Perfect Peach
Pomegranate Pizzazz
Sweet Dreams
Sweetheart Cinnamon
Tasty Tangerine

Iced Tea
  Green Tea w/Pomegranate
  Perfect Peach

Loose Tea
  Constant Comment
  Earl Grey
  English Breakfast
  Green

Organic
  Green Tea w/Pomegranate & Acai
  Rooibos w/Asian Pear
  White Tea w/Raspberry & Chrysanthemum

Celestial Seasonings -
  African Rooibos Tea
    African Orange
    Madagascar Vanilla Red
    Moroccan Pomegranate Red
    Peach Apricot Honeybush
    Safari Spice
  Black Teas
    Fast Lane
    Darjeeling (Golden Honey, Mango Organic)

Morning Thunder
Organic Black
Tuscany Orange Spice
Victorian Earl Grey Regular

Chai
Chocolate Caramel Enchantment
Decaf India Spice
Decaf Sweet Coconut Thai
Honey Vanilla White
India Spice
Vanilla Ginger Green Tea

Cool Brew Iced Tea
Blueberry Ice
Peach Ice
Raspberry Ice
Tropical Fruit

Green Tea
Antioxidant Supplement
Blueberry Breeze
Cranberry Pomegranate
Decaf (Green, Honey Chamomile, Lemon Myrtle Organic, Mandarin Orchard, Mint)
Goji Berry Pomegranate
Honey Lemon Ginseng
Lemon Zinger
Organic Green
Raspberry Gardens
Tropical Acai Berry

Herbal Tea
Acai Mango Zinger
Bengal Spice

T

Black Cherry Berry
Caffeine Free
Chamomile
Cinnamon Apple Spice
Country Peach Passion
Cranberry Apple Zinger
Honey Vanilla Chamomile
Lemon Zinger
Mandarin Orange Spice
Mint Magic
Peppermint
Raspberry Zinger
Red Zinger
Sleepytime (Regular, Vanilla)
Sweet Apple Chamomile
Sweet Clementine Chamomile Organic
Tangerine Orange Zinger
Tension Tamer
Tropic Of Strawberry
True Blueberry
Wild Berry Zinger
Holiday Tea
　Candy Cane Lane
　Nutcracker Sweet
Wellness Tea
　Diet Partner
　Honey Peach Ginger
　Sleepytime Extra
　Tension Tamer Extra
　Throat Soothers
　Tummy Mint

White Tea
  Antioxidant Supplement Plum
  Imperial White Peach
  Perfectly Pear
  Vanilla Apple White Organic

Gold Peak - Iced Tea (Diet, Green Sweetened, Lemon, Sweetened, Unsweetened)

Great Value Brand (Wal-Mart) - Tea 100% Natural (Decaf, Regular), Refrigerated (Green, Sweet Tea, Sugarfree Sweet Tea)

Hannaford Brand - Instant Iced Tea w/Lemon, Orange Pekoe Bags (Decaf, Regular)

Hansen's - All Varieties

Honest Tea - Assam Black, Black Forest Berry, Community Green, Green Dragon, Honey Green, Jasmine Green Energy, Just Black, Just Green, Lemon Black, Lori's Lemon, Mango Acai, Mango Green, Moroccan Mint Green, Peach Oolalong, Peach White, Pearfect White, Pomegranate Red, Pomegranate White

Hy-Vee - Decaf (Green, Tea Bags), Family Size Tea Bags, Green Tea Bags, Instant, Orange & Spice Specialty

Inko's White Tea - Apricot, Blueberry, Cherry Vanilla, Energy, Honeydew, Lemon, Lychee, Original, Unsweetened Hint O'Mint, Unsweetened Honeysuckle, Unsweetened Original, White Peach

Kettle Brewed - Unsweetened Green & White Tea

Lipton -
  Diet Ice Tea Mix (Lemon (Decaf, Regular), Peach, Raspberry)
  Ice Tea Drinks
    Acai Mixed Berry Red
    Asian Pear Green
    Diet (Lemon, Lime Green, Mango Green, Peach, Plum-A-Granate, Raspberry)
    Earl Grey Black
    English Breakfast Black
    Lemon

    Lemonade Iced

    Mango Green

    Mint Tea

    Nectarine White

    Original (Diet Green, Green)

    Peach Pomegranate Red

    Raspberry (Regular, White)

Regular

    Calorie Free Ice Tea Mix (Lemon)

    Green Tea Bags (Regular)

    Instant Ice Tea (100% Instant & Decaf)

Meijer Brand - Instant, Tea Bags (Decaf, Green, Green Decaf, Regular)

Nestea - Iced Tea Mix (Lemon, Lemonade Flavor), Unsweetened (Decaf, Regular)

Newman's Own - Lemonade Iced Tea

Oregon Chai -

Chai Tea Latte Concentrate

    Caffeine Free Original

    Matcha Green Tea

    Peppermint Original

    Slightly Sweet Original

    Sugar Free Original

    The Original

    Vanilla

    Vegan Original

Pacific Natural Foods -

Organic Iced Tea (Lemon, Peach, Raspberry, Sweetened, Unsweetened Green)

Simply Teas (Kiwi Mango, Peach, Tangerine, Wild Berry, Unsweetened)

Prairie Farms - Sweetened Iced Tea

Publix -
  Iced Tea (Sweetened, Unsweetened)
  Instant (Lemon, Regular)
Red Rose - All Varieties
Republic Of Tea - All Varieties●
Rishi Tea - All Varieties
Safeway Brand - Iced Tea Mix (All Flavors)
Safeway Select - Chai Tea, Earl Gray, Herbal Tea (Chamomile, Evening Delight, Lemon, Peppermint), Quiet Morning, Specialty Tea, Tea (Black, Green, Orange Spice)
Salada Tea - All Varieties
Snapple - All Varieties
SoBe - Green
Spartan Brand -
  Orange Pekoe (Decaf, Regular)
  Green
  Instant
Stash Tea - All Varieties *(Except Ginger Teas)*
Twinings Tea - All Varieties
Wegmans Brand -
  Black Tea
  Decaf (Black Tea, Green Tea)
  Earl Grey (Black, Black Decaf, Green, Supreme)
  English Breakfast (Black, Organic)
  Green Tea
  Iced Tea Lemon
  Iced Tea Mix (Decaf, Regular, w/Natural Lemon Flavor & Sugar (Decaf, Regular))
  Organic (Chai, Chamomile, Earl Grey, English Breakfast, Jasmine Green, Peppermint, Rooibos Strawberry Cream)
  Sencha (Pure Japanese Green)
Winn Dixie - Regular & Family (Decaffeinated, Tea Bags)

T Teff

    Bob's Red Mill▲ - Flour, Whole Grain Teff
    La Tortilla Factory - Gluten Free Teff Wraps (Dark●, Ivory●)
    Shiloh Farms - Brown, Ivory

Tempeh

    Lightlife - Flax, Garden Veggie, Organic Soy, Wild Rice
    White Wave - Original Soy, Soy Rice

Tequila... *All **Distilled** Alcohol Is **Gluten/Casein Free** [2]

Teriyaki Sauce

    LaChoy - Teriyaki Marinade & Sauce
    Moore's Marinade - Teriyaki
    Organicville - Organic (Island Teriyaki, Sesame Teriyaki)
    Premier Japan - Wheat Free
    San-J - Gluten Free Teriyaki Stir Fry & Marinade●
    Simply Boulder - Truly Teriyaki Culinary Sauce●

Tilapia... see Fish... *All **Fresh** Fish Is **Gluten/Casein Free** (**Non-Marinated, Unseasoned**)

Tofu

    Amy's - Indian Mattar Tofu
    Lightlife - Tofu Pups
    Mori-Nu - All Silken Tofu
    Nasoya Foods - Cubed, Extra Firm, Firm, Lite Firm, Lite Silken, Silken, Soft
    Trader Joe's - Tofu Organic (Extra Firm, Firm)
    Wegmans Brand - Asian Classic, Firm, Organic Extra Firm
    White Wave -
        Extra Firm Tofu
        Fat Reduced Tofu
        Organic Tofu (Extra Firm Vacuumed Pack, Firm Water Pack, Soft Water Pack)
    Woodstock Farms - Organic Tofu (Extra Firm, Firm)

Tomatillos... *All **Fresh** Fruits & Vegetables Are **Gluten/Casein Free**

    Las Palmas - Crushed Tomatillos

Tomato Juice... see Drinks/Juice

Tomato Paste

  Albertsons - Regular

  Contadina - Italian Paste w/Roasted Garlic, Tomato Paste

  Del Monte - Organic Tomato Paste

  Hy-Vee - Regular Tomato

  Meijer Brand - Domestic, Organic

  Muir Glen - Organic

  Publix

  S&W

  Spartan Brand - 26% Tomato

  Wegmans Brand

  Woodstock Farms - Organic

Tomato Puree

  Contadina

  Dei Fratelli

  Hunt's

  Meijer Brand

  Muir Glen - Organic

  S&W

  Wegmans Brand

Tomato Sauce... see Sauces

Tomatoes... *All Fresh Fruits & Vegetables Are **Gluten/Casein Free***

  Albertsons -

    Canned

      Celery & Bell Peppers

      Diced Tomatoes & Green Chilies

      Diced w/Jalapenos

      Stewed (Italian, w/Onions)

      Whole (No Salt, Regular)

T **Contadina** -
Crushed
Crushed w/(Italian Herbs, Roasted Garlic)
Diced (Petite Cut, Regular)
Diced w/ (Burgundy Wine & Olive Oil, Italian Herbs, Roasted Garlic, Roasted Red Pepper, Zucchini Bell Pepper & Carrots)
Stewed w/(Italian Herbs, Onions Celery & Green Peppers)

Dei Fratelli -
Canned
Chili Ready Diced
Chopped (Italian, Mexican, w/Onion & Garlic)
Crushed (Regular, w/Basil & Herbs)
Diced (In Hearty Sauce, Low Sodium, Seasoned)
No Salt Whole
Petite Diced (Regular, w/Onion & Celery & Pepper)
Stewed
Whole (In Puree, Regular)

Del Monte -
Diced Tomatoes
Pasta Style
Regular
w/Green Pepper & Onion
w/Mushrooms & Garlic
w/Zesty Mild Green Chiles
Garden Select
Petite Diced Tomatoes
Sliced Tomatoes
Organic
Crushed Tomatoes
Diced Tomatoes (Basil, Garlic & Oregano)

Petite Cut Tomatoes
  Regular
  w/Garlic & Olive Oil
  w/Zesty Jalapenos
Stewed Tomatoes
  Italian Recipe
  No Salt Added
  Original Recipe
Tomato Sauce
  No Salt Added
  Regular

Eden Organic - Crushed (Regular, w/Basil, w/Onion & Garlic), Diced (Regular, w/Basil, w/Chilies, w/Green Chilies, w/Roasted Onion), Whole Tomatoes (Regular, w/Basil)

Hannaford Brand -
  Crushed (In Puree, Regular)
  Diced (Italian, Regular, No Salt, w/Green Chilies, w/Roasted Garlic & Onion)
  Puree
  Stewed (Italian, Mexican, No Salt, Regular)
  Whole Peeled

Hunt's -
  Crushed
  Diced (Fire Roasted, Fire Roasted w/Garlic, Petite, Regular, w/Balsamic Vinegar Basil & Oil, w/Green Pepper Celery & Onions, w/Roasted Garlic, w/Sweet Onions)
  Organic Diced
  Paste (Basil Garlic & Oregano, Regular)
  Puree
  Stewed (No Salt Added, Regular)
  Whole (Basil, No Salt Added, Regular)

T

Hy-Vee - Diced (Chili Ready, Regular, w/Garlic & Onion), Italian Style (Diced, Stewed), Original Diced & Green Chilies, Petite Diced (Regular, w/Garlic & Olive Oil, w/Sweet Onion), Stewed, Tomato Paste, Whole Peeled

Meijer Brand - Crushed In Puree, Diced (Chili Ready, Green Chilies, Italian, In Juice, Organic, Petite), Stewed (Italian, Mexican, Regular), Whole (Organic, Peeled, Peeled No Salt, w/Basil Organic)

Midwest Country Fair - Diced, Stewed, Whole Peeled

Muir Glen - Organic Crushed (Fire Roasted, w/Basil), Organic Diced (Fire Roasted, No Salt Added, Regular, w/Basil & Garlic, w/Garlic & Onion, w/Green Chilies, w/Italian Herbs), Organic Stewed, Organic Whole (Fire Roasted, Peeled, Peeled Plum, Peeled w/Basil)

Publix - Crushed, Diced, Diced No Salt, Diced w/Green Chilies, Diced w/Roasted Garlic & Onion, Paste, Peeled Whole, Pureed, Sauce, Sliced & Stewed

Publix GreenWise Market - Organic (Crushed, Diced, Diced w/Basil Garlic & Oregano, Fancy Sliced, Fancy Sliced Italian, Paste, Pureed, Sauce)

S&W - All Canned Tomatoes

Safeway Brand - Crushed, Diced (Fire Roasted, Peeled, Peeled No Salt, Petite), Italian Style Stewed, Mexican Style Stewed, Whole Peeled

Spartan Brand - Diced (For Chili, Italian, Mexican, Regular, w/Green Chilies, w/Roasted Garlic & Onions), Italian Stewed, Specialty Crushed, Whole

Trader Joe's - Whole Peeled Tomatoes w/Basil

Wegmans Brand -

Coarse Ground

Crushed (w/Italian, Style Herbs, Regular)

Diced (Chili Style, Italian Style, Petite, Regular, Roasted Garlic & Onion)

Italian Classics San Marzano Tomatoes Whole Peeled

Italian Style (Diced Tomatoes, Stewed, Whole w/Basil)

Kitchen Cut w/Basil

Organic (Diced, Diced In Juice)

Peeled Whole

Petite Diced Tomatoes w/Garlic Olive Oil & Seasoning

Puree

Stewed

Whole Peeled

Winn Dixie - Canned (Crushed, Diced, Diced w/Chilies, Italian Style (Diced, Stewed), Paste, Petite Diced, Petite Diced w/Onion Celery Green Peppers, Puree, Sauce, Stewed, Whole Peeled)

Woodstock Farms -

Organic

Crushed (Basil, Original)

Diced (Basil & Garlic, Italian Herbs, No Salt, Original)

Paste

Tomato Sauce (No Salt Added, Original)

Whole Peeled (In Juice, w/Basil)

Tonic... see Soda Pop/Carbonated Beverages

Toppings... see Baking Decorations & Frostings

Tortilla Chips... see Chips

Tortilla Soup... see Soup

Tortillas

Don Pancho - Gluten Free Flour Tortillas

Food For Life - Brown Rice, Sprouted Organic Corn

Bakery - Gluten Free Tortillas●

La Tortilla Factory - Gluten Free Teff Wraps (Dark●, Ivory●)

Manny's - Corn Tortillas

Mission - Corn Tortillas (Extra Thin, Super Size White, Super Size Yellow, White, Yellow)

Que Pasa - Corn Tortillas

Trail Mix... see also Nuts

Eden Organic - All Mixed Up, All Mixed Up Too

Enjoy Life▲ - Not Nuts! (Beach Bash●, Mountain Mambo●)

T Frito Lay - Nut & Fruit

Hy-Vee - Berry, Raisin & Nut, Tropical

Mareblu Naturals -

Crunch (Almond, Almond Coconut, Cashew, Cashew Coconut, CranMango Cashew, Pecan Cinnamon, Pistachio)

Trail Mix Crunch (Blueberry Pomegranate, Cranberry Pomegranate, Cranblueberry Trail, Cranstrawberry Trail, Pecan Trail, Pistachio Trail)

Nonuttin' Foods▲ - Energy Explosion Trail Mix

Oskri Organics -

Almond Honey Crunch

Cashew Honey Crunch w/Cranberries

Pecan Honey Crunch w/Cinnamon

Winn Dixie - Energy Snack Trail Mix

Trek Mix... see Trail Mix

Tuna... see also Fish... *All Fresh Fish Is Gluten/Casein Free (Non-Marinated, Unseasoned)*

Albertsons - Canned Tuna (Albacore, Chunk Light)

Bumble Bee -

Chunk Light

Solid White Albacore In (Oil, Water)

Tuna In (Oil, Water)

Tuna Touch of Lemon In Water

Chunk White Albacore In (Oil, Water)

Premium

Albacore Tuna In Water Pouch

Light Tuna In Water Pouch

Prime Fillet Solid

Light Tuna Tonno In Olive Oil

White Albacore In (Very Low Sodium In Water, Water)

Solid White Albacore (In Oil, In Water)

Chicken Of The Sea -
  Canned
    Light Tuna (In Canola Oil, In Oil, Regular)
    Low Sodium Chunk Light Tuna In Water
    Solid White Albacore Tuna (In Oil, In Water, Regular)
    Solid White Longline Albacore In Water
  Pouch
    Premium Albacore Tuna In Water
    Premium Light Tuna In Water
Crown Prince Natural - Solid White Albacore Tuna (No Salt Added Packed In Spring Water, Packed in Spring Water)
Grand Selections - Solid White Albacore Tuna
Great Value Brand (Wal-Mart) - Premium Chunk Light Tuna In Water
Hy-Vee - Chunk Light Tuna In (Oil, Water)
Member's Mark - Highest Quality Solid White Albacore Tuna In Water
Midwest Country Fare - Chunk Light Tuna Packed In Water
Publix - Tuna Fillets
Safeway Brand - Chunk Light
Safeway Select - Solid White Albacore
Spartan Brand - Chunk Light, Solid White Albacore
Starkist -
    Chunk Light In (Vegetable Oil, Water)
    Chunk White Albacore Tuna In Water
    Gourmet Choice Solid Light Tuna Fillet In (Olive Oil, Water)
    Low Sodium Chunk Light In Water
    Pouch (Albacore White Tuna In Water)
    Pouch Chunk Light In (Sunflower Oil, Water)
    Solid White Albacore Tuna
    Tuna Creations (Hickory Smoked, Lemon Pepper, Sweet & Spicy)
    Tuna Salad Sandwich Ready (Albacore, Chunk Light)

T   **Wegmans Brand** - Albacore In Water, Yellowfin Light In Water

Winn Dixie - Canned Tuna (Albacore, Chunk Light In Water)

Turkey... see also Deli Meat ... *All Fresh Meat Is Gluten/Casein Free (Non-Marinated, Unseasoned)*

Applegate Farms -

Organic (Herb Turkey Breast, Roasted Turkey Breast, Smoked Turkey Breast)

Organic Turkey Burgers

Organic Uncured Turkey Hot Dogs

Natural (Herb Turkey Breast, Honey & Maple Turkey Breast, Roasted Turkey, Smoked Turkey Breast, Turkey Bologna, Turkey Salami)

Natural Uncured Turkey Hot Dogs

Butterball -

All Natural Turkey (Cutlets, Filets, Strips, Tenders)

Fresh Li'l Butterball Turkey *(Except Gravy Packet w/Wheat Flour)*

Fresh Whole Turkey *(Except Gravy Packet w/Wheat Flour)*

Frozen Fully Cooked Li'l Butterball Baked Turkey *(Except Gravy Packet w/Wheat Flour)*

Frozen Fully Cooked Turkey (Baked, Smoked) *(Except Gravy Packet w/Wheat Flour)*

Frozen Li'l Butterball *(Except Gravy Packet w/Wheat Flour)*

Frozen Whole Turkey *(Except Stuffed Turkeys & Gravy Packet w/Wheat Flour)*

Ground Turkey (Italian Style, Regular, Seasoned, White)

Turkey Bacon (Lower Sodium, Regular, Thin & Crispy)

Turkey Breasts (Fresh, Frozen)

Turkey Burgers (All Natural, Seasoned)

Turkey Drumsticks

Turkey Mignons

Turkey Sausage (Fresh Bratwurst, Fresh Breakfast, Fresh Hot Italian, Fresh Sweet Italian)

Turkey Thighs

Turkey Wings

Dietz & Watson -

Black Forest Turkey

Fire Roasted Breast of Turkey

Glazed Honey Cured Turkey Breast

Italian Turkey

London Broil Turkey

Maple & Honey Cured Turkey Breast

Mesquite Turkey Breast

Oven Classic Turkey Breast

Smoked Peppercorn Turkey Breast

Garrett County Farms -

Frozen Turkey Maple Breakfast Links

Turkey Andouille

Turkey Breast (Pan Roasted, Sliced (Roasted, Smoked, Turkey Ham, Turkey Ham Steak), Smoked)

Turkey Franks

Turkey Kielbasa

Turkey Tom Tom Snack Sticks

Honeysuckle White -

Estate Recipe Turkey Deli Meat

Buffalo Style

Canadian Brand Maple

Dry Roasted

Hickory Smoked (Honey Pepper, Original)

Honey Smoked

Mesquite Smoked

Fresh

Breast (Bone In, Cutlets, Roast, Strips, Tenderloins, Thin Cut Slices)

Drumsticks

Neck Pieces

Split Breast

T

Thighs

Wing (Drumettes, Portions)

Wings

Frozen (Boneless Turkey w/Gravy, Turkey Burgers)

Fully Cooked Hickory Smoked Bone In Turkey Breast

Ground Turkey

    All (85/15, 93/7, 97% Fat Free, 99% Fat Free, Italian Style Seasoned, Patties, Roll, Taco Seasoned, Value Pack)

Hardwood Smoked (Bacon, Franks)

Hickory Smoked (Cooked Turkey Salami, Turkey Ham, Turkey Pastrami)

Lunch Meat Deli Sliced

    Hickory Smoked (Honey Turkey Breast, Turkey Breast)

    Oven Roasted Turkey Breast

    Turkey Pastrami

Marinated Turkey Selections

    Creamy Dijon Mustard Breast Tenderloins

    Homestyle Breast Tenderloins

    Italian Herb Rotisserie Boneless Breast Roast

    Lemon Garlic Breast Tenderloins

    Original Style Rotisserie Boneless Breast Roast

    Rotisserie Breast Tenderloins

    Zesty Italian Herb Breast Tenderloins

Sausage

    Bratwurst

    Links (Breakfast, Chipotle Smoked, Hot Italian, Original Smoked, Poblano Pepper, Sweet Italian)

    Patties

    Roll (Breakfast, Mild Italian)

Simply Done

    Split Turkey Breast (Lemon Garlic, Mesquite, Rotisserie)

    Whole Young (Turkey, Turkey Breast)

Turkey Bologna
Turkey Breast Deli Meats
  Cajun Style Hickory Smoked
  Golden Roasted
  Hickory Smoked Peppered
  Hickory Smoked
  Honey Mesquite Smoked
  Oil Browned
  Oven Prepared
Whole Young Turkeys
  All Natural
  Cajun Style
  Fresh
  Frozen
  Fully Cooked (Hickory Smoked, Oven Roasted)
  Honey Roasted
Hormel -
  Deli Sliced (Oven Roasted, Smoked)
  Chunk Meats Turkey
  Natural Choice Deli Oven Roasted
Hy-Vee -
  Deli Thin Slices Turkey Breast (Honey Roasted, Oven Roasted)
  Thin Sliced (Honey Turkey, Turkey)
Isaly's - Oven Roasted Breast Of Turkey
Jennie-O Turkey Store -
  Fresh
    Extra Lean Boneless Turkey Breast Tenderloins
    Extra Lean Turkey Breast Cutlets
    Breakfast Sausage (Mild Links, Mild Patties)
    Ground Turkey (Extra Lean, Lean, Regular)

T

Grand Champion Turkey Breast (Hickory Smoked, Honey Cured, Mesquite Smoked, Oven Roasted, Pan Roasted, Tender Browned)

Natural Choice Deli Counter Turkey Breast (Applewood Smoked, Honey Roasted, Peppered, Tender Browned)

Premium Fresh Deli Counter Turkey Breast (Golden Classic Herb Roasted, Hickory Smoked Honey Roasted, Honey Cured, Mesquite Smoked, Oven Roasted)

Premium Seasoned Deli Counter Turkey Breast (Bourbon Maple, Cajun Style, Cracked Pepper, Cranberry Sage, Italian Style Roasted Garlic, Sun Dried Tomato, Sweet Maple)

Refrigerated (Dark Turkey Pastrami)

Kayem - Turkey Breast (Homestyle, Homestyle Skin-On Buffalo Style)

Meijer Brand -

Gold Turkey (Hen, Tom)

Hen Turkey

Frozen (Breast Tenders, Duckling, Split Breast, Young)

Regular Turkey Breast

Tom Turkey

Turkey Basted w/Timer

Turkey Breast (Fresh, Fresh Natural)

Organic Prairie -

Fresh Organic

Sliced Roast Turkey Breast 6 oz.

Sliced Smoked Turkey Breast 6 oz.

Frozen Organic

Ground Turkey 12 oz.

Whole Young Turkey (10-14 lbs.), (14-18 lbs.)

Oscar Mayer -

Deli Fresh Meats (Oven Roasted (98% Fat Free Turkey, Turkey Breast), Smoked Turkey Breast)

Shaved Deli Fresh Meats (Cracked Black Peppered Turkey Breast, Honey Smoked Turkey Breast, Mesquite Turkey Breast, Oven Roasted Turkey Breast, Smoked Turkey Breast)

Thin Sliced Deli Fresh (Honey Smoked Turkey Breast, Mesquite Turkey Breast, Oven Roasted Turkey Breast, Smoked Turkey Breast)

Publix -

Deli Fully Cooked Turkey (Breast, Whole)

Deli Pre Pack Lunch Meats (Extra Thin Sliced Oven Roasted Turkey Breast, Extra Thin Sliced Smoked Turkey Breast, Smoked Turkey, Turkey Breast)

Fresh Young Turkey (Breast, Whole)

Shelton's - Free Range Ground Turkey (#1 Chub Pack, #3 Chub Pack), Free Range Ground White Turkey (#1 Chub Pack), Free Range Whole Turkey (8-15 lbs., 16-26 lbs.), Organic (Large, Whole Small), Turkey Burgers

SPAM - Classic, Less Sodium, Lite, Oven Roasted Turkey, Smoked Flavored

Valley Fresh - 100% Natural Premium White Turkey

Wegmans Brand -

Lean Ground Turkey (94%, 99%)

Organic Turkey Breast (Honey Roasted, Oven Roasted)

Sliced Turkey Breast (Hickory Smoked, Oven Browned)

Split Turkey Breast

Thin Sliced Turkey Breast Cutlets

Turkey (Breast Tenders, Drumsticks, London Broil, Thighs, Wings)

Wellshire Farms -

All Natural Turkey Breast (Pan Roasted, Smoked)

Morning Maple Turkey Breakfast Link Sausage

Sliced (Oven Roasted Turkey Breast, Smoked Turkey Breast, Turkey Bologna, Turkey Ham)

Turkey (Andouille Sausage, Franks, Kielbasa)

Turkey Dinner Link Sausage Mild Italian Style

Turkey Ham (Ham Steak, Nuggets, Whole)

Turkey Tom Toms (Hot & Spicy, Original)

T
U
V

    Wellshire Organic - Organic Turkey (Andouille, Bacon, Franks, Kielbasa)

    Winn Dixie - Thin Sliced Turkey (Oven Roasted, Smoked, Smoked Honey)

Turkey Bacon... see Bacon

Turkey Breast... see Turkey

Turkey Burgers... see Burgers... see Turkey

Turkey Ham... see also Ham... see also Turkey

    Honeysuckle White - Hickory Smoked Turkey Ham

    Jennie-O Turkey Store - Extra Lean, Lean

    Perdue - Deli Turkey Ham Hickory Smoked

    Wellshire Farms - Turkey Ham (Ham Steak, Nuggets, Whole)

Turkey Jerky... see Jerky/Beef Sticks

Turkey Lunch Meat... see Deli Meat

Turnips... *All **Fresh** Fruits & Vegetables Are **Gluten/Casein Free***

    C & W - All Plain Frozen Vegetables

    Pictsweet - All Plain Frozen Vegetables

    Safeway Brand - Frozen Chopped

    Winn Dixie - Frozen Chopped

U

V

Vanilla Extract... see Extract

Vanilla Powder

    Authentic Foods ▲

Vegenaise

    Follow Your Heart - Grapeseed Oil, High Omega 3, Organic, Original, Flaxseed & Olive Oil Reduced Fat

V

Vegetable Juice... see Juice/Drinks
Vegetable Oil... see Oil
Vinegar
   Albertsons - Apple Cider, Red Wine, White Distilled
   Bakers & Chefs - White Distilled
   Bionaturae - Balsamic
   Bragg - Organic Apple Cider
   Di Lusso - Red Wine
   Eden Organic - Organic (Apple Cider, Brown Rice, Red Wine, Ume Plum)
   Food Club Brand - Cider, White
   Full Circle - Organic Balsamic Vinegar
   Grand Selections - Balsamic Of Modena, Red Wine, White Wine
   Great Value Brand (Wal-Mart) - Apple Cider, Distilled White
   Hannaford Brand - Apple Cider, Red Wine, White
   Heinz -
      Apple Cider
      Distilled White
      Garlic Wine
      Red Wine
   Holland House - All Vinegars *(Except Malt Vinegar)*
   Home Harvest Brand - White
   Hy-Vee - Apple Cider Flavored Distilled, White Distilled
   Lowes Foods Brand - Cider, White
   Marukan - Rice Wine Vinegar
   Nishiki - Sushi Vinegar
   Meijer Brand - Balsamic Aged (4 Yr, 12 Yr), Cider, Red Wine, White Distilled, White Wine
   Musselman's - Apple Cider, White Distilled
   Newman's Own Organics - Balsamic
   O Organics - Balsamic

Publix - Apple Cider, Balsamic, Red Wine, White Distilled

Regina - Fine (Balsamic, Red Wine, White Wine), Raspberry Balsamic

Safeway Select - Apple Cider, Distilled, Red Wine, Rice, White Wine

Spartan Brand - Cider, White

Spectrum - Balsamic, Organic (Balsamic, Brown Rice, Distilled White, Filtered Apple Cider, Golden Balsamic, Red Wine, Seasoned Brown Rice, Unfiltered Apple Cider, White Wine)

Stop & Shop Brand -

    Cider

    Simply Enjoy (Balsamic of Modena, White Balsamic)

    White

    Wine

Wegmans Brand - Apple Cider, Asian Classic Rice Vinegar, Chianti Red Wine, Italian Classic Balsamic Vinegar Of Modena (Four Leaf, Three Leaf, Two Leaf), Red Wine, Tuscan White Wine, White Distilled

Winn Dixie - Apple Cider, White

Vitamins... see Gluten/Casein Free OTC Pharmacy Section

Vodka... *All **Distilled** Alcohol Is **Gluten/Casein Free** [2]*

W

Wafers... see Cookies

Waffles/Waffle Mix... see Pancakes/Pancake Mix

Walnuts... see Nuts

Wasabi

    Eden - Wasabi Powder

    Dietz & Watson - Wasabi Mustard

    Hime - Powdered Sushi Wasabi

    Spectrum - Organic Wasabi Mayonnaise

    Sushi Sonic - Real Wasabi

Water

W

Aquafina -

    Flavor Splash (Grape, Lemon, Peach Mango, Raspberry, Strawberry Kiwi, Wild Berry)

    Purified Drinking Water

    Sparkling (Lemon Lime, Original)

Crystal Geyser - Alpine Spring

Dasani - Essence (Black Cherry, Lime, Strawberry Kiwi), Purified

Deja Blue - Purified Drinking Water

Evian

Fiji - Natural Artesian

Food Club Brand - Distilled, Drinking, Spring

Hannaford Brand - Sparkling (Black Cherry, Key Lime, Kiwi Strawberry, Peach, Raspberry, Tropical Punch, White Grape)

Hy-Vee - 10 oz. Fun Pack (Flavored, Regular), Mother's Choice Infant Water w/Fluoride, Natural Spring, Premium Distilled, Purified, Spring, Tonic

Ice Mountain

Lowes Foods Brand - Distilled, Drinking, Spring

Meijer Brand - Calcium, Distilled, Natural Calcium, Spring

Poland Spring - Sparkling Spring

Publix - Spring Water

Safeway Brand - Drinking, Purified Drinking, Spring

San Pellegrino - Sparkling Water

Snapple - All Flavored Water

Spartan Brand -

    Distilled

    Drinking

    Natural Spring

    Spring

Sweet Bay - Distilled, Drinking Water w/Minerals, Natural Spring Water Sodium Free

Wegmans Brand -
Aqua V Vitamin Infused Lemonade
Sparkling Water (Berry, FYFGA Natural, Lemon, Lime, Mandarin
Orange, Mineral, Mixed Berry, Orange, Raspberry, Tangerine Lime)
Spring (Regular, w/Fluoride)
Winn Dixie - Distilled, Drinking, Purified, Spring

Water Chestnuts
Reese - Diced, Sliced, Whole
Spartan Brand - Canned

Watermelon... *All **Fresh** Fruits & Vegetables Are **Gluten/Casein Free**

Whipping Cream
Soyatoo - Rice Whip, Soy Whip

Whiskey... *All **Distilled** Alcohol Is **Gluten/Casein Free** 2

Wine... *All Wine **Made In The USA** Is Gluten/Casein Free 2

Wing Sauce
Frank's RedHot - Chile 'N Lime, Original, Xtra Hot
Moore's Marinade - Honey BBQ Wing
Mr. Spice Organic - Salt Free Hot Wing! Sauce & Marinade

Wings... *All **Fresh** Chicken Is **Gluten/Casein Free (Non-Marinated, Unseasoned)**
Wegmans - Chicken Wings, Jumbo Buffalo Style

Worcestershire Sauce
French's - Classic, Reduced Sodium
Great Value Brand (Wal-Mart)
Hannaford Brand
Lea & Perrins - Original
Meijer Brand
Safeway Brand
Spartan Brand
The Wizard's - Organic CF/GF Vegan Worcestershire
Winn & Lovett

X

Xanthan Gum
   Authentic Foods▲
   Bob's Red Mill▲
   El Peto▲
   Ener-G▲
   Gluten-Free Essentials▲
   Kinnikinnick▲

Y

Yams... *All Fresh Fruits & Vegetables Are Gluten/Casein Free*
   S&W - Candied Yams
   Spartan Brand - Yams
Yeast
   Bob's Red Mill▲ - Yeast (Active Dry, Nutritional T6635)
   El Peto▲
   Fleischmann's - All Varieties
   Hodgson Mill▲ - Active Dry, Fast Rise
   Red Star - Active Dry, Bread Machine, Cake, Quick Rise
Yellow Squash... see Squash
Yogurt
   Nogurt -
      Organic
         Banana Cinnamon
         Blueberry
         Chocolate
         Orange
         Pomegranate

Y
Z

Ricera -
Organic
Blueberry
Peach
Strawberry
Vanilla

Silk Live! - All Soy Yogurts

So Delicious - Coconut Milk (Blueberry, Chocolate, Passionate Mango, Plain, Pina Colada, Raspberry, Strawberry, Strawberry Banana, Vanilla)

Sol Cuisine - Organic Solgurt (Lowfat Blueberry, Lowfat Strawberry, Lowfat Vanilla, Unsweetened Natural)

Trader Joe's - Soy Yogurt (All Varieties)

WholeSoy & Co. - All Products (Frozen Yogurts, Smoothies, Yogurts)

Z

Zucchini... *All **Fresh** Fruits & Vegetables Are **Gluten/Casein Free**

Gluten/Casein Free
Over The Counter (OTC)
Pharmacy Guide

Rx   After Shave/Shaving Gel

Arbonne - NutriMinC RE9 Resurface Shave Gel
Burt's Bees - Men's Natural (Aftershave, Cream)

Allergy/Sinus/Cold/Flu Relief

Afrin - Nasal Spray (All)
Airborne - Lemon Lime, On The Go Lemon Lime, Original, Pink
  Grapefruit, Very Berry
California Baby - Colds & Flu Massage Oil
Claritin - D24, Ready Tabs
Cold-Eeze - Cold Remedy Lozenges (All Flavors)
Dayquil -
  Cold & Flu Liquid
  Cough Liquid
  Mucus Control Expectorant Liquid
  Mucus Control DM Expectorant Cough Suppressant Liquid
Halls - All Varieties
Meijer -
  Apap
    Cold Child Suspension Grape
    Cough Cold (Child Suspension Cherry, Infant Drops Cherry)
    PE Allergy Sinus Caplets
    PE Cold Flu Day Cool Caplets
    PE Cold Severe Congestion Caplets
  Daytime 6hr (Liquid, Liquid Gels)
  Dibromm (DM Grape Elixir, Grape Elixir)
  Diphedryl (Tablets)
  Loratadine (D 24hr Tablets)

allergy/sinus/cold/flu relief

Nasal Spray (Extra Moist Liquid, Liquid, Multi Symptom Liquid, No Drip Pump Liquid) **Rx**

Nitetime 6 hr (Cherry Liquid, Liquid Gels, Original Liquid)

Nitetime Cough 6 hr (Cherry Liquid)

Pedia Cough Decongestion Drops

Tri Acting Nitetime Grape Liquid

Tussin (CF Liquid, CS Liquid, Cough Cold Softgels, DM Clear Liquid, DM Liquid, Pedia Cough Cold Liquid)

Nature's Baby Organics - Ah Choo Chest Rub

Nyquil -

Cold & Flu Liquid (Cherry, Original)

Cough Liquid (Cherry)

D Cold & Flu Liquid (Original)

Less Drowsy Cold & Flu Liquid (Original)

Primatene - Mist

Safeway Select -

Allergy Relief

Mucous Relief (DM & PE)

Theraflu -

Hot Liquids (Cold & Cough, Cold & Sore Throat, Daytime Severe Cold, Nighttime Severe Cold)

Thin Strips (Daytime Cold & Cough, Nightime Cold & Cough)

Warming Relief Syrups (Daytime)

Vicks -

Formula 44 Custom Care Sore Throat Spray (Berry Burst, Honey Lemon Burst)

Formula 44 Liquid

Body Aches

Chesty Cough

Congestion

Cough & Cold PM

Dry Cough

Rx   Antacids

Lactaid - Dietary Supplement (Fast Act Caplets, Fast Act Chewables)
Meijer -
  Antacid Calcium (Peppermint Chewables, Ultra Fruit Chewables, XS Berry Chewables, XS Chewables, XS Fruit Chewables, XS Tropical Chewables, XS Wintergreen Chewables)
  Antacid Fast Acting Liquid (Maximum Strength Cherry, Maximum Strength Original, Regular Strength Original)
  Cimetidine Tablets
  Effervescent Antacid Pain Tablets
  Milk Of Magnesia (Cherry Liquid, Mint Liquid, Original Liquid)
  Pink Bismuth (Chewables, Maximum Strength Liquid, Regular Strength Liquid)
  Ranitidine
Pepto Bismol - All Varieties
Safeway Select -
  Antacid Tablets (Fruit Flavored, Peppermint, Wintergreen)
Tagamet - HB

Antibiotic/Analgesic Ointment & Spray

Cortaid - All Varieties
Hy-Vee -
  First Aid
    Allergy Creme 2%
    Antibiotic Ointment
    Hydrocortisone Cream 1%
  Isopropyl Alcohol

Anti-Diarrhea

Rx

Lactaid -
  Dietary Supplement
    Fast Act Caplets
    Fast Act Chewables
Meijer -
  Loperamide (Liquid)
  Pink Bismuth (Chewables, Maximum Strength Liquid, Regular Strength Liquid)
Pepto Bismol - All Varieties

Anti-Fungal

Meijer -
  Miconazole Cream (3 Day Preapp. Combo, 3 Day Disapp. Combo, 7 Day Disapp., 7 Day Reapp.)
  Tioconazole 1 Day Ointment (Disapp.)

Anti-Gas

Lactaid -
  Dietary Supplement
    Fast Act Caplets
    Fast Act Chewables
Meijer -
  Gas Relief Ultra Softgels
  Simethicone Nonstaining Drops
Phazyme - Ultra Strength Softgels

Rx   Cosmetics

Afterglow Cosmetics▲ - All Products
Arbonne -
   About Face
     Blusher
     Brow Wax
     Cream Concealer
     Eye Pencil
     Eye Shadow
     Line Defiance Liquid Foundation SPF 15
     Lip Pencil
     Mineral Powder Foundation SPF 15
     Sheer Shine
     Translucent Powder (Loose, Pressed)
     Wipe Out Eye Makeup Remover
   Before Sun No Sun Intended Bronzing Powder

Cough Drops/Sore Throat Spray/Lozenges

Cold-Eeze - Cold Remedy Lozenges (All Flavors)
Halls - All Varieties
Hy-Vee - Cherry Eucalyptus Flavor Drops, Honey Lemon Cough Drops, Sugar Free Black Cherry Drops
Meijer - Cherry Sore Throat Spray
Nature's Baby Organics - Ah Choo Chest Rub
Organix - Organic Cough & Sore Throat Drops (Golden Honey Lemon, Orchard Cherry)
Safeway Select -
   Cough Drops (Cherry, Honey Lemon)

Rx

Vicks -
Formula 44 Custom Care Sore Throat Spray (Berry Burst, Honey Lemon Burst)

Walgreens -
Cough Drops (Sugar Free Menthol)

Deodorant

Burt's Bees - Herbal Deodorant
Tom's Of Maine -
Natural Long Lasting Deodorant (Roll On, Stick)
Natural Original Deodorant Stick
Natural Sensitive Care Deodorant Stick

Hair Care

Arbonne - Sea Source Detox Spa Fortifying Hair Mask
Burt's Bees -
Color Keeper (Conditioner, Shampoo)
Super Shiny Grapefruit Sugarbeet (Conditioner, Shampoo)
Very Volumizing (Conditioner, Shampoo)
California Baby -
Calendula (Hair Conditioner, Shampoo & Bodywash)
Calming Hair Conditioner
Calming Hair Detangler
Calming Shampoo & Body Wash
Super Sensitive (Hair Conditioner, Shampoo & Bodywash)
Swimmer's Defense Shampoo & Body Wash
Tea Tree & Lavender Shampoo & Body Wash

Rx Desert Essence Organics -
> Conditioner (Fragrance Free, Green Apple & Ginger, Italian Red Grape, Lemon Tea Tree, Red Raspberry)
> Shampoo (Fragrance Free, Green Apple & Ginger, Italian Red Grape, Lemon Tea Tree, Red Raspberry)

Fleurish Beauty - Premium (Conditioner, Shampoo)

Gluten-Free Savonnerie▲ - All Products

Hy-Vee -
> Baby Shampoo
> Extra Body Shampoo Plus Conditioner
> Le Techniq (Truly Clean Pro Vitamin Shampoo)
> Lice (Killing Shampoo, Shampoo & Cream Rinse, Treatment Kit)
> Normal Vitamin Shampoo & Conditioner

Johnson's - Baby Shampoo

Keys - All Products

Meijer - Minoxidil 5% Liquid (30 Day, 90 Day)

Pantene Pro-V -
> Always Smooth (Conditioner, Shampoo)
> Anti Frizz (Conditioner, Shampoo)
> Beautiful Lengths (Conditioner, Shampoo)
> Classic Care (Conditioner, Shampoo)
> Color Revival (Conditioner, Shampoo)
> Daily Moisture Renewal (Conditioner, Shampoo)
> Full & Thick (Conditioner, Shampoo)
> Sheer Volume (Conditioner, Shampoo)

Laxatives/Hemorrhoidal Relief

Citrucel - Fiber Therapy Powder (Orange Regular, Orange Sugar Free)

Fleet - Fiber Gummies

Konsyl - Original Natural Fiber Supplement　　　　　　　　**Rx**

Meijer -

    Fiber Therapy Caplets

    Hemorrhoidal (Cream, Ointment, Suppository)

    Laxative Tablets (Natural MS, Senna)

    NVP (Capsules, Original Orange Powder, Original Regular Powder, Smooth Orange Powder, Sugar Free Smooth Orange Powder)

Metamucil -

    Capsules

    Capsules Plus Calcium

    Powder Coarse Milled Original Texture (Orange, Unflavored)

    Powder Smooth Texture (Orange)

Pedia-Lax -

    Chewable Tablets (Watermelon)

    Liquid Stool Softener (Fruit Punch)

    Quick Dissolve Strips

Tucks - Hemorroidal Ointment, Hydrocortisone Anti Itch Ointment, Medicated Pads, Take Along Medicated Pads

Lip Care

Arbonne -

    Before Sun Lip Saver SPF 30

    Bio Nutria Herbal Lip Ointment

    Bio Nutria Lip Service Dietary Supplement

    F.Y.I. It Shines Lip Gloss

Blistex -

    Clear Advance

    Complete Moisture

Rx   DCT SPF 20
Deep Renewal
Fruit Smoothies (Berry Explosion, Melon Medley, Triple Tropical)
Gentle Sense
Herbal Answer Gel
Lip Balm (Berry, Medicated, Mint)
Lip Infusions (Cherry Splash, Moisture Splash, Soothing Splash)
Lip Medex
Lip Ointment
Lip Revitalizer
Lip Tone
Raspberry Lemonade Blast
Silk & Shine
Ultra Protection

Burt's Bees -
Lip Balm (Bees Wax, Honey, Medicated, Replenishing, Sun
Protecting)
Lip Gloss (All Shades)
Lipshimmer (All Shades)

Desert Essence Organics - Lip Tints (Coconut, Italian Red Grape, Red
Raspberry, Vanilla Chai)

Miscellaneous Products

Band-Aid - Flexible Fabric
Burt's Bees -
Bug Bite Relief
Herbal Blemish Stick
Insect Repellent
Therapeutic Bath Crystals

Rx

Elmer's - All Products *(Except Finger Paints)*
Meijer - Nicotine Gum (Mint, Regular)
Nature's Baby Organics - All Purpose Deodorizer
Nicorette -
   Chewing Gum
     Fresh Mint (2 mg, 4 mg)
     Fruit Chill (2 mg, 4 mg)
     White Ice Mint (2 mg, 4 mg)

Motion Sickness

Meijer - Anti Nausea Liquid

Oral Hygiene

Aquafresh - Toothpaste (Cavity Protection, Extra Fresh, Sensitive)
Colgate -
   Toothpaste
     Cavity Protection (Regular Flavor)
     Luminous (Crystal Clean Mint)
     Tartar Protection Whitening
     Total Fresh Stripe
     Total Plus Whitening
Crest -
   All Mouthrinses
   All Toothpaste Varieties
   All Whitestrips
Glide - Floss
Kirkman Labs - Toothpaste Gel

Rx Listerine -

    Agent Cool Blue Tinting Rinse

    Antiseptic Mouthwash (All Varieties) *(Except Citrus)*

    Pocket Paks Oral Care Strips

        Cinnamon

        Cool Mint

        Fresh Burst

    Tooth Defense Anticavity Fluoride Rinse

    Totalcare Anticavity Mouthwash

    Whitening Pre Brush Rinse

    Whitening Quick Dissolving Strips

    Whitening Vibrant White Rinse

Polident - Denture Cleanser

Scope - Mouthwash (Original, Peppermint)

Sensodyne - Pronamel Toothpaste

Tom's Of Maine -

    Children's Natural Anticavity Fluoride Toothpaste

    Children's Natural Fluoride Free Toothpaste

    Floss Antiplaque Flat

    Floss Antiplaque Round

    Maximum Strength Sensitive Fluoride Toothpaste

    Natural Anticavity Fluoride Mouthwash

    Natural Anticavity Fluoride Toothpaste

    Natural Antiplaque Fluoride Free Toothpaste w/Propolis & Myrrh

    Natural Antiplaque Plus Whitening Gel Fluoride Free Toothpaste

    Natural Antiplaque Tartar Control & Whitening Fluoride Free Toothpaste

    Natural Clean & Gentle Care SLS Free Anticavity Plus Dry Mouth Soother Fluoride Toothpaste

    Natural Clean & Gentle Care SLS Free Anticavity Plus Whitening Fluoride Toothpaste

Natural Clean & Gentle Care SLS Free Antiplaque Plus Whitening **Rx**
  Fluoride Free Toothpaste

Natural Cleansing Mouthwash

Natural Sensitive Toothpaste

Natural Tartar Control Mouthwash

Natural Whole Care Toothpaste

Natural Whole Care Toothpaste Gel

Sensitive Care SLS Free

ZOOM - Whitening Gel *(At The Dentist)*

Pain Relief

Meijer -

Apap (Caplet, Cool Caplet, ER Caplet Red, ER Caplet White, ETS
  Tablet, Gelcap, Geltab, Tablet)

Apap Child (Bubblegum Suspension, Cherry Suspension, Grape
  Suspension)

Apap Infant Cherry Suspension

Aspirin (Adult Orange Chewables, Child Orange Chewables)

Headache Tablets

Ibuprofen (Caplets Brown, Caplets Orange, Child Suspension
  Bubblegum, Junior Caplets, Tablets Brown, Tablets Orange)

Migraine Caplets

Naproxen Sodium (Caplets, Tablets)

Safeway Select -

Ibuprofen (Liquid Softgels)

Non Aspirin Extra Strength (Capsules)

Pain Reliever Fever Reducer Tablets

Rx   # Play Dough

Aroma Dough - All Natural Playing Dough
Bloom Putty - Play Putty (Scented, Unscented)
Bluedominoes - Organic Activity Dough●
Crayola - Air Dry Clay, Model Magic, Model Magic Fusion, Modeling
    Clay *(Crayola Dough is NOT Gluten/Casein Free)*
Max's Mud - Organic Sculpting Dough

Skin Care

Arbonne -
    ABC Baby Care (Body Oil, Herbal Diaper Rash Cream)
    Aromassentials
       Awaken Sea Salt Scrub 16 oz.
       Unwind Bath Salts
       Unwind Massage Oil
    Bio Nutria
       Herbal Muscle Massage Gel
       Herbal Vapor Rub
       Leg Vein Formula
    Clear Advantage
       Acne Lotion
       Refining Toner
       Skin Support Supplement
       Spot Treatment
    FC5
       Exfoliating New Cell Scrub
       Hydrating Eye Crème

skin care

Rx

Moisturizing Night Crème
Nurturing Day Lotion w/SPF 20
Oil Absorbing Day Lotion w/SPF 20
Purifying Cleanser + Toner
Skin Conditioning Oil
Ultra Hydrating Hand Crème

F.Y.I.

Body Better Body Cream
Eye Q Cream Eye Shadow
Get Even Tinted Moisturizer SPF 15
Sugar Slush Body Scrub

Figure 8

Vanish Pre Shower Cellulite Scrub
Vanish Water Relief Treatment Serum

NutriMinC RE9

Regain Illuminating Enzyme Peel
Retaliate Wrinkle Filler

Revelâge

Age Spot Brightening Day Cream w/SPF 30
Age Spot Brightening Hand Therapy w/SPF 30
Concentrated Age Spot Minimizer
Intensive Pro Brightening Night Serum

SeaSource Detox Spa

5 In 1 Essential Massage Oil
Foaming Sea Salt Scrub
Purifying Sea Soak
Remineralizing Body Lotion 24 Hr.
Renewing Body Gelée
Sea Mud Face and Body Mask

Rx Burt's Bees -

   After Sun Soother

   Almond Milk Hand Crème

   Baby Bee (Diaper Ointment, Dusting Powder)

   Beeswax & Banana Hand Crème

   Beeswax Moist (Day Creme, Night Crème)

   Carrot Nutritive Body Lotion

   Citrus & Gingerroot Citrus Body Wash

   Deep Pore Scrub

   Garden Tomato Toner

   Hand Salve

   Hand Sanitizer

   Healthy Treatment (Evening Primrose Overnight Crème,
      Marshmallow Vanishing Crème, Pore Refining Mask, Royal Jelly
      Eye Crème, Shea Butter Hand Repair)

   Lemon Butter Cuticle Crème

   Lemon Poppy Seed Facial Cleanser

   Radiance (Body Lotion, Day Cream, Eye Cream)

   Soothingly Sensitive Lotion

   Thoroughly Therapeutic (Body Butter, Foot Cream, Hand Cream,
      Lotion)

California Baby -

   Aloe Vera Cream

   Botanical Moisturizing Cream

   Calendula (Cream, Everyday Lotion)

   Calming (Diaper Rash Cream, Everyday Lotion, Massage Oil, Non
      Talc Powder, Soothing & Healing Spray)

   Citronella (SPF 30+ Sunscreen Lotion, Summer Lotion)

   Colds & Flu Massage Oil

   Everyday/Year Round SPF 30 (Sunblock Stick, Sunscreen Lotion)

   I Love You Aromatherapy Massage Oil

No Fragrance Sunblock Stick (SPF 30+)   **Rx**
No Fragrance Sunscreen Lotion (SPF 18, SPF 30+)
Overtired & Cranky Massage Oil
Sunblock Stick SPF 30 (No Fragrance)
Sunscreen SPF 30 (Citronella, No Fragrance)
Super Sensitive (Everyday Lotion, Massage Oil)
Clear & Clear - Foaming Facial Cleaner (Oil Free, Sensitive Skin)
Coppertone -
    Kids Sunblock Lotion (SPF 50, SPF 70)
    Oil Free Lotion (SPF 15, SPF 30, SPF 30 Faces)
    Sport Lotion (SPF 15, SPF 30, SPF 50, SPF 50 Faces, SPF 70)
    Suncreen Tanning Lotion (SPF 4, SPF 8)
    Waterbabies Sunblock Stick (SPF 30)
    Waterbabies Sunscreen Lotion (SPF 50, SPF 50 Pure & Simple, SPF 70)
Desert Essence Organics -
    Age Reversal Pomegranate (Eye Serum, Face Serum)
    Age Reversal SPF 30 Mineral Sunscreen
    Almond Hand & Body Lotion
    Bulgarian Lavender Hand & Body Lotion
    Coconut Hand & Body Lotion
    Pistachio Foot Repair Cream
    Pumpkin Hand Repair Cream
    Spicy Citrus Hand & Body Lotion
    Vanilla Chai Hand & Body Lotion
Eucerin - Original Lotion
Fleurish Beauty - Luxe Lotion
Gluten-Free Savonnerie ▲ - All Products
Hy-Vee -
    Skin Cream (Total Moisture)
    Therapeutic Skin Lotion

Rx **Johnson's** - Baby Oil, Head To Toe Fragrance Free Baby Lotion

Keys - All Products

Lubriderm -

Daily Moisture Lotion

Advanced Therapy

Fragrance Free

Regular

Sensitive Skin

w/SPF 15

w/Sea Kelp Extract

w/Shea & Cocoa Butters

Nature's Baby Organics - Ah Choo Chest Rub, Baby Oil, Diaper Ointment, Face & Body Moisturizer, Silky Dusting Powder, Soothing Stick

Sleep Aids

Meijer -

Apap PM (Caplets, Gelcaps, Geltabs)

Sleep Aid Nitetime (Caplets)

Soap

Arbonne -

Aromassentials

Awaken Sea Salt Scrub 16 oz.

Unwind Bath Salts

Bio Nutria Herbal Vapor Soak

Rx

Clear Advantage (Acne Wash, Refining Toner)
FC5
  Exfoliating New Cell Scrub
  Purifying Cleanser + Toner
F.Y.I. Sugar Slush Body Scrub
Figure 8 Vanish Pre Shower Cellulite Scrub
SeaSource Detox Spa
  Detoxifying Rescue Wash
  Foaming Sea Salt Scrub
  Purifying Sea Soak

Burts Bees -
Baby Bee Shampoo & Body Wash
Bay Rum Bar Soap
Carrot Complexion Soap
Citrus & Gingerroot (Bar Soap, Body Wash, Hand Soap)
Green Tea & Lemongrass Hand Soap
Men's Natural (Bar Soap, Body Wash)
Peppermint & Rosemary Body Wash
Tomato Soap

California Baby -
Bubble Bath (Calendula, Calming, Chamomile & Herbs, Colds & Flu, I Love You, Light & Happy, Overtired & Cranky, Party, Super Sensitive)
Calendula Shampoo & Body Wash
Calming Shampoo & Body Wash
Diaper Area Wash
Handwash (First Aid Moisturizing, Natural Antibacterial Blend Moisturizing, Super Sensitive)
Natural Pregnancy Body Wash
Swimmer's Defense Shampoo & Body Wash
Tea Tree & Lavender Shampoo & Body Wash

Rx Desert Essence Organics -
    Age Reversal Pomegranate Facial Cleansing Gel
    Almond Body Wash
    Bulgarian Lavender Body Wash
    Coconut Body Wash
    Fragrance Free Body Wash
    Green Apple & Ginger Body Wash
    Italian Red Grape Body Wash
    Red Raspberry Body Wash
    Vanilla Chai Body Wash

Dial - Liquid Hand Soap

Fleurish Beauty - Aloe & Shea Body Wash, Bar Soap (Ambrosia, Cassia Clove, Lavender, Lemongrass, Patchouli, Peppermint, Sandalwood)

Gluten-Free Savonnerie▲ - All Products

Goodnight Moon Soaps - All Soaps & Sprays

Johnson's - Head To Toe Baby Wash

Keys - All Products

Tom's Of Maine -
    Body Bar
        Natural Clear
        Natural Deodorant
        Natural Moisturizing

Stay Awake

Meijer - Stay Awake Tablets
Ultra Pep-Back

Supplements

Rx

Aqua Flow - Enzymatic Therapy

Arbonne - Smart Nutritional Hybrids Daily Nutritional Chews For Teens, Smart Nutritional Hybrids Daily Power Punch For Kids

Blaine - MagOX 400

Carlson -

Able Eyes

Aces (Gold, Plus Zinc, Regular)

Acetyl L Carnitine (Capsules, Powder)

Aloe Vera Gel

Alpha Lipoic Acid Tablets

Bioflavonoids

Blood Nutrients

Buffalo Liver

Cardi Rite

Carlson For Kids Chewable DHA

Carlson For Kids Cod Liver Oil

Carlson For Kids Very Finest Fish Oil (Lemon, Orange)

Cod Liver Oil (Lemon, Regular, w/Low Vitamin A)

Co Q 10

Cranberry Concentrate

Creatine

DLPA

Digestive Aid

Easy Soy

E Gem Lip Care

E Gem Oil Drops

E Gem Shampoo

Rx
E Gem Skin Care Soap
Empty Gelatin
EPA Gems
Eye Rite
Fish Oil Q
Folic Acid
GLA
Garlic
Glucosamine Sulfate Capsules
Glutathione Booster
Glycine
Golden Aloe
Golden Primrose
HCL & Pepsin
Healthy Mood 5 HTP Elite
Heartbeat Elite Scientifically Complete
Hi Fiber
Homocysteine Guard
Kelp
Key E Cream
Key E Ointment
L Alanine
L Arginine Capsules
L Arginine Powder
L Asparagine
L Aspartic Acid
L Carnitine
Leci Key
Lecithin
L Glutamic Acid

supplements

Rx

L Glutamine (Capsules, Powder)
Lightly Lemon
L Lysine (Capsules, Powder)
L Methionine (Capsules, Powder)
L Proline (Capsules, Powder)
L Serine
L Threonine
Lutein 6 MG
Lutein 15 MG + Kale
Lycopene (Tomato Free)
MSM Sulfur
Medomega Fish Oil
Mellow Mood
Mild C (Capsules, Chewable, Crystals, Timed Release)
Mini Multi
Moistur Eyes
Moly B
Mother's DHA
NAC (Capsules, Powder)
Nutra Support Diabetes
Nutra Bone Support
Nutra Support Joint Cartilage Builder
Nutra Support Memory
Nutra Support Prostate
P5P
Pantethine Time
Pantothenic Acid Time
Phospatidyl Choline
Phosphatidyl Serine
Pro Rite
Psyllium

Rx Rhythm Right
Ribose
Right For Cholesterol
Right For The Liver
Right For The Macula
Rutin Quercetin
Salmon (Oil, Oil & GLA)
Selenium (Capsules, Tablets)
Super Beta Carotene
Super Cod Liver Oil
Super Daily Amino Blend (Capsules, Powder)
Super DHA Gems
Taurine
Tocotrienols
Tri B Homocysteine Formula
Very Finest Fish Oil Lemon Flavor (Liquid, Softgels)
Very Finest Fish Oil Orange Flavor (Liquid, Softgels)

Country Life -
7 Ketotrim●
Activated Charcoal Caplets●
Bee Propolis Veg Caplets●
Bio Active Hyaluronic Acid●
Brewer's Yeast Tablets●
Celadrin●
Clatonalin●
Cod Liver Oil●
CoQ10●
Daily Dophilus●
Daily Fiber X Veg Caplets●
Easy Iron●
Enhanced QM 1●

supplements

Rx

Estro G Balance●
Evening Primrose Oil●
Genaslim●
Go Less●
Green Edge II Powder●
Lecithin●
Lecithin Granules (Super Strength)●
Lipotropic metabolizer●
Maxi Sorb Carni Q Gel +E●
Maxi Sorb CoQ10●
Maxi Sorb CoQ10 Mega Q Gel●
Maxi Sorb Ultra CoQ10●
Natural Acidophilus w/Pectin Veg Caplets●
Nature's Garlic●
Norwegian Kelp●
Omega 3●
Phosphatidyl Choline Complex●
Power Dophilus Veg Caplets●
RNA/DNA●
R esveratrol Plus●
Shark Cartilage Veg Caplets●
Shark Liver Oil●
Sharp Thought●
Stress Shield●
Super Fiber Psyllium Seed Husk Powder●
Super Omega 3●
Total Lipid Control●
Ultra (Oils, Omegas DHA/EPA)●
VaricoVein●
Zinc Picolinate●

Rx Kirkman Labs -

    Acetyl L Carnitine

    Acidophilus Powder

    Alpha (Ketoglutaric Acid, Lipoic Acid)

    Amino Support (Capsules, Powder)

    Bifido Complex (Regular)

    BioCore Dairy

    Buffered Magnesium (Glycinate Bio Max Series Powder, Oxide)

    Carb Digest w/Isogest

    Chromium

    Cod Liver Oil (Lemon Lime Liquid, Regular Liquid, w/Vitamins A & D)

    Coenzyme Q10 (Capsules, Chewable Tablets, Tablets)

    Colostrum Gold (Flavored, Unflavored)

    Creatine (Capsules)

    DMAE (Capsules, Chewable Wafers)

    DMG (Capsules, Capsules w/Folic Acid & B12, Capsules w/Folinic Acid & B12, Liquid, Maximum Strength, w/B12 & Folinic Acid Liquid)

    DPP- IV Forte

    DRN (Detoxification Booster Capsules, Lithium, Vitamin/Mineral Basic Supplement Powder, Vitamin/Mineral LDA Basic Supplement)

    Detox Aid Advanced Formula

    Detoxification Aid Pro Support II

    EFA Powder

    EnZym Aid Multi Enzyme Complex

    EnZym Complete DPP IV II (Regular, w/Isogest)

    Everyday Multi Vitamin (Regular, w/o Vitamins A & D)

    Folic Acid (Chewable Tablets, w/B12 Capsules, w/B12 Liquid)

    Folinic Acid (Capsules, w/B12 Liquid)

    GABA (Plain, w/Niacinamide & Inositol)

    Gastro Support

Gastromune AI Support **Rx**

Ginkgo Biloba

Glucosamine Sulfate

Glycine

Grape Extract

Grapefruit Seed Extract

Idebenone

Immuno Aid

Inositol Pure Soluble Powder

Iron Bio Max Series (Capsules, Liquid)

L Glutamine

L Taurine

Lactobacillus Acidophilus

Lactobacillus Duo

Magnesium (Citrate Soluble Powder, Glycinate Bio Max Series, Malate, Sulfate Cream)

Maximum Spectrum Enzyme Complete/DPP IV Fruit Free w/Isogest

Melatonin (Chewables, Plus Magnesium, Slo Release Tablets)

Methylcobalamin Concentrated Powder

Milk Thistle

Mito Cell Support

Molybdenum

Multi (Enzyme Formula, Flora Spectrum)

N Acetyl Cysteine

Nordic (Berries, Omega 3 Gummies)

Nordic Naturals (Balanced Omega Combination, Cod Liver Oil Soft Gels, DHA Junior Strawberry, ProDHA, ProEFA Capsules, ProEFA Soft Gels, ProEPA, ProOmega Soft Gels)

Nu Thera (Everyday, Everyday Companion, w/P5P, w/o Vitamins A & D)

P5P (Regular, w/Magnesium Glycinate)

Peptidase Complete

Rx Phenol Assist (Companion, Regular)

Pro (Culture Gold, EFA Junior, Immune Support)

Pro Bio (Chewable Wafers, Defense, Gold, Inulin Free)

Reduced L Glatathione (Capsules, Lotion)

Saccharomyces Boulardii

Selenium

Spectrum Complete (Capsules, Powder Flavored, Powder Regular)

Super Cranberry Extract (Capsules, Chewables)

Super NuThera (Caplets, Capsules, Challenge Powders, Lemon Lime Liquid, New Improved Powder, Powder, Raspberry Flavored Concentrate, Tropical Fruit Liquid, w/P5P Caplets, w/P5P Lemon Lime Flavored Concentrate, w/P5P Liquid, w/P5P New Improved Powder, w/P5P Powder, w/o Vitamins A & D (Cherry Liquid, Regular, Tropical Fruit Liquid))

Super Pro Bio (Bio Max Series)

TMG (Capsules, Capsules w/Folic Acid & B12, Liquid w/Folinic Acid & B12, Powder w/Folic Acid & B12, w/Folic Acid & B12, w/Folinic Acid & B12, w/Folinic Acid & Methyl B12)

Thera Response

Threelac

Vanadium

Yeast Aid (Capsules, Powder)

Meijer -

Antioxidant

Astaxanthin

Biocosinol

CLA (Conjugated Linolenic Acid)

Chromium Picolinate

Cod Liver Oil

CoQ10

Cranmax

supplements

DHA

Rx

EPA (Eicosapentaenoic Acid)

Echinacea

Estroplus Extra Strength

Fish Oil (Concentrate, Enteric Coated, Extra Strength, Extra Strength Enteric Coated, w/CoQ10)

Focus smart

GLA (Gamma Linolenic Acid)

Gingko Biloba

Glucosamine & Collagen & HA

Glucosamine Chondroitin (3X, Extra Strength, Plus MSM)

Glucosamine Sulfate Caplets

Green Tea

Hair Skin Nail

Lutein

Lycopene Capsules

Memory & Mood Supplement

Odorfree Garlic

Panax Ginseng

Phytosterol Esters

Saw Palmetto Softgels

Soy Isoflavones

Super Omega

Vision Formula w/Lutein

Member's Mark (Sam's Club) -

CoQ10

Cranberry Extract

Fish Oil

Flaxseed Oil

Garlic

Gingko Biloba

Rx Glucosamine +MSM

Glucosamine HCL

Glucosamine Chondroitin Triple Strength

Lutein

Omega 3 6 9

Nature's Bounty -

Glucosamine Chondroitin Complex Xtra Strength

Os-Cal - Calcium Supplement (500+ D, 500 + Extra D, 500 + Extra D Chewable)

Osteo Bi-Flex - (Double Strength Softgels, Double Strength Tablets, Triple Strength Tablets)

Schiff - Probiotics Acidophilus (Tablets)

Vitamins & Minerals

Carlson -

Aqua Gem E

B 12 SL

B 12 Time

B 50 Gel

B Compleet

Baby Drops Vitamin D

Biotin

C Gel

Carlson For Kids Chewable Calcium

Carlson For Kids Chewable Vitamin C

Chelated Cal Mag

Chelated Calcium

Chelated Chromium

Chelated Copper

Chelated Iron

Rx

Chelated Magnanese
Chelated Magnesium
Chelated Mineral Compleet
Chelated Zinc
Chew Iron
Chewable Calcium Citrate
Chewable Vitamins & Minerals
Complexed Potassium
D Alpha Gems
D Drops (1000 IU, 2000 IU)
E Gems
E Gems Elite
E Gems Plus
E Sel
Gamma E Gems
Key E 400 IU
Key E Kaps
Key E Powder
Liquid Cal 600
Liquid Cal Mag
Liquid Calcium
Liquid Magnesium
Liquid Multiple Minerals
Magnesium
Niacin
Niacin Amide
Niacin Time
One Gram C
Potassium

Rx Solar D Gems
Super 1 Daily
Super 2 Daily
Super C Complex
Super D Omega 3
Super Omega 3 Gems
Time C
Time C Bio
Veg E Gems
Vitamin A Pamitate
Vitamin A Solubilized
Vitamin A w/Pectin
Vitamin B 1
Vitamin B2
Vitamin B6 (Liquid, Tablets)
Vitamin C Crystals
Vitamin D
Vitamin K
Zinc
Zinc Ease

Country Life -
Action B Caplets●
Basic B Caplets●
Bio Rutin Complex●
Biotin●
Buffered Vitamin C●
Cap C Veg Caplets●
Cellular Active Coenzyme B Complex Veg Caplets●
Chewable Acerola C Complex●
Chewable Orange Juice●

vitamins & minerals

Rx

Chewable Vitamin E●
Choline●
Choline Inositol Complex●
Citrus Bioflavonoids●
Coenzyme Active B6●
Dry Vitamin D 1000 IU●
Ester C●
Ester C Veg Caplets●
Flush Free Niacin Veg Caplets●
Folic Acid●
Grape Complete Caps●
Grape Seed Extract Veg Caps●
Hi Potency Biotin●
Hi Potency Biotin Veg Caps●
Hi Potency Maxi B Caps●
Inositol Powder●
Lutein●
Maxi C Complex Vitamin C●
Natural Beta Carotene●
Natural Dry Vitamin E●
Natural E Complex●
Natural Vitamin A●
Natural Vitamin A & D●
Natural Vitamin D●
Natural Vitamin E●
Niacin●
Niacinamide●
Paba●
Pantothenic Acid●

Rx Phyto Nutrient Carotenoid Complex●
Rutin●
Special C Complex●
Stress M●
Sublingual Vitamin B12●
Super Potency Action B●
Super Potency Hi B●
Superior Vitamin C●
Supreme Hi B●
Tall Tree Children's Chewable Vitamin C●
Vitamin A Dry●
Vitamin B1●
Vitamin B2●
Vitamin B6●
Vitamin B6 Veg Caplets●
Vitamin B12●
Vitamin C●
Vitamin C Crystals●
Vitamin D3●
Vitamin E Complex●
Vitamin K1●

Kirkman Labs -
Advanced Adult Multi Vitamin
Advanced Mineral Support
B Complex w/CoEnzymes Pro Support (Capsules, Powder)
Buffered Vitamin C Powder
Calcium Bio Max Series
Calcium Magnesium Liquid
Calcium w/Vitamin D (Chewable Tablets, Powder Unflavored)
Calcium w/o Vitamin D Bio Max Series
Children's Chewable Multi Vitamin/Mineral (Capsules, Wafers)

vitamins & minerals

D Biotin

Rx

Multi Mineral Complex Pro Support

Multi Vitamin Pro Support

Mycellized Vitamin A Liquid

Perry Prenatal

Vitamin B6 (Magnesium Vitamin/Mineral Chewable Wafers, Regular)

Vitamin C (Bio Max Series Buffered Powder Flavored, Bio Max Series Buffered Powder Unflavored, Capsules, Chewables, Tablets)

Vitamin D

Vitamin D3

Vitamin E

Zinc (Bio Max Series, Liquid, Sulfate, w/Vitamin C & Slippery Elm Lozenges)

Meijer -

50 Plus w/Ester C

Advanced Formula w/Ester C

Calcium (Citrate Chewable, Coral, Phosphorus Plus D, Plus D)

Central Vitamin Select

Ester C

Multivitamin (Hi Potency Men, Hi Potency Women, Inov., Inov. Prenatal)

Slow Release Iron

Vitamin A

Vitamin B Complex w/Vitamin C

Vitamin B6 Natural

Vitamin B12

Vitamin C Natural

Vitamin E

Vitamin E Oil

Vitamin E Synthetic Softgels

Vitamin E w/Fish Oil

Vitamin E w/Vitamin C

Rx **Member's Mark (Sam's Club)** -
  Children's (Chewable Multi Complete, Multivitamin Gummies)
  Complete Multi
  Iron Slow Release
  Niacin
  Potassium
  Super B Complex w/Vitamin C
  Vitamin B Complex w/Vitamin C
  Vitamin B12
  Vitamin C w/Natural Rose Hips
  Vitamin D3
  Vitamin E 400 IU
  Ocuvite - Lutein (Capsules, Tablets)
  Safeway Select -
  Calcium (w/ Vitamin D)
  Central Vite (Multi Vitamin, Senior Formula)
  One Tablet Daily Vitamin
  Prenatal Vitamins
  Vitamin C
  Woman's One Tablet Daily
  Schiff - Niacin Flush Free (Tablets)
  Slice Of Life - Gummy Vitamins For Adults (All Varieties)
  Yummi Bears - All Varieties (Organic, Regular)

Weight Loss

Alli
Arbonne - Figure 8 On the Go! Weight Loss Chews (Berry Burst, Chocolate, Creamy Caramel, Peanut Butter)
CitriMax Plus

index

index

Gluten/Casein Free OTC Pharmacy

NOTES

NOTES

NOTES

Making Gluten-Free Living Easy!

Cecelia's Marketplace

Kalamazoo, Michigan

www.CeceliasMarketplace.com

Quick Order Form

Online Orders: www.CeceliasMarketplace.com

✉ **Mail Orders:** Kal-Haven Publishing
P.O. Box 20383
Kalamazoo, MI 49019
U.S.A.

Cecelia's Marketplace	Quantity	Price	Total
Gluten-Free Grocery Shopping Guide	_____	(x $24.95) =	_____
Gluten/Casein Free Grocery Shopping Guide	_____	(x $24.95) =	_____
Gluten/Casein/Soy Free Grocery Shopping Guide	_____	(x $24.95) =	_____

Sales Tax: Michigan residents please add 6% sales tax   _____

Sub Total: _____

Shipping: (quantities 1-2 add $5.25)
(quantities 3-6 add $9.95)   _____

Total: _____

*Please make check or money order payable to Kal-Haven Publishing

Name: _____

Address: _____

City: _____State: _____Zip: _____

Email address: _____

Making Gluten-Free Living Easy!

Cecelia's Marketplace

Kalamazoo, Michigan

www.CeceliasMarketplace.com

Quick Order Form

Online Orders: www.CeceliasMarketplace.com

Mail Orders: Kal-Haven Publishing
P.O. Box 20383
Kalamazoo, MI 49019
U.S.A.

Cecelia's Marketplace	Quantity	Price	Total
Gluten-Free Grocery Shopping Guide	_____	(x $24.95) =	_____
Gluten/Casein Free Grocery Shopping Guide	_____	(x $24.95) =	_____
Gluten/Casein/Soy Free Grocery Shopping Guide	_____	(x $24.95) =	_____

Sales Tax: Michigan residents please add 6% sales tax _____

Sub Total: _____

Shipping: (quantities 1-2 add $5.25)
(quantities 3-6 add $9.95) _____

Total: _____

*Please make check or money order payable to Kal-Haven Publishing

Name: _____

Address: _____

City: _____ State: _____ Zip: _____

Email address: _____

Making Gluten-Free Living Easy!

Cecelia's Marketplace

Kalamazoo, Michigan

www.CeceliasMarketplace.com

Quick Order Form

Online Orders: www.CeceliasMarketplace.com

✉ Mail Orders: Kal-Haven Publishing
P.O. Box 20383
Kalamazoo, MI 49019
U.S.A.

Cecelia's Marketplace	Quantity	Price	Total
Gluten-Free Grocery Shopping Guide	_____	(x $24.95) =	_____
Gluten/Casein Free Grocery Shopping Guide	_____	(x $24.95) =	_____
Gluten/Casein/Soy Free Grocery Shopping Guide	_____	(x $24.95) =	_____

Sales Tax: Michigan residents please add 6% sales tax _____

Sub Total: _____

Shipping: (quantities 1-2 add $5.25)
(quantities 3-6 add $9.95) _____

Total: _____

*Please make check or money order payable to Kal-Haven Publishing

Name: _____

Address: _____

City: _____State: _____ Zip: _____

Email address: _____

Making Gluten-Free Living Easy!

Cecelia's Marketplace

Kalamazoo, Michigan

www.CeceliasMarketplace.com

Quick Order Form

 Online Orders: www.CeceliasMarketplace.com

✉ **Mail Orders:** Kal-Haven Publishing
P.O. Box 20383
Kalamazoo, MI 49019
U.S.A.

Cecelia's Marketplace	Quantity	Price	Total
Gluten-Free Grocery Shopping Guide	_____	(x $24.95) =	_____
Gluten/Casein Free Grocery Shopping Guide	_____	(x $24.95) =	_____
Gluten/Casein/Soy Free Grocery Shopping Guide	_____	(x $24.95) =	_____

Sales Tax: Michigan residents please add 6% sales tax _____

Sub Total: _____

Shipping: (quantities 1-2 add $5.25)
(quantities 3-6 add $9.95) _____

Total: _____

*Please make check or money order payable to Kal-Haven Publishing

Name: _____

Address: _____

City: _____ State: _____ Zip: _____

Email address: _____